DILEMMAS OF CHANGE IN BRITISH POLITICS

Institute of Anglo-American Studies

The Institute of Anglo-American Studies is an academic collegium co-sponsored by the University of Southern Mississippi and the University of South Alabama under the aegis of the USM Center for International Education. The purpose of the Institute is to promote a more profound understanding of Anglo-American culture through scholarly and cultural activities in both the United Kingdom and the United States.

A scholarly publications series will be an integral part of the Institute's programme. We are extremely pleased to have this volume as our initial endeavour in this area. Professors Studlar and Waltman have assembled an outstanding array of scholars and have performed their jobs of editing and guiding the manuscript to fruition with the highest degree of professionalism. They have produced a book with an important theme and have done it justice. Our hope is that future volumes will live up to the standard of excellence found here.

The Institute takes no official position on any matter. The opinions expressed herein, therefore, are those of the authors.

WILLIAM B. TAYLOR
Director

Dilemmas of Change in British Politics

Edited by
Donley T. Studlar
and
Jerold L. Waltman

in association with
the Institute of Anglo-American Studies
Center for International Education
University of Southern Mississippi
University Press of Mississippi, Jackson

First published in 1984 in the United States of America
by the University Press of Mississippi
Printed in Hong Kong

Library of Congress Cataloging in Publication Data

Main entry under title:
Dilemmas of change in British politics.
Includes index.
1. Great Britain—Politics and government—1979–
—Addresses, essays, lectures. I. Studlar, Donley T.
II. Waltman, Jerold L., 1945– . III. University
of Southern Mississippi. Institute of Anglo-American
Studies.
JN231.D55 1984 320.941 83–14782
ISBN 0–87805–195–3

For our parents

Joe and Irene Studlar
O.L. and Carletta Waltman

Contents

Foreword: Political Change and the 1983 Election

Political science is not journalism. It does, however utilize the insights and findings of journalism in developing longer term analyses of political institutions and political behaviour. The papers in this volume were completed before the British General Election of 1983; yet events surrounding the General Election support the continuing relevance of the perspectives herein.

Most evidently, the party system remains in flux, but without a clear direction of change. Electorally there now exists a three-party system reminiscent of the 1920s. The largest party rules as a minority in terms of popular votes and the electorate as a whole, thanks to an almost evenly split opposition. The workings of the electoral system have, nevertheless, generated a strong majority for that party in the House of Commons and a large disparity in seats between the other two.

The agonies of the Labour Party have deepened, and the potential for party realignment seems closer to realization than at any time in the post World War II period. Adoption of a more democratic method of selecting the party leader and deputy leader, involving a drawn-out compaign, has provided another opportunity for recurring policy wrangles within the party. Whether the new procedures are sufficiently democratic is also a question of considerable concern.

Tensions within the Social Democratic–Liberal Alliance over structure and policies, however, make it uncertain whether this grouping is the true successor to Labour on the left. Espousing constitutional reform as a major part of its manifest, the Alliance secured one-fourth of the vote in the General Election, insufficient to break the mould of British politics as of yet.

In the immediate aftermath of the election, even the Labour left appeared reconciled to continuing British membership of the European Community. But if the 1975 referendum did not settle the question, the 1983 General Election may not have done so either.

Almost unnoticed, the political consequences of judicial decisions grow. The Labour Party used its scarce financial resources to challenge the redistribution decisions of the Boundary Commission in the courts, where the party was ultimately rebuffed. Some of the internal Labour Party disputes have also landed in the courtroom. Perhaps more significantly, one contender for the parliamentary nomination of the Conservative Party in Clwyd Northwest successfully petitioned the courts for an injunction to prevent the victory of his principal rival, whereupon the challenger eventually secured the nomination for the safe Conservative seat. The 1983 redistribution of seats was exceptional in its impact, and several ferocious fights for nomination occurred. Clwyd Northwest was an unusual episode (although a similar situation occurred in Bridgend), but it raises the question of whether involving the courts in candidate selection is preferable to party primaries in Britain.

The 1983 election revealed some interesting developments in territorial politics. Northern Ireland continues to be an awkward problem, and Scotland (but not Wales) has steadfastly resisted the advance of Thatcherite Conservatism. Nationalist redoubts remain in Wales and Scotland; both present the phenomenon of four-party politics within the nation. Norman Furniss identifies the SDP–Liberal Alliance as a potential carrier of Scottish Nationalism in the 1980s. The 1983 election gave signs of just such an emergence.

Local government continues to be subject to the partisan initiatives of central government. One of the few specific Conservative proposals in its manifesto was to abolish the Metropolitan County Councils and the Greater London Council. Since the legislation is not to be brought forward in the first session of Parliament after the election, this proposal will hang like a Sword of Damocles over the activities of these bodies for the next several years. The complicated, time-consuming implementation of such a sweeping rearrangement of local government functions means that the GLC elections may be postponed from 1985 until 1986, thus preserving Ken Livingstone as a convenient symbol for all that the present Government finds objectionable in local government. Meanwhile concerted attempts by central government to hold down local authority spending persist.

Legislatively, Labour remains the major opposition party. Asserting the Commons' power against the Government however, depends not simply on dissenting Conservative Party MPs, but on truly massive revolts to overcome the nominal 140-seat majority of the Government. The episodes involving selection of the Speaker, MP's pay, and hanging in the summer of 1983 are not necessarily auguries for further substantial dissent, since all of these are, in one fashion or another, House of Commons matters. The refusal to consider seriously a referendum on hanging (or any other issue) shows that the sway of Parliamentary sovereignty is still strong. Select Committees can be embarrassing, but they are not yet powerful. There are few signs that the prevalent legislative ethos of the twentieth century is moving beyond the changes described in this book.

The implication of a legislature only slightly altered is that strong executive control will continue for the foreseeable future. Ostensibly, one reason for the abolition of the Central Policy Review Staff was that too many leaks of its reports occurred. Since leaks have been proliferating in other areas of government as well in recent years, this argument is not convincing. Much more persuasive is the notion that the Prime Minister is attempting to dominate sometimes recalcitrant sections of the executive. Accusations about the assignment of higher Civil Servants on the basis of enthusiasm for the Thatcher programme have been rife. Whether Mrs Thatcher can have as large an impact on the nature of the executive in Britain as she has had on the economy and society, however, remains to be seen.

The situation after the General Election of 1983 closely resembles that before the election. The most significant indications of change are emanating from the party system (still a major channel of participation), and, to lesser degrees, Parliament and the judiciary. Usually several elections rather than one are necessary to bring about and confirm fundamental change. This book stands or falls on its analysis of long term, not short term, trends.

August 1983
D.T.S
J.L.W.

Notes on the Editors and Other Contributors

Donley T. Studlar is Associate Professor of Government at Centre College of Kentucky. His articles on British politics have appeared in the *American Political Science Review, British Journal of Political Science, Comparative Political Studies, Political Studies*, and elsewhere.

Jerold L. Waltman is Associate Professor of Political Science at the University of Southern Mississippi. He is the author of *Copying Other Nations' Policies* (1980).

Douglas E. Ashford is Andrew Mellon Professor of Comparative Politics at the University of Pittsburgh. His books include *Politics and Policy in Britain* (1980) and *British Dogmatism and French Pragmatism: the Politics of Central-Local Relations in the Welfare State* (1982).

James B. Christoph is Professor of Political Science at Indiana University and a former president of the British Politics Group. The author of several articles on the British civil service, he has also published *Capital Punishment and British Politics* (1962) and *Cases in Comparative Politics* (3rd edn, 1976).

Norman Furniss is Professor of Political Science and Director of the West European Studies Program at Indiana University. His publications include *The Case for the Welfare State* (1977) as well as work on nationalism and decentralization in Britain.

Harry Lazer is Associate Professor of Political Science at City College of New York. A long-time student of British populism, he is the author of a forthcoming book on the subject, in addition to articles in *Political Science Quarterly* and *Publius*.

Hans J. Michelmann is Associate Professor of Political Science at the University of Saskatchewan. A member of the editorial board of the *Journal of European Integration*, he is the author of *Organisational Effectiveness in a Multinational Bureaucracy* (1979).

Jorgen S. Rasmussen is Professor of Political Science at Iowa State University and Executive Secretary of the British Politics Group. His books include *Retrenchment and Revival: a Study of the Contemporary Liberal Party* (1964), *The Process of Politics* (1969), and *Major European Governments* (6th edn, 1982).

Kenneth D. Wald is Associate Professor of Political Science at the University of Florida. His book *Crosses on the Ballot*, a study of British voting behaviour since 1885, was published in 1983.

Acknowledgements

Without the encouragement, assistance, and financial support of several individuals and organizations, this book would not have been written. We especially thank William B. Taylor, Director, and the Publications Committee of the Institute of Anglo-American Studies, University of Southern Mississippi; President E.C. Reckard and the Faculty Development Committee of Centre College; the Department of Politics, University of Warwick; and the British Politics Group.

1 Introduction: Dilemmas of Change in British Politics

Donley T. Studlar

> Governments are praised when their nations are great. How much of the success of a nation is caused by the structure of its government and how much by other conditions is difficult to determine.
>
> Kenneth Waltz, *Foreign Policy and Democratic Politics*

BRITAIN'S PROBLEMS

The last quarter century has witnessed a radical shift in the reputation of the British polity. For a long time the United Kingdom had a reputation as a bulwark of political stability. British institutions were considered to possess a rare capacity to reconcile the demand for change with the maintenance of political order. A major five-country study of democratic political attitudes concluded that Britain was a 'civic culture', combining the requisite amounts of political participation and obedience to authority.[1] The British party system of unified, disciplined legislative voting on proposals from the Executive was highly touted as a superior means of combining debate and governing.[2] These views were not the domain of foreigners only. The British population as a whole manifested a high degree of contentment with its institutions,[3] and members of the British élite were only too eager to share their institutions with the newly-emerging states of the former Empire.

From being a positive political model, the United Kingdom has increasingly become a negative model, both in the eyes of the Queen's subjects and of foreigners. The most popular view of this deterioration of Britain's reputation has focused on economic problems. The 'British (or English) disease', once referring to problems of management–union relations which led to low productivity, has now become generalized to cover all of Britain's economic problems – strikes, inflation, unemployment, loss of export markets, etc. The persistence of serious social problems in Northern Ireland and in non-white areas of the United Kingdom has also led people to question the efficacy of British institutions. A third theme of the critics has been Britain's loss of international power.

In the face of these and other problems, a spate of books and articles has appeared in recent years on the general difficulties of British public life. Usually referred to as 'the state of Britain' literature, the first round of these was published in the early 1960s and mainly questioned social and cultural aspects of British life.[4] The second round has flourished in the last half-decade. The titles of these works are often an informative guide to the contents: *Britain in Decline*;[5] *The Future That Doesn't Work*;[6] *Britain Against Itself*;[7] *British Government and Its Discontents*[8] 'A Report on England: The Future That Never Was';[9] *Alas, Alas for England*;[10] *The Death of British Democracy*;[11] and *Is Britain Dying?*[12] Large doses of criticism are also contained in the following works: 'Why Has Britain 'Failed'?'[13] *Britain: Progress and Decline;*[14] *Britain's Economic Prospects;*[15] and *The United Kingdom in 1980.*[16] The one recent optimistic account is *Britain: A Future That Works.*[17]

Most of these works concentrate on the economic and social problems of Britain and recommend various changes of behaviour to deal with them. Furthermore, some of them argue that not much can be done domestically to improve matters because the main influences are international, especially international economic forces. Surprisingly, political institutions come in for relatively little criticism, even from the political scientists involved. The basic theme seems to be 'if only Britain can get its economy right, everything else will fall into place'.

Of course, it is possible to argue with the recent negative view of Britain, just as it is possible to question whether British stability ever really met the historical image set out for it. Accounts of previous British stability often conveniently ignore the half century of problems associated with the rise of Irish nationalism in the late nineteenth century. The eventual secession of the Irish Republic was not the culmination of an episode of consensual, effective governance. The hangover of the Irish problem in Ulster has also not been an example which devotees of a civic culture would cherish. Further abroad, the transfer of British political institutions and practices to former colonies has not had the felicitous results expected. Former British colonies have had their share of the political disruptions and instability characteristic of much of the Third World. Few of them manifest the effective governance with consent that Britain was supposedly transferring with its institutions.

Even if one acknowledges, however, that the United Kingdom never quite fulfilled its reputation as an island of stability in a politically turbulent sea, its contemporary difficulties do seem forbidding. Some of them, such as massive unemployment, have occurred before, as has the Irish problem, difficulties associated with immigration, and problems with strikes. Slow economic growth has been the historical norm. The conjunction of all of these problems, however, with some recent questioning of political institutions makes the situation seem especially critical.

One particular manifestation of these combined difficulties was the series of riots across Britain in the long summer of 1981. Like Dr Johnson's prospect of hanging, they concentrated the minds of political observers on what was wrong with the system and how it could be changed. The depth of alienation revealed by the riots could not be attributed to the effects of economic factors alone. The inability of the government to forestall the riots showed that its authority was weak. When one considers all of the foregoing problems, it is difficult to disagree with the contention that 'Britain at the moment seems less endowed with political stability than was previously assumed to be the case.'[18]

The message of recent scholarly and journalistic critiques, then, is that Britain is in trouble. But how much of that trouble is due to defects in political institutions? As has been indicated, the thrust of most of the general critiques has been that the problems are economic, social, and/or international. These problems can be considered political insofar as they are policy problems with which political leaders are called upon to cope. After problems have accumulated to this extent, however, and have resisted initiatives by Governments of various political persuasions, a critical examination of political institutions is needed. While defects in political institutions may be related to policy problems in a society, the two are not connected in a deterministic manner. The fact that Saudi Arabia does not have the economic difficulties of the United Kingdom is no reason to conclude that the institutional problems of the latter are greater.

The examination of political institutions is a task pre-eminently suited for political scientists. Accordingly, in this book several political scientists will examine the recent performance and prospects for change of some of the major governmental institutions in the United Kingdom.[19] Given the widespread study and admiration of British poltical institutions by North American political scientists, it does not seem inappropriate that this task be undertaken by American and Canadian scholars.[20] This perspective should be especially valuable in light of the fact that recent re-evaluations of British political institutions have been carried out almost exclusively by British scholars.

The rest of this chapter will set out some of the controversy about British political institutions and posit four models that purport to explain recent institutional developments in the United Kingdom. The remainder of the book will examine the political institutions more carefully and will assess how appropriate these models are to the reality of British politics.

Throughout the book emphasis will be placed on the notion of dilemmas of change. A dilemma means a difficult choice. 'A dilemma, by definition, implies both stasis and movement.'[21] Changes are always occurring to some degree in political institutions, but choices remain about accelerating, retarding, or diverting change. Fundamental change is more frequently advocated than implemented. Uncertain consequences are an occupational hazard for politicians. This book analyses the institutional problems facing them.

POLITICAL INSTITUTIONS AND POLITICAL CHANGE

Recently there has been an upsurge of interest in British institutional change and some actual implementation of change, in stark contrast to earlier in the twentieth century. In an influential article, Dennis Kavanagh has noted the following 'old chestnuts' of British politics now seriously open to question:[22]

British politics is about class,
  all else is embellishment and detail;
the deferential political culture;
the unitary political system;
collective Cabinet responsibility;
the supremacy of Parliament;

the homogeneity of Britain, the
absence of nationality disputes and
serious constitutional disagreements,
which have been "resolved" in the flux of time;
the classic two party system and secure one party
majority government.

Instead of the old chestnuts, recent years have seen the development of ethnic politics, use of the referendum, devolution proposals, publicly dissenting Cabinet ministers, a more active judiciary, the impact of the European Community, minority government, coalition government, proposals for a Bill of Rights and/or a written Constitution, an ombudsman, demands for more open government, Parliamentary specialized committees, increased Parliamentary dissent, advocacy of proportional representation, and suggested reforms of the House of Lords. Most of these changes are institutional ones. In this environment, only the monarchy seems safe from challenge, secure in its substantive weakness.

Why, then, do the general critiques discussed above de-emphasize these developments? First, in fairness, they do not completely ignore institutional change. Beer strongly argues that changes in British political culture have been reflected in political institutions and behaviour; a new mobilization of political consent is necessary to cope with the whole range of Britain's problems.[23] Heren advocates sweeping political reforms, including proportional representation, the referendum, devolution, stronger Parliamentary committees, and open government.[24] Some of the contributors to the Gwyn-Rose and Kramnick volumes also argue for the significance of political institutions.[25] Haseler attributes many of the problems of Britain to defects within the Labour party.[26] Smith and Polsby see a strengthened role for Parliament as a significant improvement.[27] Even the Hudson Report concludes that reform of the House of Lords is necessary for the United Kingdom to reobtain dynamic economic growth.[28] Yet for the most part these are secondary themes in the state of Britain literature. The general focus is clearly elsewhere. Partly this is due to the 'problem orientation' of journalists and many in the scholarly community. Economic problems and international problems make headlines; only rarely do political institutions. Furthermore, politicians themselves often talk as if economic problems, in particular, were the major concern of governments. Political institutions are often assumed to be the 'givens' through which policies are worked out. Scholars and journalists also often operate on the materialistic assumption that human beings place economic concerns above all others.[29] For all of these reasons, political institutions usually assume a secondary importance in the recent state of Britain critiques.

Several British political scientists, journalists, and politicians, however, have not been so sanguine about the structure of British government. Since the early 1960s, a small but growing number of observers have questioned the effectiveness and/or representativeness of particular political institutions.[30] Advocates of change have proliferated in recent years, partially because of the worsening economic problems and a perception of bipartisan policy failures in economic and other fields. Whatever the inspiration, institutional change has become a major concern rather than a deviant inclination, for both political leaders and political analysts. An outline of the main features of this institutional ferment, both proposed and implemented, may be helpful.

A perennial favourite for institutional reform is the Civil Service. A host of academic commentators and Royal Commissions have criticized the Civil Service on grounds of élitism, amateurism, and unacknowledged policymaking influence.[31] Moreover, some changes have been made in Civil Service procedures, especially recruitment, promotion, and accountability. Whether the reforms that have been made have actually had the intended effect is questionable.[32] The optimist would say it is too early to tell; the pessimist would say that the Civil Service is capable of absorbing almost any reform without real change resulting. Unlike many British political institutions, however, the Civil Service has been the object of serious reform efforts. Perhaps for that reason it has not been so severely criticized lately. The major remaining thrust of the critics at the Civil Service concerns the general problem of accountability to the public and to Parliament. Despite Richard Crossman, executive secrecy is still the norm in Britain. Much of the suspicion of unwonted Civil Service influence on policymaking arises from the lack of information about how policies are made within the executive. Suspicions were further aroused rather than quieted when the Thatcher Government's abortive bill on secrecy was announced. There have been suggestions that the doctrine of individual ministerial responsibility for the policy actions of the department be modified to allow public acknowledgment of the role of Civil Servants in policymaking.[33] If the role of Select Committees in the House of Commons was expanded to include requisition of government personnel and papers, accountability would be enhanced.

Second only to the Civil Service as a target of institutional reform efforts has been Parliament. The House of Commons has been the scene of considerable institutional tinkering. Changes in both procedures and in the behaviour of members have been well documented, and various explanations have been offered for these changes.[34] As with Civil Service reform, the major question is how effective the changes are in producing the desired results. So far it seems that an unexpected behavioural change, namely the increase of dissent within the Parliamentary parties, has been more important than the structural changes involving the expansion of the Select Committee system. The former, however, has been of longer duration than the latter.

The expansion of Select Committees occurred during 1979 after a fifteen-year experiment with 'select' Select Committees. The Select Committees do not have power to deliberate over legislation but are intended to help members of Parliament perform their oversight duties through better information and the acquisition of greater legislative expertise. This reform has excited many observers through its potential for increasing the power of the legislature to challenge the executive's control of information. Since the powers of Select Committees are relatively circumscribed, however, one wonders whether the expansion of Select Committees has been a substantively effective reform or one that is merely cosmetic.

Despite two major reforms in the twentieth century, the House of Lords continues to be a target of critics, especially within the Labour party, for its unrepresentative influence on government policy. While this concern is understandable, the reluctance to change, much less to abolish, such a venerable institution has heretofore been stronger than the desire for change. Although the urge to reform the House of Lords is bipartisan,[35] resistance to change also crosses party lines. The failure to undertake reform of the House of Lords does not augur well for significant changes in more influential institutions. On the other hand, one could argue that House of Lords reform would be diversionary from more important concerns.

Closely connected to the power of Parliament, especially the House of Commons, is the role of political parties. Recent internal developments, especially within the Labour party, have provoked much discussion about the direction of British parties. The emergence of the Social Democrats, their by-election victories, and their high ratings in the opinion polls have led to speculation that the basic two-party system may be at an end, that single-party majority governments may be passé, and that a Social Democratic–Liberal Alliance may be the source of a future government. All of these things have yet to be demonstrated. It is not that unusual for party splits and coalition governments to occur, as a brief perusal of the inter-war years would indicate. The birth of a new party with a substantial representation in the House of Commons is, however, more unusual. It is also best not to put too much weight on poll ratings or by-elections as guides to what will happen in a General Election.[36] When people are forced to make a choice for the next five years at the ballot box, they will often vote, however reluctantly, for a party of which they have been intensely critical previously. The Liberals have always done better in by-elections and opinion polls than they have at general elections. Even when one is properly cautious about the long-term impact of the Social Democrats or a Social Democrat–Liberal Alliance, it is still remarkable that, in the face of the immense unpopularity of the Conservative Government in the early 1980s, the Labour party also remained relatively unpopular. That the two-party see-saw in popularity ratings no longer seems to have as wide an arc may bespeak a coming party realignment.

The formation of the Social Democratic party is related, of course, to other Labour party internal strife over the selection procedure for a leader, reselection procedures for sitting party MPs, and how the election manifesto will be drawn up. In all three of these cases, the general perception has been that the Left of the party has scored victories in having the rules changed in recent years. Yet these victories are tentative at best. Early indications of the effects of the reselection procedures are ambiguous.[37] The impact of the Left on leader selection and manifesto make-up depends upon the influence of the Left on the trade union vote, which has varied considerably over the years. One must also remember that in spite of the birth of the Social Democrats, most of the Labour Right has remained within the party. Two permanent socialist parties are not foreordained.

As long as the British electoral system remains one of first-past-the-post plurality, the flux of political parties is likely to continue. Small shifts in votes can result in large differences in Parliamentary seats. In view of the disparity between the voting support of the two major parties and their Parliamentary seats, plus the radical shifts in certain policies when parties changed office, several commentators have questioned the utility of maintaining the present electoral system.[38] According to this argument, the electoral system misrepresents public opinion by rewarding the two major parties with much more legislative and executive power than their standing with the public merits. Then once in office, the undeserved majority party claims a mandate for all of its policies and may pursue them far beyond what the public really wants, only to be replaced at the next election by the other party, which may then reverse government policy to the far opposite pole. The corollary of the over-represented majority parties is the under-represented minority ones. In a classic case of catch-22, the Liberals have been advocating proportional representation for years, to no avail against the major parties. Proportional representation was rejected by the major parties as the method for choosing deputies to devolved assemblies and to the European Parliament, in addition to their refusal to consider it for Parliamentary elections. The use of PR in Northern Ireland points to the continued separate treatment for that province. If PR were to be adopted throughout the United Kingdom, perhaps through a Liberal – Social Democratic coalition government, it would tend to institutionalize present party divisions and would lead to continual inter- and intra-party bargaining. Whether such an arrangement would result in more moderate policies and more effective governance is debatable.

Among the parties that might be affected by the adoption of PR are the Scottish Nationalists and the Welsh Nationalists (Plaid Cymru), which represent the forces of devolution and, to some degree, separatism in the United Kingdom. After the technical defeat of the Scottish devolution proposal and the overwhelming defeat of the more limited Welsh measure in 1979 referenda, many people have assumed that devolution is dead. Similar assumptions, however, were made about the decline of nationalism in the early 1970s after its brief flurry in the late 1960s. Aside from its expression of ethnic politics, nationalism presents the highly centralized British polity with a profound structural problem. How can one decentralize an island equitably? Every time that home rule or devolution has become a pertinent issue, the solution to the problems has foundered on just that difficulty.[39] One begins to suspect that the famed consensus of the residents of the United Kingdom may be a somewhat artificial one if it can only be held together by a strongly centralized authority.

Another persistent territorial problem is local government reform. Major change was proposed in this area in the late 1960s and early 1970s, culminating in the Local Government Act of 1972. The consequences of this act, however, have stimulated almost universal disapprobation.[40] The failure of such a widely discussed and carefully considered proposal to result in beneficial change has led some commentators to question whether British institutions are capable of meeting contemporary political needs.[41] Political decentralization, in both local government and regional government forms, is likely to appear on the political agenda again.

The referendum is a major structural change in British politics which has only been introduced in the last fifteen years, although it was discussed seriously as a device far earlier.[42] In contrast to devolution legislation, which took up the better part of two Parliamentary sessions in being passed (only to be stifled by the 1979 referenda results), the referendum has become a part of British government with relatively little controversy. Contrary to common belief, the first referendum in the United Kingdom was not the one on the European Community in 1975, but the Border Poll on Northern Ireland remaining in the United Kingdom in 1973. Before and after the poll, the pledge has frequently been made that Ulster will not be forced to leave the United Kingdom without the consent of its population. The 1975 referendum was a convenient method for the internally divided Labour party to settle the issue of British membership in the EC without endangering its ever-fragile party unity. Even though the issue of Community membership has arisen again, this use of the referendum must be viewed as a success in realizing its goals. The 1979 referenda in Scotland and Wales, like the Ulster referendum, were less than statewide. The results of these consultative referenda, however, eventually led to the defeat of the Labour Government on a motion of confidence. Once again, the referendum was embraced as a device which would enable the sitting government to avoid full responsibility for a deeply divisive issue. In this case, however, the attempt boomeranged.

The referendum seems to have stirred less controversy than devolution because of its use as a lesser of evils in situations where the government prefers to have its actions ratified by the most affected section of the public rather than risk a continuing source of intra-party division. Heretofore, governments have employed the referendum only as a means of settling constitutional issues. Despite Mrs Thatcher's threat to use it as an instrument of labour relations, its most likely future use is also to decide constitutional questions. Lacking an explicit written constitution, political leaders can justify use of the referendum on such issues much easier than they can on the normal socioeconomic issues which Parliament has always handled. If more constitutional questions arise (or are revived), then the popularity of the referendum may become more firmly established in the

United Kingdom.

Joining the European Community was widely perceived as a major change not only for British foreign and economic policy, but also for domestic political institutions. Despite all of the forebodings about erosion of Parliamentary sovereignty, nobody has yet made a convincing demonstration that such an erosion has occurred. One could grant that it would take a while before firm conclusions could be drawn on a matter such as this, but it has now been over ten years since Britain joined. Politicians and the public complain not about loss of sovereignty, but about the questionable economic payoffs of joining the EC. As has been shown time and again, public opinion on the EC is very unstable, and the public basically would rather not be bothered about the matter.[43] Direct elections for the European Parliament failed to excite people.[44] How much change, in both British institutions and British policy, has really occurred as a result of Community membership?

One way in which the Community could have an impact on British institutions is through the judiciary. So far the supposedly inevitable clash between United Kingdom law and Community law, to the detriment of the former, has been avoided. Those who see the EC as a threat to British domestic sovereignty might contend that this clash has been avoided by the compliance of Parliament to the demands of Community law, which involves no less an erosion of sovereignty. Nevertheless, the courts have not been the main agent of the European Community. The domestic courts, however, have expanded their political role somewhat in recent years.[45] Even this extension of judicial power, however, has not satisfied those who have called for a British Bill of Rights to guarantee civil liberties and/or a written Constitution.[46] Demands for a bill of rights or a written Constitution imply a suspicion of Parliament, political parties, and the consensual nature of the political culture. Lack of respect for the law and violent clashes between the antagonistic groups do seem to have increased recently, although still nowhere near the levels of the United States, for instance. Can the courts shore up a tattered political consensus? Can they exercise a role of political leadership?

The preceding survey of some of the major developments in British political institutions indicates that this aspect of British life has been in flux at the same time as the more publicized economic and social problems have occurred. In focusing on political institutions, several questions need to be assessed. How have institutions been changing? Why have these changes come about? Are these changes interconnected? What effects do these changes have? What are the prospects for further change? In order to understand these changes in broader perspective, several general models utilized to explain British political change will be examined.

MODELS OF POLITICAL CHANGE

A model is 'a pattern or mode of structure or formation'.[47] Less complex and rich than a theory, it offers an abstraction of interconnected patterns of behaviour. Specifically, we shall be concerned with four models of change: (1) incrementalism, (2) archaism, (3) overload, and (4) post-industrialism.[48] The incremental model, long beloved of political scientists, is often thought to be particularly applicable to Britain.[49] In this model change is adaptive and non-comprehensive. Individual institutions develop at their own pace as demands for change become irresistible. Political leaders are able to cope with demands by artfully blending the old and the new in a pragmatic manner. Although some periods of time may present severe challenges to the polity, these challenges are successfully met. Incremental change is most readily associated with a non-event, lack of a revolution. Since Britain has not had a statewide revolution since the seventeenth century,[50] incremental change must be successful there, according to the proponents of this model. The blending of the old and the new – royalty with aristocracy, aristocracy with liberal democracy, liberal democracy with mass democracy – is seen as further evidence of successful adaptation and political stability. But is this model still applicable to the United Kingdom (if it ever was)? Are political institutions developing at their own pace in adaptive ways? Is the current period simply one of the eras of sustained challenge to the incremental model?

The second model, archaism or grudging adaptation, is a variation of the first model. Archaism is less sanguine about the adaptive powers of the British polity.[51] Although the United Kingdom has managed to make necessary institutional changes and avoid revolutionary upheaval, it frequently does so in an agonizingly slow and painful manner. The supposedly pragmatic changes that result often have to be further adjusted later because of incompatible elements. Rather than leading in political change, Britain is usually a laggard in change. The conservatism and patience of the British population, rather than the skills of leaders, are largely responsible for the continuation of such a system. Instances of grudging adaptation would include the two twentieth century reforms of the House of Lords, the attempt to introduce more specialists into the Civil Service, and the recent embrace of Select Committees by the House of Commons. Devotees of archaism could even go further and contend that Britain resembles the situation often depicted as typically French, wherein the demand for change is normally so stifled by centralized institutions staffed by insensitive personnel that rapid change bursts forth at selective periods. Arguably, there have been only two major periods of policy innovation in twentieth century Britain, 1906–11 and 1945–50. Only in the earlier period was there substantial institutional change, in the form of the 1911 Parliament Act. Subsequent party realignments have had little effect on government institutions. The difference between the French and the British cases, however, lies in the fact that a turnover of regime is not necessary to achieve change in Britain. If archaism is the applicable model, is Britain in a crisis period? What kinds of innovations will alleviate the problems?

The third model of political change, overloaded government, has become a significant interpretation of British politics within the last decade.[52] According to this model, political institutions have difficulty in coping with contemporary problems because government has taken responsibility for too much – there are too many issues on the agenda, the issues are tremendously complicated, and government often lacks the necessary expertise and consensus to solve them. Most of the work on overload focuses on economic responsibilities that government has assumed with the growth of the welfare state and interventionist economic principles. Much of the British political agenda and Parliamentary timetable in recent years, however, has been devoted to constitutional issues, not economic ones.[53] The weakness of the overload model, aside from its concentration on economic issues, is that it never explains what a normal load entails. One could argue, for instance, that British government was 'overloaded' in the 1945–50 period with the re-establishing of peacetime political practices, building the welfare state, rebuilding the economy, and negotiating foreign alliances and withdrawals. Today the government has fewer foreign responsibilities and has only to maintain, not build, the welfare state apparatus. Yet it suffers, so we are told, from overload. Perhaps it does, but the dimensions of overload in the general sense remain to be specified. For instance, what role does lack of public confidence in leaders play in creating overload? Or is lack of public confidence a consequence of overload? Do the several interrelated problems outlined here constitute an example of political overload?

The fourth model of political change that can be applied to recent British politics is that of post-industrialism. This model is not one that Britons normally apply to themselves. 'Americans write about the problems of living in a technologically advanced post-industrial society; in England the greater worry is de-industrialization.'[54] Yet post-industrialism is worth considering, if for no other reason than that so many commentators have chosen to view the United Kingdom in these terms.[55] What does 'post-industrialism' mean? Briefly, it refers to a society which is characterized by mass economic abundance, a growing service sector of the economy, a premium on specialized knowledge, importance of technological communication, and social complexity.[56] Empirical studies have indicated that the United Kingdom belongs in such a post-industrial classification.[57] The politics of a post-industrial society, however, are far from clearly delineated.[58] As older political cleavages give way to newer ones, uncertainty and confusing conflict abound. If post-industrialism is eroding the importance of industrially-related cleavages and is bringing new cleavages to the fore, politicians will have difficulty in coping. In the British case, the contemporary difficulties of political institutions may stem from just such a change in the nature of society and its problems. De-industrialization and post-industrialization may not be all that different. Faced with shifting political values, the old institutions and the old methods do not work well. Most of the writers on post-industrialism see this model as incorporating demands for greater responsiveness and democracy in government rather than greater efficiency. If this is true, then it would seem that demands for open government, proportional representation, strengthened local government, referenda, devolution, and constitutional guarantees of civil liberties are the wave of the future. Perhaps the difficulty of birth for many of these proposed reforms indicates that the United Kingdom's post-industrial path is uncertain.[59] Is the United Kingdom really a post-industrial society? What are the elements of post-industrial political institutions?

Although these four models have been posited as independent explanations for contemporary political change in Britain, they could also be combined in various ways. Post-industrialism, for instance, could contribute to overloaded government. Alternatively, grudging adaptation could lead to a period of overloaded government. Incremental change could still be working, even in a period of post-industrialism and/or overloaded government. One combination of these models which seems to be gaining headway in discussions of British politics is the idea of over-institutionalization. As first articulated by Kesselman in his study of French local government and applied to British politics by Kavanagh and Rose, over-institutionalization encompasses elements of all four models.[60] Although political institutions earlier may have adapted successfully to change (Model I), in late industrial or post-industrial societies (Model IV) they have become rigid, defensive, and ill-equipped to cope with change. Therefore political demands may multiply (Model III) without adequate responses from political institutions, which act to stifle change (Model II). Over-institutionalization is a suggestive concept, but it has not been utilized to analyse British politics in a systematic, empirical manner.

The presentation of these models is not intended to be definitive. Instead, they are intended as organizing devices to aid in thinking about the broader implications of specific institutional changes. The authors of the papers in this volume are not asked to agree with any of the above formulations. If these models stimulate alternative and better ones, they will have served their purpose.

NOTES

1. Gabriel Almond and Sidney Verba, *The Civic Culture* (Boston: Little, Brown, 1963).
2. Leon Epstein, 'What Happened to the British Party Model?', *American Political Science Review*, LXXIV (Mar. 1980) 9–22.
3. Almond and Verba, *op. cit.*
4. See James B. Christoph. 'Consensus and Cleavage in British Political Ideology', *American Political Science Review*, LIX (Sept. 1965) 629–39; William B. Gwyn, 'Jeremiahs and Pragmatists: Perceptions of British Decline', in *Britain: Progress and Decline*, ed. William B. Gwyn and Richard Rose (New Orleans: Tulane University Press, 1980) 1–25.
5. Andrew Gamble, *Britain in Decline* (Boston: Beacon Press, 1982).
6. R. Emmett Tyrrell, ed., *The Future That Doesn't Work* (Garden City, N.Y.: Doubleday, 1977).
7. Samuel H. Beer, *Britain Against Itself* (New York: Norton, 1982).
8. Geoffrey Smith and Nelson Polsby, *British Government and Its Discontents* (New York: Basic Books, 1981).
9. Daniel Bell, 'A Report on England: I. The Future That Never Was', *Public Interest*, LI (Spring 1978) 35–73.
10. Louis Heren, *Alas, Alas for England* (London: Hamish Hamilton, 1981).

11. Stephen Haseler, *The Death of British Democracy* (Buffalo, N.Y.: Prometheus Books, 1976).
12. Isaac Kramnick, ed., *Is Britain Dying*? (Ithaca, N.Y.: Cornell University Press, 1979).
13. Ralf Dahrendorf, 'Why Has Britain 'Failed'?' (Washington, D.C.: American Friends of the London School of Economics, n.d.).
14. Gwyn and Rose, *op. cit.*
15. Richard Caves and Lawrence Krause, ed., *Britain's Economic Performance* (Washington, D.C.: Brookings Institution, 1980).
16. The Hudson Report, *The United Kingdom in 1980* (London: Associated Business Programmers, 1974).
17. Bernard Nossiter, *Britain: A Future That Works* (Boston: Little, Brown, 1978).
18. Dennis Kavanagh, 'New Bottles for New Wines: Changing Assumptions About British Politics', *Parliamentary Affairs*, XXXI (Winter 1978) 7.
19. The essays in this volume are concerned with governmental institutions with one exception, political parties. The British party system, however, has been so closely linked with the formal governmental institutions through the party government model that an assessment of governmental institutions would be incomplete without its inclusion.
20. Dennis Kavanagh, 'An American Science of British Politics', *Political Studies*, XXII (Sept. 1974) 251–70.
21. Richard Rose, *Do Parties Make a Difference*? (Chatham, N.J.: Chatham House, 1980) 111.
22. Kavanagh, 'New Bottles for New Wines: Changing Assumptions About British Politics', p. 6.
23. Beer, *op. cit.*
24. Heren, *op. cit.*
25. See especially Richard Rose, 'From Steady State to Fluid State: the United Kingdom Today', in Gwyn and Rose, *op. cit.*, 129–54; Stephen Blank, 'Britain's Economic Problems: Lies and Damn Lies', in Kramnick, *op. cit.*, 66–88; Jorgen Rasmussen, 'Was Guy Fawkes Right?', in Kramnick, *op. cit.*, 97–125.
26. Haseler, *op. cit.*
27. Smith and Polsby, *op. cit.*
28. The Hudson Report, *op. cit.*
29. Nathan Glazer and Daniel P. Moynihan, 'Introduction', in *Ethnicity*, ed. Nathan Glazer and Daniel P. Moynihan (Cambridge, MA: Harvard University Press, 1975) 1–26.
30. Bernard Crick, *The Reform of Parliament* (Garden City, NY: Doubleday Anchor Books, 1965); Brian Chapman, *British Government Observed* (London: Allen & Unwin, 1963); W. J. Stankiewicz, ed., *Crisis in British Government* (London: Collier-Macmillan, 1967); Trevor Smith, *Anti-Politics* (London: Charles Knight & Co., 1972); Frank Stacey, *British Government, 1966 to 1975* (London: Oxford University Press, 1975); Samuel Brittan, *Left or Right: The Bogus Dilemma* (London: Secker & Warburg, 1968).
31. Chapman, *op. cit.*; Michael R. Gordon, 'Civil Servants, Politicians, and Parties: Shortcomings in the British Policy Process', *Comparative*

Politics, IV (Oct. 1971) 29–58; Richard Rose, 'The Making of Cabinet Ministers', *British Journal of Political Science*, I (Oct. 1971) 393–414.

32. Anthony H. Birch, 'Westminster and Whitehall', in Gwyn and Rose, *op. cit.*, 57–72.
33. Gordon, *op. cit.*, Nevil Johnson, *In Search of the Constitution* (New York: Pergamon Press, 1977) 207; Brittan, *op. cit.*, 167.
34. Philip Norton, *Dissension in the House of Commons, 1945–74* (London: Macmillan, 1975); Philip Norton, *Conservative Dissidents* (London: Temple Smith, 1978); Philip Norton, *Dissension in the House of Commons, 1945–1979* (New York: Oxford University Press, 1980); Rasmussen, *op. cit.*; John E. Schwarz, 'Exploring a New Role in Policy Making: The British House of Commons in the 1970's', *American Political Science Review*, LXXIV (Mar. 1980) 23–37.
35. Lord Hailsham, The *Dilemma of Democracy* (London: Collins, 1978); Johnson, *op. cit.*
36. William L. Miller and Myles Mackie, 'The Electoral Cycle and the Asymmetry of Government and Opposition Popularity', *Political Studies*, XXI (Sept. 1973) 263–79.
37. 'Do Not Ask for Whom the Bell Tolls', *British Politics Group Newsletter*, no. 25 (Summer 1981) 3–4; 'Reselection Is Taking Its Toll', *British Politics Group Newsletter*, no. 28 (Spring 1982) 3–5; 'Labour Party: Where Militant Matters', *The Economist* (3 Apr. 1982) 23–4.
38. Samuel E. Finer, *Adversary Politics and Electoral Reform* (London: Wigram, 1975); Lord Hailsham, *op. cit.;* 'Blowing Up a Tyranny', *The Economist* (5 Nov. 1977) 11–16; Samuel E. Finer, *The Changing British Party System, 1945–1979* (Washington: American Enterprise Institute, 1980); Johnson, *op. cit.*; Vernon Bogdanor, *The People and the Party System* (New York: Cambridge University Press, 1981).
39. Vernon Bogdanor, *Devolution* (New York: Oxford University Press, 1979).
40. 'Does Local Democracy Exist?', *The Economist*, 2 Feb. 1980, 26–7; Douglas E. Ashford, *Politics and Policy in Britain* (Philadelphia: Temple University Press, 1981) 167–98; Alan Alexander, *Local Government in Britain Since Reorganization* (London: Allen & Unwin, 1982).
41. Douglas E. Ashford, *British Dogmatism and French Pragmatism* (London: Allen & Unwin, 1981).
42. Bogdanor, *The People and the Party System*, pp. 9–93.
43. Anthony King, *Britain Says Yes* (Washington, D.C.: American Enterprise Institute, 1977).
44. David Butler and David Marquand, *European Elections and British Politics* (London: Longman, 1981).
45. Ashford, *Politics and Policy in Britain*, 49–50. For an interpretation somewhat at variance with this one, see Gillian Peele, 'The Developing Constitution', in *Trends in British Politics Since 1945*, ed. Chris Cook and John Ramsden (New York: St. Martin's Press, 1978) 1–27.
46. Johnson, *op. cit.*; Hailsham, *op. cit.*; 'Blowing Up a Tyranny', *op. cit.*
47. *Random House College Dictionary* (rev. edn; New York: Random House, 1975) p. 857. See Richard Rose, 'Models of Governing', *Comparative Politics*, V (July 1973) 465–96.

48. Other models are, of course, possible. Various Marxist models are offered by Tom Nairn, *The Break-Up of Britain* (Atlantic Highlands, N.J.: Humanities Press, 1977); Robert Moss, *The Collapse of Democracy* (New Rochelle, N.Y.: Arlington House, 1976); and Haseler, *op. cit*. A recent popular model can be variously labeled – 'ungovernable interests', 'pluralistic stagnation', or 'corporatism'. See W.J.M. Mackenzie, 'Models of English Politics', in *Studies in British Politics*, ed. Richard Rose (3rd edn, New York: St. Martin's Press, 1976) 5–15; Samuel H. Beer, *British Politics in the Collectivist Age* (New York: Vintage Books, 1969); Beer, *Britain Against Itself*; Haseler, *op. cit*.; Anthony Burgess, *1985* (Boston: Little, Brown, 1978). Aside from increased trade union power, what this model implies is unclear. A useful survey and critique of corporatism is Alfred Diamant, 'Bureaucracy and Public Policy in Neocorporatist Settings: Some European Lessons', *Comparative Politics*, XIV (Oct. 1981) 101–24.
49. David Braybrooke and Charles E. Lindblom, *A Strategy of Decision* (New York: Free Press, 1963). Samuel H. Beer, *The British Political System* (New York: Random House, 1974); Richard Rose, 'England: a Traditionally Modern Political Culture', in *Political Culture and Political Development*, ed. Lucien W. Pye and Sidney Verba (Princeton, N.J.: Princeton University Press, 1965) 83–129; Richard Rose, *Politics in England* (3rd edn, Boston: Little, Brown, 1980) 374–5.
50. Once again, Irish exceptionalism exists.
51. Kenneth N. Waltz, *Foreign Policy and Democratic Politics* (Boston: Little, Brown, 1967); Max Nicholson, *The System* (London: Hodder & Stoughton, 1967); Keith Thomas, 'The United Kingdom', in *Crises of Political Development in Europe and the United States*, ed. Raymond Grew (Princeton University Press, 1978) 41–97; Ashford, *op. cit*.; Smith, *op. cit*.
52. Anthony King, 'Overload: Problems of Governing in the 1970's', *Political Studies*, XXIII (Sept. 1975) 284–96; Richard Rose and B.G. Peters, *Can Government Go Bankrupt*? (New York: Basic Books, 1978).
53. Kavanagh, 'New Bottles for New Wines: Changing Assumptions About British Politics', p. 9.
54. Rose, *Politics in England*, p. 1.
55. Nossiter, *op. cit*.; Leslie Lenkowsky, 'Welfare in the Welfare State', in Tyrrell, *op. cit*., 144–66; Ronald Inglehart, *The Silent Revolution* (Princeton University Press, 1977); Alan Marsh, 'The 'Silent Revolution', Value Priorities, and the Quality of Life in Britain', *American Political Science Review*, LXIX (Mar. 1975) 21–30.
56. Daniel Bell, *The Coming of Post-Industrial Society* (New York: Basic Books, 1973); Zbigniew Brzezinski, *Between Two Ages: America's Role in the Technetronic Era* (New York: Viking Press, 1971); Inglehart, *op. cit*.
57. Roger W. Benjamin, *The Limits of Politics* (University of Chicago Press, 1980); John Robertson, 'Post-Industrial Development and the Implications for International Trade and Public Authority', paper presented at meeting of International Studies Association, Los Angeles, 1980.

58. Samuel Huntington, 'Post-Industrial Politics: How Benign Will It Be?', *Comparative Politics*, VI (Jan. 1974) 163–91.
59. Even some of the writers who argue that Britain is moving in a post-industrial direction view this development as being not as rapid as similar movements in other states. See Inglehart, *op. cit.;* Marsh, *op. cit*.
60. Mark Kesselman, 'Over-institutionalization and Political Constraint: The Case of France', *Comparative Politics*, III (Oct. 1970) 21–44; Kavanagh, 'An American Science of British Politics', p. 265; Rose, *Politics in England*, p. 1. See also William B. Gwyn, 'The Ombudsman in Britain: a Qualified Success in Government Reform', paper presented at meeting of British Politics Group, New York, 1981.

2 Is Parliament Revolting?

Jorgen S. Rasmussen

'I'd die to get into Parliament. If I could get elected and serve only six months, I'd die happily.' When a former Liberal candidate said this to me in 1960, I took the words simply as a bit of hyperbole. Now I would be hard pressed to suppress incredulous laughter. Can there be anyone in Britain in the 1980s who holds Parliament in that esteem? If Britain has become a negative model – an example of what other political systems should seek to avoid – no institution of the British political system has suffered a greater fall in prestige than has Parliament.

In the mid-19th century when revolutions swept Europe, the revolutionaries sought not a Marxist proletarian dictatorship, but a British parliamentary system. Now the British Parliament comes closer to revolting people than to having people revolt for it. When pollsters asked Britons to rate 'the honesty and ethical standards' of people in seven different occupations, while 70 per cent rated doctors high, only 13 per cent were willing to do the same for MPs.[1] Young people – those 15 to 24 – held an even more jaundiced view. Although more than half of them (54 per cent) mentioned the police(!) as among the two or three groups of people for which they had the most respect, only five per cent felt that way about MPs.[2]

These negative public attitudes may well have undermined MPs' self-confidence. Little more than half (53 per cent) of the MPs interviewed consider MPs themselves to be an occupational group 'essential to Britain's prosperity', while two-thirds of them regard accountants this way and 93 per cent accord this label to chartered engineers.[3] This suggests that MPs see themselves as contributing little to meliorating Britain's most important problem. Even more damning is the fact that little more than a third (36 per cent) of the MPs feel that MPs 'perform their job to a high standard'.

BRITISH THEORIES OF REPRESENTATION

So basic and prevalent is the dissatisfaction with Parliament that, although Britain is known for a piecemeal, patching approach to governmental reform, a fundamental examination of the institution in the context of representational theory is required. Beer's classic work on British politics traces the development of British thought on representation.[4] The Old Tory view permitted MPs little or no policy role and confined them to being local ombudsmen. In the 19th century both the Old Whig and the Liberal conception expanded MPs' role to include a policy component. Although the former stressed representation of the interests of corporate bodies and the latter of individuals, yet both agreed that MPs were not merely to transmit the will of the people, but were to deliberate for the common good of the whole community.

Radical thought, or what we now would call participatory democracy or Bennite Labourism, provided a divergent view. It saw local party organization not as a help to MPs in gaining re-election, but as a channel through which people could play a role in policy-making and have greater control over who served in Parliament. Although the mainstream of representational theory was to flow in other channels in 20th century Britain, in one respect Radical thought proved to be a precursor of the theories that did become predominant. Just as Radicalism de-emphasized Parliament's policy role, so Socialist and Tory Democracy rejected it. Both regard MPs as party representatives, thus confining their role to support for the policy decisions made by party leaders.

Beer's historical analysis can be enhanced by combining it with Loewenberg and Patterson's more theoretical discussion of the linkages between legislator and constituent. They offer a taxonomy of three dimensions – component, style, and focus. The first dimension deals with the substance of legislator responsiveness – whether the legislator seeks to provide policy, symbolic, public goods, or service output.[5] Style deals with the extent to which a legislater feels bound by his or her constituents.[6] Focus is the nature and location of the group which the legislator attempts to represent.[7]

The symbolic component has a fair amount in common with the service one, both being affected to a considerable extent by an MP's availability to constituents. Parliament's defects do not appear to lie in these areas. The negative feelings discussed earlier seem to be directed mainly toward Parliament as an institution or MPs as a collectivity. When Britons are asked whether they are satisfied with their own MP, more than half are (56 per cent) and only a fifth are dissatisfied (the rest don't know).[8] A study of the electoral value of constituency service makes clear that the criteria used by most constituents in rating their MP were primarily the MP's personal characteristics and availability – the latter clearly a measure of the MP's industriousness in serving the constituency, in peforming the ombudsman role.[9]

Thus Parliament's failures are the product of lack of MP policy and public goods responsiveness. Since these two components have some aspects in common and since MPs can provide some public goods responsiveness under the private bill procedure, confining the discussion to the policy component is desirable for the sake of clarity. Figure 2.1 indicates how the representational theories discussed by Beer can be fitted into an adapted version of the Loewenberg and Patterson taxonomy.

Two features of this classification are especially noteworthy: (1) only the Radical theory is concerned with representation of a subnational constituency and (2) all three of the most recent theories confine MPs to the delegate style, thus permitting them little input in the policy process. The full significance of these features can best be explained by contrasting the behaviour of MPs a century and a half ago with now and by examining how this behaviour was modified by changes in British political and governmental institutions, which changes in turn produced the development of representational thought which Beer has traced.

REPRESENTATION DURING 'THE GOLDEN AGE'

Once Governments no longer were able to control Parliament by patronage and corruption (as had been the practice under the Old Tory theory of representation), 'no one could be sure how a member would vote on a particular issue except that he would please himself. . . . He regarded himself as sent to Parliament to use his best judgement about the *country's* [emphasis added] affairs and to vote accordingly'.[10]

Prior to the first Reform Act, little value was accorded to representation of local interests. Dunwich had slid into the sea and Old Sarum was a vacant field where sheep grazed. Both returned two members to Parliament, while the growing industrial towns of Manchester and

FIGURE 2.1 *Representational theories classified by types of legislative responsiveness*

<table>
<tr><th rowspan="3">style</th><th colspan="6">focus</th></tr>
<tr><th colspan="2">geographical area</th><th colspan="2">party</th><th colspan="2">group</th></tr>
<tr><th>local</th><th>national</th><th>local</th><th>national</th><th>national</th><th>local</th></tr>
<tr><td>trustee</td><td></td><td>Liberal</td><td></td><td></td><td>Old Whig</td><td></td></tr>
<tr><td>delegate</td><td>Radical</td><td></td><td></td><td>Tory Democracy</td><td colspan="2">Socialist Democracy</td></tr>
</table>

Birmingham had none. Such rotten boroughs did not greatly trouble the political élite because they believed in the idea of virtual representation. Despite lacking MPs, Manchester and Birmingham were said to be represented in Parliament because they were part of the country and Parliament worked for the good of the nation. Any particular local interests that the people of Manchester and Birmingham might wish to have considered in the policy-process not only did not need voicing, but would be inappropriate to inject into the process.

Such an argument should sound especially familiar to Americans. The same views had been pressed on the colonists in the previous century to try to convince them that they indeed were represented in the British Parliament even though they could not vote for a representative. Their interests were being taken into consideration, indeed were voiced by some members. So what need was there for them to have to vote for someone to be their representative? The residents of Manchester and Birmingham found the argument little more convincing than had the colonists before them. None the less, the fact that such an argument was made indicates the prevalence of the view that no necessary connection exists between geography and membership in the national legislature.

After the first Reform Act, however, MPs did begin to represent local policy interests. 'It was no longer possible for a candidate merely to offer them his services in Parliament. Electors began to wish to know what a candidate stood for. The custom became general of getting out in a printed election address the policies which the candidate proposed to support in Parliament'.[11] Aydelotte's study of Parliamentary dissent during the period between the first and second Reform Acts found that the ' 'focus' of representation . . . appears to have been, for most of these MPs, more local than national'.[12] MPs took positions on bills 'appropriate for the needs of their own constituencies . . . differences in policy between Members of Parliament reflected the circumstances of the different kinds of constituencies that they represented'.[13]

While some of these MPs were Radicals, the representative role which Aydelotte found MPs to be playing during this period does not fall in same category as Radical representational theory in Figure 2.1. He was unable to find evidence that MPs were constrained to take the policy positions which they did, that they felt bound in any way to serve as delegates for constituency policy preferences. The relationship was one in which MPs were in tune with the desires of their constituents and represented their preferences of their own volition as a matter of course.[14] The key institutional point about this pattern of behaviour is that it was the absence of disciplined Parliamentary parties that permitted MPs to link themselves to their constituents in this fashion. The constituents to which they were linked, the interests which they represented, however, were élite, not mass ones.

None the less, linked to constituents in a trustee, rather than a delegate, style and unconstrained by party discipline, MPs wielded considerable power. This was the almost mythological golden age of Parliament. 'Only in the period between the two Reform Acts can it be said·that the House of Commons constitued a regular part of the decision-making process.'[15] 'The private members could monopolize the lion's share of such parliamentary time as existed, and monopolize it they did.'[16] Evidence of the diverse local interests being represented in this process is the growth of non-party votes from a quarter of all divisions in 1836 to a third in 1850 and a half in 1860.[17] The type of votes which we now regard as normal – those in which the overwhelming majority of the Government party votes in one lobby and the overwhelming majority of the Opposition in the other – occurred in little more than fifth of all divisions in 1836 and then declined even lower – 16 per cent in 1850 and 6 per cent in 1860.

Furthermore, the Government could not obtain the unified support of its nominal followers even when it put on the whips, which it did only half to two-thirds of the time. In 1836 a party vote occurred only in half of the divisions in which the Government issued a whip; by 1850 the proportion had declined to little more than a third and in 1860 it was a quarter. Party votes, in fact, occurred more often in those divisions which the Government did not whip. The result was that in both 1850 and 1860 the Government actually whipped a greater proportion of the non-party votes than it did of the party votes.[18]

In the light of current legislative–executive relations in Britain one wonders how the system managed to function at all during the mid-19th century. Stalemate like that of Third and Fourth Republic France was avoided by the 'amazing' fact "that when faced with a straight plea by the government for special treatment the general consensus of opinion in the House supported that request."[19] 'Faced with ministers pleading the need for time to facilitate the expedition of official business . . . the House constantly gave way.'[20] Also important was the nature of dissent. In both parties rebellions tended to be extremist ones – votes in which a group on a wing of the party voted against the leaders of both parties, who agreed on their position – rather than cross-votes in which part of a party broke off to vote with its opponents.[21] None the less, during the 1850s the Government was defeated on whipped divisions 106 times and during the 1860s 97 times.[22]

In the latter part of the 19th century several developments altered MPs' representational role. Before examining these, however, it is worth inquiring just what the Commons accomplished with its great power during the golden era. The high esteem in which Parliament was held in the 19th and early 20th centuries derived not so much from its specific policy output – unfamiliar to most people both at home and abroad – as from Britain's reputation for stability. Other European countries had monarchs, cabinets, and so forth, but none a parliament like Britain's. So that must be the missing ingredient in stability. Ironically, the British reputation for stability was a relatively recent acquistion. Not until Britain escaped being engulfed by the revolutionary excesses unleashed by the French Revolution in 1789 was Britain regarded as having a talent for responding adaptively to pressures for change so as to diffuse discontent and maintain political stability. The events of the 19th century reinforced this new image of the British. During the period between the two Reform Acts Britain not only managed to avoid the political upheavals that troubled the Continent, but also was able to transform its economy by becoming the first industrial nation. More than any other British political institution, Parliament was credited with the ability to process demands for change so efficiently that political order could be maintained even during a period of major social and economic change.

In the last quarter of the 20th century most people have forgotten that despite the maintenance of the political order, the 19th century hardly was a tranquil time for Britain. Before the first Reform Bill could be passed to extend the franchise, Britain had had to experience both urban and rural riots, London troops put on alert prepared to defend the government from mobs, and an attempt to break the monetary system as a means to prevent rule by a military hero, the Duke of Wellington.

The temper of the times is nicely summed up in a comment related to rebuilding the House of Commons. When an accidental fire destroyed the Commons in 1834, the decision was to rebuild in the same location. One of the chief reasons, cited by Robert Peel (not only Prime Minister during this period, but also the founder of the London police), was 'the facility which the Thames offered for escaping from inflamed mobs'.[23] Sir Robert's precautions probably were well taken. The years of the building of the new Commons chamber were the period of Chartism. The demands of the Chartists produced widespread disorders.

How did Parliament respond to such turmoil? It did pass electoral reform bills and prosperity did occur from time to time to improve the condition of the workers. Parliament hardly was in the forefront of reform, however, actively processing demands so as to maintain satisfaction with the existing system. Gilbert and Sullivan's judgement levied upon the House of Lords during the Napoleonic wars seems not inappropriate: Parliament 'did nothing in particular and did it very well'. Should this be regarded as too harsh a judgement, we must at least conclude that Parliament's activity during its so-called golden age corresponds more closely to the grudging adaptation model of change in Britain than it does to the piecemeal, gradual evolution one.

THE TRANSFORMATION OF THE MP'S ROLE

Perhaps it was the political élite's underlying recognition that the accomplishments of the Commons were not that remarkable that facilitated a change in its procedures. The growing complexity of an industrializing society greatly expanded Parliament's business, as did the developmental problems of a worldwide empire. The political executive felt the need for some means other than merely relying on the goodwill of MPs to process this business effectively.[24]

The expansion of the electorate led to fully developed national party organizations and these, in turn, were another major factor in altering the representational role of MPs. Norton argues that voters newly enfranchised by the second Reform Act were 'too ill-educated to appreciate the discriminating political judgement of independently minded Members in parliamentary cross-voting. Members of Parliament increasingly became reliant upon their newly developed constituency associations . . . while at the same time having to support the general policy of one of the political parties with which sections of the electorate could identify'.[25] Thus elections came to turn on the promises for legislation which Governments and Oppositions – not individual MPs – made during elections with the winner being conceded a mandate to implement those promises.[26]

While these general trends provided pressure for reform of the Commons' procedures, the main impetus for fundamental change came from a specific problem – Irish obstructionism. The nationalist MPs were unwilling to play by what everyone else understood to be the rules of the game – that a minority in the Commons ultimately would give way and would allow the Cabinet's bills to get through. The nationalists employed Parliament's permissive rules to bring the body to a complete halt. They sought to prevent any action on any matter until such time as they were able to coerce the majority into granting what they, the minority, sought. The shared values, the restraint which had made the system operable earlier in the century no longer existed.

From 1877 to 1882 and again from 1896 to 1902 major changes were made in the Commons' procedures.[27] These included closure and guillotine motions to limit debate so that decisions could be taken on bills and rules concerning the agenda designed to give a high priority to the Government's legislative program. That nationalism – an issue dealing with the adequacy of representation of regional interests in central decision-making – should have been the ultimate catalyst responsible for changes in the Commons' procedure greatly restricting the role of the individual Member is instructive.

The changes in procedure were accompanied by changes in party cohesion. Berrington argues that Government control over the business of the Commons produced high cohesion rather than high cohesion being the factor that gave the Government control over the timetable.[28] Whatever the causal sequence, party cohesion did begin to grow during the 1870s and by the 1880s had become quite high. Non-party votes fell to only 18 per cent of all divisions in 1871 and subsequently accounted for only a few percentage points of all divisions.[29] Opposed party votes did not become the predominant type of vote, however, until the 1890s.[30] None the less, the Government had come to whip the vast majority (80 per cent or more) of the divisions and by the 1880s when it did so was able to get a party vote in the great majority of cases (85 per cent or more).[31] Thus Government defeats in whipped divisions fell to only 38 during the 1870s, remained virtually at that same level during the next decade, and dropped to only 13 during the final decade of the century.[32]

Although dissent had declined, it appears to have continued to be motivated to a considerable extent by an attempt to represent constituency interests. Berrington notes 'the large part played by territorial interests in the crossbench deviations from party rule. The agricultural interest and the Londoner . . . , the dairy lobby . . . and the graziers . . . these examples show that the material claims of the constituency were often more urgent than the promptings of conscience'.[33]

While representation of constituency interests of these types still could be tolerated to some extent, representation of Irish nationalism could not. Britain would not permit anything analogous to the filibuster of the US Senate. The British were not conversant with J. C. Calhoun's ideas concerning concurrent majorities. The Cabinet's job was to govern; local interests were not to impede implementation of the mandate which the Cabinet had won on the national issues in the election. This was the crucial point, for although the procedural changes were intended to deal specifically with the problem of Irish obstructionism, underlying them was an unarticulated theory of representation of considerable importance.

The procedural changes implicitly asserted that Parliament should not be regarded as an institution representing the detailed policy preferences of the people organized in constituencies. Its role instead was to be that of a validator or legitimator. It was to be a forum in which the *Cabinet's* policies could be challenged and defended. Once this had occurred, their implementation could be regarded as legitimate; having endured the trial of public discussion the vote to approve them should be virtually automatic.

The key aspect of this conceptualization of Parliament's role is that it did not provide for representation of constituency interests. The general principles of Cabinet policies and their general effect were to be discussed: localism was out of place in such debates. MPs were elected in local constituencies simply as a matter of convenience of electoral mechanics, not because of any desire to inject local policy preferences into the decision-making process. Thus, for example, what had been detailed examination of government spending in the Commons' debates in the first part of the 19th century had become general discussion of policy questions selected by Opposition leaders in the latter part of the century.[34] As these views came to be accepted toward the close of the 19th century the Commons lost its elective function to the voters and its legislative function to the Cabinet.[35] The mess of pottage which it got in return was the ability to talk about what the Cabinet was doing – an activity that occurred as well with equal impact in a great many pubs.

THE REASONS FOR FAILING TO PERCEIVE THE PROBLEM

While the growth of a modern party system and the expansion of the franchise severed the links which gave local élites representation in the policy-process, no equivalent links for mass or popular views developed in their place. Ironically, the growth of democracy helped to curtail public participation in policy-making by undermining the foundations of representational theory. The British never adequately conceptualized the representational role in a mass democracy. This failure has gone largely unnoticed for three reasons, the first of which is the pace of reform.

Party organization developed gradually; the franchise was expanded in five installments over a period of a century. Such evolutionary growth usually is regarded as one of the hallmarks of the British genius for stable political development. Incremental change is thought to be less dislocating, more easy to digest. But when first a room, and then a wing, and then a second story is added to the old house, the change never is great enough at any time for someone to recognize that the nature of the structure has been transformed and the time has arrived for a thorough remodeling. The pace of reform in Britain meant that the political system never felt required to come to grips with a modern theory of mass representation.

Secondly, the British long have pretended that significant regional differences of political importance do not exist in their country. Since it is difficult to believe that they really think Britain is homogeneous, this pretence may have been a means of trying to deny the problems of diversity – Ireland, for instance – they knew only too well existed. Whatever the reason, the product was functional representation – representation of particular social groups regardless of their geographical location, a view most fully embodied in the Socialist Democracy theory of representation. In so far as one denies the existence of important regional interests of contrasting views, one obviously will perceive little need to conceptualize mass representation so as to provide adequate channels for voicing local diversity.

The third reason why the inadequate conceptualization of representation attracted little comment derives from the nature of the party system. For most of the century since the Reform Act of 1884 created something approaching a mass electorate in Britain (only then could half of the *men*, to say nothing of the women, vote) Britain has *not* had a two-party system. This was not only because the Labour party replaced the Liberal party (a development related to the class conception of representation), but also because of such groups as the Irish Nationalists, the Liberal Unionists, the Asquithian Liberals, the Lloyd George Liberals, the Liberal Nationals, and others. These were not just factions within parties, like the Tribune Group in the Labour party, but distinct separate party organizations. Only once in 14 elections from 1885 through 1931 did the two largest parties manage to win 90 per cent or more of the seats in the Commons between them and on one occasion dropped as low as controlling only 66 per cent. Although the two-party share of the Commons seats never has fallen below 90 per cent since 1935, yet in the last three general elections the two leading parties have won only three-quarters or four-fifths of the popular vote. Thus by even a generous definition Britain has had a two-party system for only about a third of the last century. Whatever the British may have pretended about their political homogeneity, the reality was a party system expressing diversity. The greater the fractionalization of the party system the greater the scope for representation of diverse interests. Since these interests were in fact being represented, whatever the theory, there was little pressure to develop a more realistic and comprehensive conceptualization of representation.

Fractionalization is a likely result of any attempt to implement a mandate theory of elections by means of extraordinarily disciplined legislative parties. Those who argued against trying to reform American parties along the lines of the so-called British responsible party system stressed the diversity of the United States and pointed out the problems this would produce should we attempt to maintain high party cohesion. Canada was a highly instructive example.[36] Where a country of continental dimension and diversity tried to operate the British Parliamentary system, the result was to fractionalize the party system. The nation's diversities could not be contained within only two highly disciplined parties. What was lost sight of in Britain, but which has become increasingly apparent in the last decade, is that the United Kingdom as well is too diverse for all relevant political interests to be contained within only two highly cohesive parties, especially when the electorate (unlike the situation in most of the 19th century) is a mass, well-educated one.

The excessive rigidity which highly disciplined legislative parties produced in the British party system was, in fact, already apparent before the end of the 19th century. Irish nationalism was not just a matter of the obstructionism of those MPs elected in Ireland; it was an issue that broke the Liberal party. Parliamentary party cohesiveness had developed to such a high level that the Liberal Unionists were unable to represent the local interests of their constituents on this issue and still remain within the party. Liberal Unionist strength was related to geography – their strongholds were concentrated in certain areas and types of seats.[37] The most detailed analysis of turn-of-the-century

British elections concludes that 'regional factors, then, were of considerable importance in British politics in this period . . . . In a period which was dominated by the Irish question more than any other single issue, we have to accept that British political behaviour was far more sectional than it is today, and that social class was not as much of a political watershed as it has been in recent years'.[38] At a time, then, when Britain was fully industrializing and the Labour party was being born, class was not a preeminent, nationalizing issue.

If not at such a time, then when did class function in this fashion? As Butler and Stokes' classic study indicates, the inter-war period was a transitional one in the rising importance of the class issue and not until after World War II was it clearly of predominant importance in voting behaviour.[39] But as their work and that of Rose indicates, this importance was short-lived; less than a quarter of a century later, by the close of the 1960s, class was on the wane in its impact on voting behaviour.[40] Thus only for a short time following World War II is it sensible to think of British politics as revolving around a single issue, of one class against another throughout the country. Both before and since that period local concerns have been important in British political behaviour.

The British, however, have sought ever since the latter years of the 19th century to operate a parliamentary system that has flown in the face of this fact. They have refused to permit representation of local interests. True, many MPs have developed close relations with their constituents and have responded to their needs. But they do so as ombudsmen or social workers, not as representatives. They are not permitted to represent their constituents' interests in the policy process.

Could they be permitted to do so? Such a question might seem strange since the discussion above of the operation of the Commons in the mid-19th century is evidence that MP independence can be allowed. So influential, however, are the practices which have prevailed in the Commons in the 20th century that highly cohesive parties have been made virtually a functional requisite for the British Parliamentary system. Even such a friend of increased MP dissent as Norton argues that the fusion of powers system requires high party cohesion to work effectively. In his view the structure of British Parliamentary institutions helps to 'facilitate the emergence of this cohesion'.[41]

Yet Norton's work also makes clear that such cohesion is not essential. One of his main contributions has been to establish that, contrary to widely held belief, defeat for a Government even on important legislation is not in itself withdrawal of confidence. Only defeat on a motion of confidence does this.[42] The fact that significant numbers of MPs began to realize in the 1970s that defeat for the Government need not mean its resignation is the primary reason for the great increase in dissident voting during this period. Only if one believes with Lowell that rejection of any Government measure 'indicates a general loss of confidence in the policy of the party in power and a preference for another body of leaders with a different policy'[43] does high cohesion become essential for the British system. For as Lowell himself granted, were this 'not so the Swiss system of remaining in office, but yielding on the point at issue, would be far more reasonable'.

What the Lowell conception does is to demand total unity on all issues and it is this which has led to what is increasingly being recognized as the bane of British politics – adversary politics or the business of the Opposition is to oppose. Faced with behaviour of this type, the Government, naturally, is unwilling to concede anything.[44] Thus compromise, in supposedly pragmatic and practical Britain, becomes less common than it was in the supposedly dogmatic, ideological politics of Third and Fourth Republic France. Were opposition to Government measures regarded as expression of local interests rather than partisan posturing, a Government could respond without loss of face. An adequate conceptualization of the representative role of MPs would help to buttress the insight of the 1970s that defeat on anything short of a vote of confidence is not a withdrawal of confidence and does not necessitate dissolution and elections.

POPULAR INTEREST IN A NEW REPRESENTATION ROLE

To what extent can a reform of Parliament so as to provide for more adequate representation of constituency interests be regarded as a response to popular concerns and desires? The popular sentiment to which it most obviously would respond is devolution. Although limited turnout helped to prevent implementation of devolution proposals in 1979, this should not obscure the fact that a majority of those Scots who voted favoured devolution. The point is not that they wanted Scotland to be independent – a majority believe that this either is very unlikely to happen or definitely will not happen.[45] Their dissatisfaction appears to be mainly a feeling that the distinct interests of Scotland are not adequately represented under current arrangements. The Scots clearly regard themselves as a distinct group. Asked whether they consider themselves 'first and foremost as being Scottish or as British', 77 per cent say Scottish, with the proportion being even higher among manual workers. As for securing representation for this distinctiveness in Parliament, they showed a relatively high level of support for a little discussed, fairly inchoate reform. Forty-five per cent said that were devolution to be implemented throughout Britain with each region having its own regional assembly, they would favour having these assembiles elect representatives to a reconstituted House of Lords. While a third of the Scots were uncertain whether this was a good idea, less than a quarter opposed it. This seems to suggest fairly substantial feeling that Scotland needs something like the US Senate so that its regional interests can be represented more adequately than they are at present.

Better representation of constituency interests would respond not only to nationalism; its relevance extends beyond the devolution issue. Two-thirds of the *British* population feels that MPs 'lose touch with the people pretty quickly' (nearly a fifth strongly agree with this view) and only a quarter dissent.[46] To some extent the idea of 'keeping in touch' relates to the symbolic and service components in Loewenberg and Patterson's typology of representation, as well as to the policy component, which is the particular concern here. Therefore, it is highly significant to note that when constituents were asked about their expectations of an MP's proper role, although helping people and keeping in touch were important, the most common response was protecting the interests of the constituency.[47] Here is where the dissatisfaction with Parliament seems to focus, for only two-fifths of those surveyed regarded the House of Commons as 'representative of the views of the general public as a whole'. while a third thought it was not and a quarter was uncertain.[48] Clearly the average Briton has serious reservations about the policy links between the voter and the MP. This hardly should be surprising if one recalls Norton's view that one of the factors in the decline of MPs' independence was the inability of an ill-educated electorate to appreciate the nuances of cross-voting. The British electorate now obviously is much better educated and informed than it was a century ago. Furthermore, many of these more politically aware Britons want to participate more fully in the political process. Whatever may have been the accuracy of Almond and Verba's portrait of British political culture in the 1950s, currently a contrast between a participatory United States and a deferent Britain seems misdrawn.[49]

MP RESPONSIVENESS TO LOCAL POLICY CONCERNS

The high level of Parliamentary party cohesiveness has constrained MPs from responding adequately to these concerns. Perhaps constrains is the wrong word, since, as Richards observes, 'On most issues the formation of a clear party line at Westminister *provides protection against local criticism*. [Emphasis added.]'[50] None the less, evidence of at least some MP reponse to constituent expectations regarding representational roles would help to establish that such a link is not just a matter of abstract speculation. On issues for which a party line is not formed, on matters of conscience where free votes are allowed, Richards finds a pattern of voting that varies with geographical area.[51] This is to say that when permitted to do so for this relatively narrow range of issues that come up relatively infrequently, MPs do give some evidence of attempting to represent constitutency interest.

But even for issues that are not matters of conscience and which occurred prior to the decline in party discipline in the 1970s, some evidence of MP reponse to constituency interests can be found. A case study of immigration and education policy in the late 1950s to mid-1960s led Schwarz to conclude that 'it has been known for some time that many MPs are constitency-oriented in the sense of performing service tasks for their constituents. The cases here reveal that constituency was also of importance in how Conservative backbenchers behave on questions of public policy during the formative stages of issue development'.[52]

With the growth of intra-party dissent in the 1970s, searching for evidence of MP behaviour responding to constituency interests becomes a bit more feasible. Ideology, however, rather than constituency interests, seems to have been a major factor in increased dissidence. The analyses of both Schwarz and Norton stress the Tribune Group as a persistent and sizable source of dissidence in the Labour party.[53] On the other hand, neither saw the Tribunites as the whole explanation.

Norton observes that even 'without the presence of . . . the Tribune Group, there would still have been a large number of divisions witnessing dissenting votes, but the size of the dissenting lobbies would have been significantly smaller'.[54] As for Government defeats, it was those that saw 'Members from all parts of the Parliamentary Labour Party voting with the Opposition . . . [that was] the most varied and encompassed the greatest number of defeats,' rather than those inflicted by either the party's right or left wings.[55] This is the point that this current study emphasizes; the aim is not to deny that ideology is important in dissent, may even be the most important factor. Rather the argument is that constituency interests are not unimportant and need to be taken account of in any adequate conceptualization of representation.

The key question would seem to be whether MPs from different types of constituencies behave differently in Parliament. Constituencies have been classified by a variety of methods. The most elaborate and sophisticated procedure is that developed by Richard Webber.[56] Webber used 40 variables drawn from the 1971 census to group the 623 British constituencies into 30 clusters. These clusters, in turn, were combined into six families.[57] Evidence that this procedure produces a taxonomy related to partisan political preferences appears in Table 2.1. In October 1974 the Conservatives won a majority – usually a substantial majority – of the seats in 11 of the 13 clusters in each of the first three families. The Labour party won a majority – again, usually substantial – in every cluster, with a single exception, in the last three families.

TABLE 2.1 *Partisan distribution of seats by constituency type for the October 1974 General Election*

Family and cluster	*no of seats*	*per cent held by* Lab	Con	Other
I Suburbs and service centres				
1 Centres of learning	18	17	83	0
2 Service centres with single people	23	43	57	0
3 Outer London suburbs	33	6	94	0
4 Very high status areas	31	0	100	0
II Rural areas and seaside resorts				
5 Areas extremely dependent upon agriculture	21	5	62	33
6 Agricultural areas	39	3	92	5
7 Scottish rural areas	19	11	32	57
8 Resort and retirement areas	30	0	97	3
III Growth areas				
9 Areas of intermediate status and modern housing	24	46	54	0
10 East Midlands/North West small industrial towns	30	30	67	3
11 South Midlands growth areas	35	0	100	0
12 West Midlands growth areas	15	73	27	0
13 Areas of rapid growth	19	26	68	6

IV Stable industrial areas				
14 Conurbation mining areas	18	100	0	0
15 Mining areas	20	100	0	0
16 The Black Country	12	100	0	0
17 Steel and chemical towns	20	100	0	0
18 South Wales valleys	19	89	0	11
19 Poorer urban centres with some non-manufacturing functions	19	79	21	0
20 Metropolitan inter-war suburbs	21	81	19	0
21 Textile areas	40	98	0	2
V Areas dominated by local authority housing				
22 Maritime industrial areas	13	100	0	0
23 Peripheral conurbation council estates	11	100	0	0
24 Scottish industrial areas	20	95	0	5
25 Scottish city constituencies	13	77	15	8
26 Clydeside	10	100	0	0
VI Metropolitan inner areas				
27 Low status inner-London	23	100	0	0
28 Provincial inner areas	19	100	0	0
29 High status central London	6	17	83	0
30 Multi-occupied inner London	12	75	25	0

In some senses some of the constituencies can be regarded as deviants. For example, although the great majority of the constituencies in the centres of learning cluster were held by the Conservatives in October 1974, three went Labour. The Parliamentary behaviour of these three Labour MPs could be expected to be subject to a certain tension – a desire on their part on the one hand to vote with their party and on the other hand to respond to the views of their constituents, whose socioeconomic characteristics typically inclined them toward the Conservatives. Thus they would appear to have a high potential for dissident voting. This would be likely to be dissident voting of a particular type, however. They would be likely to engage in cross-voting, in voting in the Conservative lobby, rather than in left-wing voting – voting in a dissident lobby when the leaders of both Government and the Opposition were united in their stand.

To investigate whether such behaviour occurred, the 218 Labour backbenchers of the 1974–9 Commons were divided into three groups – those from Labour type constituencies, from Conservative type, and from mixed type.[58] The instances of Labour MPs cross-voting in the Conservative lobby were tabulated for the entire Parliament; the results appear in Table 2.2.[59] Labour MPs representing Labour type constituencies were somewhat more loyal to their party than were Labour MPs from other types of constituencies. Not only were Labour MPs not sitting for Labour type seats more likely to dissent, they also were more likely to do so frequently.

TABLE 2.2 *Cross-voting by constituency type*

	Labour type		*mixed*		*Conservative type*	
	no.	*%*	*no.*	*%*	*no.*	*%*
none	46	26.3	2	20	15	15.2
1–5 times	85	48.6	5	50	17	51.5
6 or more times	44	25.1	3	30	11	33.3
	175		10		33	

This analysis can be carried one step further by breaking down the Labour type constituencies into two groups. In some of these clusters – 19, 20, 25, 30 – the Conservatives did manage to win some seats, while in the others they were shut out entirely. Following the current line of argument, Labour MPs from the former clusters might be slightly more subject to some tension in their Parliamentary behaviour than would be those MPs from totally Labour clusters. Table 2.3 indicates that Labour MPs from constituencies in the four specified clusters were no more likely to cross-vote than were Labour MPs from the totally Labour clusters; they were however, more likely to be frequent cross-voters – the proportion doing so being exactly the same as among those Labour MPs representing constitutencies of the Conservative type.

TABLE 2.3 *Cross-voting by constituency sub-type within Labour type*

	no Conservative victories		*some Conservative victories*	
	no.	*%*	*no.*	*%*
none	37	26.1	9	27.2
1–5 times	72	50.7	13	39.4
6 or more times	33	23.2	11	33.3
	142		33	

Thus variations in constituency socioeconomic characteristics and related partisan political preferences do appear to be linked with MP behaviour and were able to gain some limited expression as the incidence of dissent became more prevalent in the Commons in the latter part of the 1970s.

The relatively limited differences in the percentages in Tables 2.2 and 2.3 may not seem sufficient to be of importance.[60] That they are noteworthy becomes quite evident when a similar analysis is done for the other type of dissident voting – left-wing dissent.[61] In this case MPs representing Labour type constituencies might be expected to dissent more frequently as they tried to represent the interests of a limited section of the population and thus came in conflict with their Governmental leaders, who would need to be more concerned with the general good. But as Table 2.4 indicates this did not occur; constituency type was unrelated to incidence of left-wing dissent.[62] That is to say that left-wing dissent is primarily ideological behaviour and not representation of constituency interests. In such instances the MP would seem to be adhering more to the trustee role of representation rather than the delegate role. (Were the MP functioning as a delegate, it would be of the local party activists rather than of the electorate of the constituency.)

TABLE 2.4 *Left-wing dissent by Constituency type*

	Labour type		*mixed*		*Conservative type*	
	no.	*%*	*no.*	*%*	*no.*	*%*
none	25	14.3	0	0	4	12.1
1–10 times	90	51.4	3	30	18	54.5
11 or more times	60	34.3	7	70	11	33.3
	175		10		33	

Given the importance of the Tribune Group to intra-Labour dissent, the possibility that its members' behaviour accounts for the pattern of dissidence should be examined.[63] Table 2.5 indicates that Tribunite dissent did not distort the results.[64] When the voting records of only those Labour backbenchers who were not members of the Tribune Group are examined, constituency continues to be of some importance for the incidence of cross-voting but not for left-wing dissent.

TABLE 2.5 *Dissent by non-Tribune MPs by constituency type cross-voting*

	Labour type		*Conservative type*	
	no.	*%*	*no.*	*%*
none	40	33.3	5	20.8
1–5 times	61	50.8	13	54.2
6 or more times	19	15.8	6	25.0

Left-wing dissent

	Labour type		*Conservative type*	
	no.	*%*	*no.*	*%*
none	25	20.8	4	16.7
1–10 times	80	66.7	17	70.8
11 or more times	15	12.5	3	12.5

Non-Tribune Group MPs representing Conservative type constituencies were more likely to cross-vote and to do so more frequently, but were not appreciably more dissident than those representing Labour type constituencies for left-wing deviation from party voting.[65]

While the question of whether the argument presented here applies to the Opposition, as well as to the Government, backbenchers and to a party in which factions tend to be less well organized and more ephemeral is an interesting one, little can be done to study intra-Conservative dissent in the same fashion for this period. Only six of the constituencies won by Conservative backbenchers in October 1974 were of the Labour type and even adding those of the mixed type brings the total only to 13. The fact that less than a quarter of the 13 MPs from these constituencies never cross-voted during the 1974–9 Parliament, while over 40 per cent of the remaining 207 Conservative backbenchers representing Conservative type constituencies never voted in the Labour lobby in defiance of the party leaders suggests some constituency influence in their case as well. Given the small number, however, this can only be suggestive.

Thus the evidence presented here derives from an analysis of the behaviour of only Labour dissidents during a limited time period and does not utilize sophisticated multi-variate techniques. As such, the findings can only be preliminary. None the less, they are suggestive and tend to support the argument that MPs from differing types of constituencies do behave differently in some circumstances even within the highly disciplined Parliamentary party system that continues to characterize Britain despite the decline in cohesion in the 1970s. The key point that follows from this is that a theory of representation that fails to include roles concerned with representation of local policy interests – whether these be the delegate or the trustee role – is inadequate.

ESCAPING FROM THE DILEMMA OF PARLIAMENTARY REFORM

But, it may be asked, of what practical relevance are these theoretical concerns; what difference does it actually make that the British theory of representation is inadequately conceptualized? Currently the Bennite wing of the Labour party is seeking to resurrect the Radical theory of representation. Ignoring the complaints of its anti-democratic, quasi-revolutionary allies and the questionable sincerity of Benn himself, one can see that a valid point of significance lies at the heart of this conflict – while it is a struggle for personal power, it is not just that. The justifiable objective is to give British citizens a greater sense of input into the political decision-making process than they currently have. One need not go all the way with the Bennites to embrace the delegate role as the only valid one. A mix of delegate and trustee orientations, the politico role delineated by Loewenberg and Patterson,[66] properly linked to local interests, could do a great deal to eliminate much of the current ill feelings directed toward Parliament as an institution.

Adequate conceptualization of representational theory is not just a means of dealing with factionalism in the Labour party. It also is a promising approach to winning the support essential to instituting the reforms that Britain needs. The entire debate about reform of the House of Commons has been argued in an adversary context – the Commons against the Government. How, it has been asked, do we strengthen the Commons so that it can better control the Government? In such a context how can anyone expect the Government to do anything other than stonewall? Why should it concede anything of substance when the declared objective is to weaken it? This is the fundamental dilemma of change of British political institutions – reform can occur only by the support of that institution, the Cabinet, that has no motivation to want reform. There is little point in expecting that the barons of Parliament can stage a Runnymede. And even apart from the power relations involved, the truth is that to this point an adequate intellectual case has not been made for strengthening the Commons. Reform of Parliament has been advocated with little consideration of why it is desirable; strengthening the Commons has been regarded as a self-evident good.

The debate would be a more sensible one and have some hope of bearing fruit in the form of changes of substance, if it were discussed from the viewpoint that British mass democracy has developed in such a way as to distort representational roles. The Commons needs reforming in order to improve the nature, the quality of representation – it is not a matter of a power struggle between executive and legislature. What must be recognized is that Britain is diverse, not the mythical homogeneous land existing only in many American textbooks on British government. The diverse needs and interests of the British people are not being adequately served under the existing system. Pluralistic stagnation in Britain has helped to obscure the real issue by encouraging the idea that representation of large, national interests, rather than of local diversity, is what matters. Focusing on these diverse interests creates the possibility of flexible and varying majorities and thus offers a way to break out of stagnation.

Various packages of reforms can be thought of that would facilitate representation of local diversity. Thus any list is more suggestive than requisite. In terms of practices, full recognition of Norton's point that Governments fall only on no confidence votes should help to continue the loosening of party discipline so that MPs need not regard representation of constituency interests as disloyalty to party leaders. To make MPs more concerned to represent those interests, primary elections are needed. While it would not be impossible to institute these under the current British system, it could be done most easily if the Commons were to have a fixed term of office. As in Sweden, this would require the Cabinet to persuade the Commons to pass its legislation or to accept those modifications insisted upon by the Commons. Any Government which found the Commons' desires totally objectional would have to give way for one that could gain support from the Commons as currently composed. Only in cases of clear deadlock between the executive and the legislature – when no group of leaders could gain sustained support in the Commons – would an election be called ahead of schedule. Devolution, not just to Wales and Scotland, but within England as well, would produce a more flexible system able to respond to British diversity. Reform of the House of Lords could sensibly be coupled with devolution. Members in a House of the Regions could be selected by the regional assemblies with a requirement that anyone representing a region would have to be a resident there.

Changes of this nature would help to develop the link that Britons now feel is missing between them and their government. Without such reforms, steps such as the revision of the Commons' committee system are mere palliatives. They attract a good deal of attention but do little to grapple with the fundamental problem because they fail to understand that the issue is one of adequate conceptualization of representational roles. Coupled with reforms responding to the basic problem, they would make a useful contribution. Until then, however, they are insignificant constitutional tinkering. The time for further patching in British Parliamentary institutions is past; it is time to purchase a new coat even though it is cut from the same old tweed.

NOTES

1. Market & Opinion Research International (MORI), August 1981 poll, reported in *Public Opinion in Great Britain*, Oct. 1981, no. 4.
2. MORI August 1979 poll, reported in *Youth in Britain: Attitudes and Life Style*.
3. MORI summer 1980 poll, reported in *Public Opinion in Great Britain*.
4. Samuel H. Beer, *British Politics in the Collectivist Age* (New York: Knopf, 1965) chs 1–3, but especially pp. 6–7, 15, 33, 34, 40–1, 53, 70.
5. Gerhard Loewenberg and Samuel C. Patterson, *Comparing Legislatures* (Boston: Little Brown, 1979)167–91.
6. Note that in the figure on p. 169, Loewenberg and Patterson, ibid., they mention only the delegate and trustee styles, but in the discussion on pp. 179–82, they add the politico. In order not to unduly complicate the discussion here, only the first two styles will be considered.
7. The three categories provided by Loewenberg and Patterson do not adequately cover possible conflicts between center and periphery, which would make a referent unit at one level hold views in conflict with one of the same type at another level. Thus a local/national contrast needs to be provided for in the focus dimension.
8. MORI January 1981 poll, reported in *Public Opinion in Great Britain*. Although 1000 respondents were polled, only people living in the Stockton, Middlesborough, and Thornaby constituencies were interviewed. Perhaps the MPs from these constituencies were better than the average MP.
9. Bruce Cain, John Ferejohn, and Morris Fiorina, 'Partisanship and Constituency Representation', paper presented to the British Politics Group at the 76th Annual Meeting of the American Political Science Association, Washington, D.C., 28–31 Aug. 1980, pp. 7–9, 24.
10. Ivor Bulmer-Thomas, *The Growth of the British Party System*, vol. I, 1840–1923 (London: Baker, 1965) pp. 69, 80.

11. Ibid., p. 81.
12. William Aydelotte, 'Constituency Influence on the British House of Commons, 1841–1847', in Aydelotte, ed., *The History of Parliamentary Behaviour* (Princeton University Press, 1977) p. 236.
13. Ibid., p. 237.
14. Ibid., pp. 237–45.
15. Philip Norton, *The Commons in Perspective* (New York: Longman, 1981) p. 23.
16. Valerie Cromwell, 'The Losing of the Initiative by the House of Commons, 1780–1914', *Transactions of the Royal Historical Society*, 5th Series (London: 1968) vol. 18, p. 13.
17. Calculated from A. Lawrence Lowell, 'The Influence of Party upon Legislation in England and America', *Annual Report of the American Historical Association for the Year 1901*, vol. I (Washington: Government Printing Office, 1902) p. 532. A non-party vote is one in which, in the case of *both* parties, fewer than nine-tenths of those of its members voting, voted together on the same side. That is to say that in the case of both parties a tenth or more of its voting members broke off to vote in the other lobby.
18. Calculated from ibid., pp. 356, 367, 374.
19. Cromwell, op. cit., p. 18.
20. Ibid., p. 22.
21. Aydelotte, op. cit., pp. 233, 234, 236.
22. Lowell, op. cit., p. 542.
23. Speech reported in *Morning Post*, 10 Feb. 1836, quoted in M. H. Post, ed., *The House of Parliament* (New Haven, Conn.: Yale University Press, 1976) p. 20.
24. Cromwell, op. cit., pp. 15–18.
25. Norton, op. cit., p. 15.
26. Ibid., p. 17.
27. Ibid., pp. 19–20.
28. Hugh Berrington, 'Partisanship and Dissidence in the Nineteenth-Century House of Commons', *Parliamentary Affairs*, 21 (Autumn 1968) 363, 371–2.
29. Calculated from Lowell, op. cit., p. 532.
30. Ibid., and Berrington, op. cit., p. 344.
31. Calculated from Lowell, op. cit., pp. 382, 395, 404, 416.
32. Ibid., p. 542.
33. Berrington, op. cit., pp. 360–1.
34. Cromwell, op. cit., 20–1.
35. Norton, op. cit., p. 18.
36. Leon Epstein, 'A Comparative Study of Canadian Parties', *American Political Science Review*, LVIII (Mar. 1968) 46–59.
37. Michael Kinnear, *The British Voter: an Atlas and Survey since 1885* (London: Batsford, 1968) pp. 18, 98.
38. Henry Pelling, *Social Geography of British Elections 1885-1910* (London: Macmillan, 1967) p. 418. See also his comments on pp. 414 and 416.
39. David Butler and Donald Stokes, *Political Change in Britain* (2nd college edn; New York: St. Martin's Press, 1976) pp. 109–38.

40. Ibid., pp. 139–52 and Richard Rose, 'Britain: Simple Abstractions and Complex Realities', Richard Rose, ed., *Electoral Behaviour: a Comparative Handbook* (New York: The Free Press, 1974) pp. 523–33.
41. Norton, op. cit., p. 18. See also the comments of Lowell, op. cit., p. 332.
42. Ibid., pp. 68, 225–6.
43. Lowell, op. cit., p. 332.
44. *Loc. cit.*
45. MORI November 1981 poll in Scotland, reported in *Public Opinion in Great Britain*, no. 5, Oct.–Dec. 1981, p. 53. The information in the rest of this paragraph is from the same source, pp. 55, 56.
46. Alan Marsh, *Protest and Political Consciousness* (London: Sage Publications, 1977) p. 115.
47. Cain *et al.*, op. cit., pp. 6–7, 23. Protecting the interests of the constituency could be regarded, in part, as relevant to the public goods component of representation. Even if that is the case, its relevance to the policy component as well would seem unquestionable.
48. Norman Webb and Robert Wybrow, eds., *The Gallup Report* (London: Sphere Books, 1981) p. 28.
49. Gabriel Almond and Sidney Verba, *The Civic Culture* (Boston: Little, Brown, 1965) p. 315 and Dennis Kavanagh, 'Political Culture in Great Britain: the Decline of the Civic Culture', Almond and Verba, eds, *The Civic Culture Revisited* (Boston: Little Brown, 1980) pp. 133–6, 149–60.
50. Peter Richards, *The Backbenchers* (London: Faber, 1972) p. 157.
51. Ibid., p. 159. See also Richards, *Parliament and Conscience* (London: Allen & Unwin, 1970) pp. 187–8.
52. John Schwarz, 'The Impact of Constituency on the Behaviour of British Conservative MPs', *Comparative Political Studies*, 8 (Apr. 1975) 88.
53. John Schwarz, 'The Quiet Revolution: the Awakening of the British House of Commons in the 1970s', paper presented at the 75th Annual Meeting of the American Political Science Association, Washington, D.C., 31 Aug.–3 Sept. 1979, pp. 27–8 and also p. 29. Compare this with the published version of the paper, 'Exploring a New Role in Policy Making: the British House of Commons in the 1970s', *American Political Science Review*, 74 (Mar. 1980) 30–3.
54. Philip Norton, *Dissension in the House of Commons 1974–1979* (Oxford: Clarendon Press, 1980) p. 441.
55. Ibid., p. 443.
56. Richard Webber, *Parliamentary constituencies: a Socio-economic Classification* (Occasional Paper 13; London: Office of Population Censuses and Surveys, 1978).
57. The variables dealt primarily with the age structure of the population, its socio-economic status, and its employment; with the composition of households in the constituency and the type and quality of housing there; and with the transportation patterns. The first grouping lost 29.2 per cent of the original variance and the second grouping into families lost another 26.2 per cent. Ibid., p. 4.
58. The Labour type are those in which Labour won a majority of seats in the cluster and in the relevant family – specifically clusters 14 through 28 and 30. The Conservative type are where the Conservatives won a majority at

each level – constituencies in clusters 1–3, 5–7, 9, 10, and 13. The mixed type are those in which Labour won a majority in the cluster but the Conservatives won a majority in the family – cluster 12 – and those in which the Conservatives won a majority in the cluster and Labour a majority in the family – cluster 29. Clusters 4, 8, 11 are omitted, since no Labour MP was elected in these constituences. Of the 319 Labour members, 97 were excluded because they held positions in the Government or were an officer of the Commons for more than half of the Parliament. Three were excluded because they left the Labour party before the Parliament was half over and a fourth because he died early in the Parliament. In those cases in which a by-election changed the MP for a constituency, the one serving for half or more of the Parliament was included.

59. Voting records were compiled from Norton, *Dissension . . .* , *op. cit.*
60. The differences in Tables 2 and 3 are small. None the less, because the cases are a population, rather than a sample, these are real differences. Thus there is no need to test for significance. Some researchers argue, however, that significance tests are helpful in assessing the importance of the findings even when dealing with populations. See Hubert M. Blalock, Jr., *Social Statistics* (2nd ed.; New York: McGraw-Hill, 1972) pp. 238–9. For this data, the Kolmogorov–Smirnov approximation of chi-square would be most appropriate. (Ibid., pp. 262–5.) With two degrees of freedom chi-square at the 0.05 level would need to be 5.99. Neither Table 2 and 3 comes close to this, with values of 1.36 and 0.95. (The small number of mixed cases were ignored for these calculations.) This should not be particularly troubling, since the argument being made here is not that constituency type is the only, or indeed even the primary, influence upon voting behaviour in the Commons. Rather the point is that the nature of the area an MP represents is related to voting behaviour – as Tables 2.2 and 2.3 clearly show – while the British system is so structured as to thwart expression of these diverse concerns related to location. Local interests should not be dominant, but they clearly deserve greater representation than they have received in the Commons.
61. Given the large number of divisions in which such dissent occurred during the 1974–9 Parliament, only 46 divisions were selected for this analysis. Those chosen were all cases in which not only a majority of Labour and of Conservative MPs voting, voted in the same lobby, but also the number of Conservative MPs doing so exceeded 50. The dividing line used to separate MPs into moderate and frequent dissenters is higher in Table 4 than it was in Tables 2.2 and 2.3 because left-wing voting was much more common than cross-voting. The average number of cross-votes for the entire group of 218 MPs was 4.2 compared to an average of 9.9 left-wing rebellions. Excluding those who never dissented on these divisions, the average is 5.6 for 165 MPs on cross-votes and 11.4 for 189 MPs on left-wing rebellions.
62. The Smirnov test yields a miniscule chi-square value of 0.05. Again, the small number of MPs from mixed type constituencies precludes any meaningful analysis of their pattern of dissent. These constituencies were retained as a separate category to avoid any distorition of the figures

which might have occurred by assigning them to either of the other two categories.

63. Membership in the Tribune Group was ascertained from lists appearing in *The Political Companion*. Of the 71 back-benchers appearing on these lists, 64 were included for more than half of the life of the Parliament, while the other seven were members for less than half the time. Figures similar to those presented in Table 2.5 cannot be usefully discussed for the Tribune Group itself because over three-quarters of its MPs represented Labour type constituencies. Thus the N for mixed type is only 7 and for Conservative type only 9.
64. Mixed type constituencies is not a category in this table because with the removal of Tribunites, the N drops to only three. These three cases simply are excluded from Table 2.5
65. The Smirnov test chi-square for the top part of Table 5 is 1.25; again not significant at the 0.05 level, but considerably larger than the 0.13 for the bottom part of the table. Thus as with the previous tables, the significance tests help to make clear that the real differences in the case of cross-voting are of greater import than those in the case of left-wing dissent.
66. Loewenberg and Patterson, op. cit., pp. 179–82.

3 Rubbing Up or Running Down? Dilemmas of Civil Service Reform in Britain

James B. Christoph

> . . . the Civil Service is a bit like a Rolls-Royce – you know it's the best machine in the world, but you're not quite sure what to do with it. I think it's a bit too smooth: it needs rubbing up a bit.
>
> R. A. Butler to Anthony Sampson

The late Lord Butler's mild complaint about the British Civil Service has certainly been heeded in the past twenty years. There has been no shortage of efforts, by friends and foes alike, to prescribe change for the higher bureaucracy, and we can count dozens of efforts to redo or undo some of the chief features that came to characterize the Civil Service following its reshaping by the Victorian reformers. Some of these attempts have borne tangible fruit: the form the Civil Service presents to the outside world does look quite different from the days of Attlee and Macmillan. The reality of genuine and substantial change is both less clear and more controversial. Making sense out of change, sorting it out from reform, discovering that it is really development, or deciding when it is revolutionary, is no easy job. While I make no claim to add something new to theories of change or to terminological precision, I do hope to show that in politics and the world of events planned, conscious institutional reform is only one source of real change, and not often the principal one, at least so far as the British Civil Service is concerned.

My main theme is that in the period since about 1960 deliberately, centrally initiated efforts to make basic changes in British administration have been less important than the effects of broader, less direct and controllable developments in the environment in which government and its permanent officials operate. To accept this position is not to deny or ridicule some of the well-known institutional reforms that emerged in the 1960s and 1970s, or to prophesy failure for Mrs Thatcher's equally well-publicized attempts to (in her view) put Civil Servants in their proper place for the first time in decades. Nor is it to endorse the strongly advanced view that British bureaucrats are so clever, subtle and devious that they always succeed in derailing or diluting attempts by outsiders to reform the Civil Service against its will. What I do propose is that we consider the Civil Service, and changes which really do affect its character, as increasingly influenced by actions taken in an environment less and less under its own control.

My emphasis will be principally on senior officials, where the worlds of administration and politics come together and where so many of the concerns of critics has been focused. In looking at the traditional bureaucratic élite and its relationships with traditional political leaders it is easy to equate this small group of about two thousand mandarins with the Civil Service. We are apt then to overlook one of those very environmental changes that has influenced new patterns of power: the tendency for higher officials in times of economic retrenchment to associate themselves with some of the outlooks and connections of lower-level public employees, most notably by engaging in union activities and contemplating industrial action. My comments will be limited to the central government's Civil Service, which comprises today only about ten per cent of public sector employees. Once again, a simple fact masks a political statement, for one of the changing environmental elements has been the advent of related but rival structures of management and policy influence, such as nationalized industries, the National Health Service, and countless boards, tribunals, and quangos operating to some extent like some parts of the pre-Northcote-Trevelyan, pre-Treasury control bureaucracy.[1]

I

Change from what? is the usual question, just like compared to what? For my purpose, the answer is from the dominant model of the Civil

Service in the making of policy and administration. Its central features, both admired and criticized, are several. Civil Servants have their existence only through ministers of the Crown, whom they serve and counsel but not override. To the Government and the public they are connected by the concept of ministerial responsibility, which serves to ensure their political master of their loyalty and protects their individual actions from exposure to Parliament, the press or the public. In return for security of tenure, and to facilitate their need to work equally with Governments of different political parties, higher officials are to be non-political in the partisan sense. The ethos by which they work stresses intellectual skills, anonymity, flexibility, subtlety, facility in bureaucratic politics; their power derives from permanence, experience, secrecy, and brokering consensus. In this view from the inside, the Civil Service looked varied, hard-working, skilled, self-contained, sensible. To outsiders, the Civil Service appeared distant, cosy, fair-minded, given to somewhat conservative and inefficient rituals. As matters go, its morale was reasonably high and approval by the general public and the political élite was taken for granted, if not assumed to be enthusiastic. In most cases, and increasingly, key Civil Servants and their political 'masters' shared social and educational backgrounds; they also tended to have common views of the role of government, which seldom were ideological. Finally, Civil Servants were unionized only strongly at the manual and clerical levels, the Administrative Class and other higher echelons being represented by more 'professional' staff associations that were not militant or close to regular unions.

Today this depiction of the Civil Service seems out of focus – not distorted beyond recognition but decidedly blurred. This is so partly because perceptions and opinions have changed, often beyond the reality of situations but not less influential for that. Like many traditional British institutions, beginning in the early 1960s Whitehall came under attack and scrutiny for being one cause of 'what's wrong with Britain', especially for its alleged failures in economic management, technological amateurishness, and isolation from the real world of salesmanship or the shop floor.[2] Another external source of change, probably also related to a spreading consciousness of national decline, was a shift in popular attitudes, away from the older patterns of class hierarchy, admiration for and confidence in élite leadership, and belief in the virtues of traditional institutions and harmonious social relationships, to an emergent political culture which downplayed such attitudes and emphasized more self-regarding, open, and (as Samuel

Beer uses the term) populist values.[3] These shifts in patterns of support were, of course, not unique to Britain in this period, nor were their effects limited to popular support for administrative features. Another set of developments that affected the larger environment in which Civil Servants functioned was the expansion in this period of the activities of government that brought Civil Servants into closer contact with citizens and their representative groups, often with discretionary powers. The very complexity and closeness of the bureaucratic process to ordinary citizens associated with the elaboration of the welfare state bred, if not contempt, at least suspicion. Douglas Ashford has pointed out the potential this development holds for increasing adversarial relations between citizens and bureaucracies.[4]

In more proximate terms, prospects for change in the Civil Service were sharpened by two other shifts in the general climate in which government decisions are made. The first was the deepening of hard times for the public sector as economic resources available to British governments were outrun by the costs of maintaining existing programs and commitments. As the nation's largest employer, the central government felt impelled to use its leverage over its employees to control runaway inflation and set the tone for the private sector. In the 1970s governments of both parties resorted to public sector wage freezes, cash limits on the public borrowing requirement, and retrenchment of marginal services. Even before Mrs Thatcher's arrival in Downing Street Civil Servants were struggling to avoid permanent status as the Government's centre-piece for wage restraint, with initial but declining success. Awareness of their vulnerability pushed many Civil Servants for the first time into the growing white collar unions, who warned political leaders against trying to balance the economy on the backs of their own officials (to borrow a phrase from another national setting).

The second shift was the advent of Governments more committed than usual in British politics to strategies of administrative reform. Their predecessors certainly had not hesitated to make occasional changes in the structure and nomenclature of public administration; but few of them had put as much stock in the virtues of organizational reconstruction to overcome policy weaknesses as did the meritocrats Harold Wilson and Edward Heath. The amount of attention given to administrative change and the number of new structures put into place in the years 1964–74 led some observers to herald 'an administrative revolution', a concept which will be examined later in this paper.[5]

Others would reserve that term for the events of the first years of the Thatcher Government, if by it is meant a sharp break from the continuity of older patterns achieved as an act of will.

In order to assess the usefulness of various interpretations of change in the recent period I have chosen to recall four experiments in administrative reform launched in the fifteen years preceding the General Election of 1979, after which I look somewhat more closely at the assumptions and actions of the Thatcher Government in these matters.

II

The 1960s and 1970s brought fairly steady outbursts of reform activity affecting the working of the Civil Service. To mention just a few examples of institutional innovation, new ministries came and went (the Department of Economic Affairs, the Ministry of Technology, the Civil Service Department), the ombudsman came and stayed, new types of Parliamentary committees were created, new techniques of budgetary planning and control appeared and faded (PAR, PESC). In a time of national self-doubt and growing skepticism over governmental performance, it was not unnatural, and certainly reassuring, to coin new instruments to deal with unsolved dilemmas. Some of these innovations had a continuing life and impact, but many of them foundered or fizzled. Whether they were flawed from the beginning, overtaken by uncontrollable events, or deliberately scuttled by Civil Servants is difficult to settle. In most cases no single cause, or conspiracy theory, provides the sole explanation. Such is certainly true of that presumed triumph of Fabianism, the Fulton reforms, whose fate demonstrates nicely many of the dilemmas of formulating and achieving change in British government.

The story of the Fulton Committee (1966-68) is well known.[6] It owed its origin mainly to the widely held suspicion, especially by Harold Wilson and his political advisers, that the structure and composition of the Civil Service were impediments to modern policy-making in Britain. As viewed by Wilson and a majority of the committee, the problems to be solved were *within* Whitehall and not in the constitutional and political environment of which it is a part. Hence by its terms of reference the committee was prevented from taking a direct look at the role of ministers or the effects on the civil service of the doctrine of ministerial responsibility; nor did it pay much attention to the impact on the Civil Service of changes in the scope and complexity of what British government now does (or is expected to do). Rather, in its report the committee stressed shortcomings in the managerial attitudes and skills of officials, as well as barriers to the adoption of modern techniques, such as the 'cult of the generalist', the downgrading of specialists and technology, Civil Servants' isolation from the outside world, and the absence of genuine mobility between Civil Service grades and classes. The committee's proposals, too numerous to list here, centred on the introduction of the approaches of modern business management, emphasis on recruitment of specialized rather than generally trained entrants, more delegation of budgetary responsibility to units organized around objectives, simplification of the career hierarchy (especially elimination of the powerful élite Administrative Class), and systematic in-service training to replace apprenticeship learning.

Despite reservations on the part of influential Civil Servants and academics as to the Fulton Report's assumptions, the Wilson Government quickly accepted and moved to implement a number of the committee's central recommendations. Among these were the establishment of a new Civil Service Department with central authority (previously held by the Treasury) on matters of recruitment, staffing, and administrative procedures; the creation of a Civil Service College to broaden and systematize training; the dedication of more resources to personnel management; and the abolition of hundreds of departmental classes in favour of a unified grading structure, topped by an expanded Administrative Group, with more opportunities for late entry and internal mobility between grades. Decisions on the remaining Fulton recommendations, including business managerialism, de-emphasizing Oxbridge backgrounds, and new structures for accountability, were postponed until further studies to be conducted by the Civil Service Department could be completed.

Three observations about the Fulton proposals can be made. First, the recommendations that were picked out for swift implementation were those that just happened to call for extra staff and the expansion of Civil Service functions.[7] The recommendations that centered on improved efficiency and accountability were thrown into the future in-tray. Second, the central proposals did little to challenge the existing structure of constitutional authority or reorder relationships between Civil Servants and the overtly political organs of government. It is noteworthy that the one basic organizational change accepted by the Government – the creation of the CSD and the designation of the

Prime Minister as Head of the Civil Service – proved to be the most transient of the proposals adopted in 1968. Third, until the activation of interest by the Expenditure Committee of the Commons in the mid-1970s the implementation of the Fulton reforms was considered by many an internal matter for the CSD. In other words, as is often the case, politicians and reformers cannot easily sustain interest in the implementation of changes beyond a limited time period.

The fate of the Fulton changes is instructive. Most observers agree that taken together the new undertakings sparked by Fulton fell considerably short of intentions and rhetoric. For many reasons the Civil Service College did not live up to the expectation that it would revitalize training and innovation in public administration skills.[8] Experiments in 'accountable management' were launched in the Heath years but their effectiveness was blunted by uncertainties over the roles of the Treasury, the CSD, and other units charged with co-ordination from the centre, and more particularly by governments' need to respond quickly to economic crises that would not wait for new machinery and techniques.[9] The hierarchy of the Civil Service was rearranged to eliminate many of the barriers to promotion of careers begun outside the former Administrative Class, but it was not long before new distinctions and special tracks took their place, especially as many of the anti-élitist assumptions of Fulton were not as widely shared by politicians and officials as at first thought.[10]

Fifteen years after, the legacy of Fulton seems rather meagre with respect to deep-reaching change. In one sense this may be so because of intrinsic weaknesses in the presuppositions of the report itself. This view has, I believe, as much to commend it as the one (made by one of the Fulton Committee's most influential members and defenders) that 'what actually happened after the Fulton Report shows the insidious operation of Civil Service power at its most triumphant' in subverting the reform impulse for its own purposes.[11] One has difficulty in disagreeing with Nevil Johnson's comment that these developments, as with the British political system generally, show an existing institution's 'remarkable capacity to absorb and transform reform proposals, adapting them subtly to its perceptions of what is tolerable'.[12]

A closer look at one of the Fulton legacies, the Civil Service Department, shows the decisive effect of changes from the outer environment in which an institution is embedded. Formed in 1968 by splitting off the personnel management and efficiency functions from the Treasury, the CSD was envisioned as the principal change agent for the central bureaucracy.[13] In its first six years its permanent secretary was the formidable Sir William (later Lord) Armstrong, an economics mandarin who had headed the Civil Service side of the Treasury until the CSD came into being. Most of the staff he brought with him came from the Treasury, but it was rumored that many of those he had tried to get would not move because they were skeptical over the CSD's standing in the Whitehall power structure and its ability to overcome entrenched departmental autonomy to achieve its objectives.

In its early years the CSD adopted some useful innovations in the dissemination of information and set in motion the Civil Service College. There was encouraging talk of lessening the amount of secrecy in Whitehall and of letting Civil Servants speak out publicly on more questions. However, even prior to Armstrong's retirement in 1974, major structural and political weaknesses began to show, and as it approached its demise in 1981 the CSD seemed to lose the high hopes of its originators that it could make a serious dent in established ways for doing the business of government. Perhaps the problem was that none of Armstrong's successors as permanent secretary came to the job with his unique political connections. (Heath relied heavily on him for economic and industrial policy advice, which while it gave Armstrong high-level access also diverted him from his CSD responsibilities.) But there were more compelling reasons. One was the perennial difficulties central staff departments (like the CSD) encounter in getting line departments to change their ideas and their ways in the absence of real incentives and sanctions. (The Treasury at least raised and disbursed money.) As the economic situation tightened and individual departments felt stretched just to perform their programmed tasks, resentment built up against what were viewed as excessive coordination and demands for experimentation from the CSD. Another reason was that although in the Fulton reorganization the Prime Minister had been given the additional title of Minister for the Civil Service (presumably to fill the power void of separation from the Treasury), in fact prime ministers did not, and probably could not, take a close personal interest in management questions in ways that might have supported detailed CSD initiatives. To make matters worse, when the Prime Minister's attention was captured it was usually to cope with the consequences of increasing 'industrial unrest' in the Civil Service. 'After the first major strike was called in February 1973, prime ministers were much more likely to be called into CSD work by the threats of worsening staff relations than by the prestige of improved management schemes.'[14] The CSD was beginning to be perceived as a somewhat irritating lobby for the Civil Service not entirely content with the government's overall economic policies. Finally, it might be noted that in the first decade of the CSD's existence another small staff unit, the Cabinet Office, was increasing its functions and its presumed indispensability to the coordination of multi-department enterprises such as devolution and European Community affairs. By 1980 the Cabinet Office seemed at least as well equipped to take on central personnel management functions as did the CSD, and it was much more favourably regarded by ministers suspicious of the CSD's ability to stand apart from Civil Servants' interests.

The rather brief history of the CSD testifies to the difficulty of achieving substantial reforms in a unit of government which is increasingly dependent on forces and events that it cannot control effectively, and at a time when its standing with the political élite and the general public was not strong enough to give it a long period of time to live up to expectations.

III

Another thrust of reformers in this period was aimed not so much at improving the efficiency of Civil Servants as at controlling what was believed to be their potential for abusing power. Complainants included citizens' groups, the press, backbench Members of Parliament, even an occasional frustrated minister like Richard Crossman. Particularly in the first Wilson years (1964–70) pressures built up for changes that would open up bureaucratic decisions to external scrutiny and bypass the device of ministerial responsibility to extend accountability beyond the élite-to-élite level. A number of new departures were made, usually focusing on the coining of a new institutional device. As with some of the Fulton-based changes, one cannot say conclusively that they succeeded or failed. But as they found their places in the British political system it became apparent that they were not able to offer much more than marginal change and could not effectively challenge or replace fundamental authority relationships (if that indeed was ever the intention of those who set them in motion). In the case of one set of reform proposals, for 'open government', little beyond cosmetic changes occurred.

An innovation that has attracted attention was the introduction in 1967 of the Parliamentary Commissioner for Administration, or ombudsman, by whom for the first time citizen allegations of maladministration against Civil Servants could be investigated and, if verified and accepted by the Government of the day, rectified. Compared to its counterparts elsewhere, the British ombudsman's office and powers are limited and its record to present a 'qualified success'.[15] Its jurisdiction has expanded somewhat since its origins; it is no longer the exclusive preserve of retired senior Civil Servants; and versions of it have spread to the National Health Service and local government authorities. In one view the record confirms its creators' belief that the ombudsman would deflect criticism of the Civil Service and still not threaten the essence of traditional Whitehall activity or upset relations between ministers and their officials. Others have interpreted this record as potentially much more threatening to Civil Service traditions (or promising to reformers) because by giving even limited powers to the ombudsman Parliament has acknowledged that the doctrine of ministerial responsibility is no longer absolute and is really outdated.[16] By doing what the adversary character of Parliamentary proceedings seldom permits – getting ministers and officials to acknowledge error, even at the procedural level – the ombudsman has in his office the seeds of constitutional change. Whether such seeds will ever take on roots is hard to say; but it is quite imaginable that if they threatened to grow they could be cut back by an alliance of threatened ministers and senior officials, unless the thrust for change took a politically more inclusive form such as major constitutional revision.

The mixed achievements of the ombudsman are paralleled by those of the new-style Parliamentary committees set up, at least in part, to inform the House of Commons more effectively on the administration of policy. Previously it was assumed, again under the logic of ministerial responsibility, that the Commons learned about the workings of the bureaucracy either through questions on the floor or from all-purpose special committees such as those on Public Accounts and Estimates. Regular committees of the Commons were weak and usually unspecialized. Lateral contacts between MPs and Civil Servants were infrequent, discouraged, and revealing. In the period of reform there have been three different attempts to use new committee forms to allow the Parliament to move somewhat closer to the level at which most policies are made.

The first modest start came in 1969, when, as part of the Crossman reforms of Commons' procedures, sessional select committees were created on an experimental basis to supplement the normal unspecialized standing committees with a few others focussing on functional departments' policies (agriculture, overseas aid, etc.).

Sessional select committees were introduced as much to provide counterbalances against policy group pressures on Whitehall as to foster better legislation, and were not a great success. They seldom touched Civil Service matters and faded out in the Conservative years that followed. There was a renewal of interest in the reform of the bureaucracy in the third Wilson Government, this time centreing on efforts of the newly revamped Expenditure Committee to penetrate Whitehall's policy roles and the extent to which the Fulton changes were real changes. The 1976–77 (English) Expenditure Committee did serve as a forum for critics and defenders of the Civil Service, and its reports are useful sources of information and commentary, but as with many initiatives in the mid-and late-70s its work tended to erode before the tide of economizing and tensening public sector relationships. The third committee development, arising from the early Thatcher years, was the reorganization of regular Commons committees along more specialized, functional, 'American' lines. Fourteen committees to shadow government ministries were set up in 1979, but were given no effective powers or staff.

With what powers they possess (chiefly of disclosure) the newer Commons committees occasionally have shed light on questions of administration. Civil Servants rather gingerly have been allowed to appear before them, but ministers have made it clear that these officials are not to be permitted to express different policy preferences from the minister's, or to be questioned about the internal processes by which individual decisions are reached.

Another innovation popular in the 1960s was the non-career political adviser to the minister. Hopes were held out that the dependence of ministers on senior officials for policy advice could be weakened, and that more insider-outsiders could keep an eye on Civil Servants in their implementation of the minister's initiatives. Political advisers were to be a somewhat diluted version of the French *cabinets* (so disapproved of by the Fulton Committee) without forcing partisan roles on neutral officials. The prospects for tension, creative or otherwise, between these newcomers and departmental old hands were there, and there were reports of friction in those ministries where the new advisers were established prima donnas. But so far as we can tell, the famed assimilationist skills of Whitehall prevailed. As Rose has commented, 'The political advisers (typically young persons aspiring to become MPs themselves) have been accepted, because they have concentrated on doing work that Civil Servants would not in any event do. . . . The insertion of a youthful political adviser and an academic on leave has not basically altered the routines of department . . . '.[17]

British government has the deserved reputation among democracies of having in its bureaucracy one of the strongest 'cultures of secrecy'. An extensive literature on the subject of open government and administrative secrecy attest to the strength in the past two decades of popular interest in reforms that would make public all but justifiably sensitive government information or that interfering with essentially private concerns.[18] Increasing impatience with the explanations of government officials, well-publicized instances of alleged cover-ups of information embarrassing but not vital to Governments of the day, and concerted press campaigns helped put pressure on reforming Governments to shed at least the more archaic and overt supports for excessive official secrecy. A favourite target was the much-criticized Section 2 of the Official Secrets Act of 1911, which if taken seriously puts clamps on almost any piece of official information a government sees fit to withhold from public view. Unease over other conventions of Whitehall grew, fostered by the unanswerable surmise that secrecy was being invoked to blur responsibility for decisions and conceal administrative mistakes. Among these was the customary refusal of prime ministers (before Thatcher) to disclose the membership of often decisive Cabinet committees and the equally hoary practice, justified in the name of bureaucratic neutrality, of destroying all traces of the advice given by senior officials to the previous minister when administrations changed.

Information indeed is power, especially if it is possessed only by a few. Thus it is hardly surprising that despite outside pressures and the assurance of foreign examples, both ministers and Civil Servants proved most reluctant to give up the essentials of administrative secrecy. Committees sat and reported, politicians agreed that there was a need to shed some secrecy, and low-risk concessions were made by prime ministers (notably Callaghan). But ten years after the Franks Committee recommended that much of the Official Secrets Act be scrapped, it remains unaltered. Equally, attempts by backbenchers and pressure groups to gain acceptance for some modified version of the United States' Freedom of Information Act remain stillborn. If anything, Britain narrowly escaped the adoption of even more restricted public information laws. One of the first bills drafted by the Thatcher Government was a Protection of Official Information Bill which, instead of abolishing or liberalizing Section 2 would have strengthened the power of bureaucrats to deny information to the public in ways going well beyond present practice. Unexpectedly, the bill was withdrawn when it was pointed out that if passed it would have prevented the publication of a book like Andrew Boyle's *The Climate of Treason*, from which the public was able to deduce the identity of former Russian spy (and British Civil Servant) Sir Anthony Blunt. The bill expired through an accident of its timing rather than because of the conversion of the Conservative leadership to the cause of open government reforms.

IV

That brings us to Mrs Thatcher and her role in changing the bureaucracy. In politics she has been pictured as a radical of the right. Has that characterization also held true of her views and actions as they have affected Whitehall? For decades top officials had demonstrated their skills in adjusting to Governments of considerably varying political and ideological complexions, 'domesticating' inexperienced or wild-eyed ones without losing their confidence. In 1979 uncertainties arose in view of Mrs Thatcher's strongly enunciated policy views and general philosophy of government. Used to the occasional accusations from the keepers of the Labour Left (Crossman, Benn) and the sniping of rivals for the ears of ministers (Marcia Williams, Joe Haines), the mandarins were still not quite ready for savaging from the political right. Unlike the three prime ministers who had preceded her, Mrs Thatcher had never herself been a Civil Servant; nor had she had either the lengthy ministerial or even Parliamentary experience of the average twentieth-century prime minister. Her thin Whitehall background cannot in itself account for the strong degree of suspicion and impatience toward Civil Servants that she brought to the job; but it is an element in her make-up that may account for her small attachment to the traditions of bureaucracy.

It is probably true that most senior Civil Servants 'neither understood nor believed in the dogmas of the Prime Minister and those close about her'.[19] Senior Civil Servants had spent nearly all of their working lives with moderate governments and under the influence of Keynesian economics and the welfare state. They now had to come to grips with a Government bent on turning the nation away from those accustomed norms of their working lives, and with a Prime Minister apparently convinced of the necessity of reducing the size, interventionist potential, and general importance of the Civil Service. Much more than Harold Wilson in 1964, Mrs Thatcher saw

Whitehall as a large part of what's wrong with Britain. Her view of Civil Servants as a breed seemed to be based on four images. Firstly, Civil Servants believe in the special virtues of government; thus whenever they can they will assert and expand its powers. Secondly, they are infused with the Keynesian approach so dominant in economic and social decision making since 1950, and so detrimental to a vital Britain. Thirdly, Civil Servants have arrogated to themselves large parts of the policy-making responsibilities of ministers and have replaced ministerial initiatives with their own private views of what is in the best interests of the country. Fourthly, Civil Servants thrive on caution, delay, accommodation, and minced words when to solve Britain's problems what is required in its decision makers is toughness, bluntness, clear objectives, and attachment to the virtues of postponed gratification. To Mrs Thatcher, most permanent officials were at once too powerful and too 'wet'. To many of those officials, the Prime Minister was too ideological, inexperienced, and headstrong.

The corollary of Mrs Thatcher's assumption that there would be shrinkage in the roles played by Civil Servants was that the political heads of ministries were to be strengthened in their policy-making roles and toughened by, if necessary, disregarding or overruling compromisers in the ranks. Michael Lee has described how the whole strategy of the Thatcher Government for reducing public spending rested on the concept of 'ministerial management', in contradistinction to 'wetness' or warmed over Keynesianism.[20] Coupled with the assertion of this outlook have been (as will be shown later) increased prime ministerial involvement in the promotion and assignment of top Civil Servants and downgrading in importance the tradition of staff-government consultation through forums such as the Whitley Councils.

It would still be a mistake to describe the Thatcher approach to the central bureaucracy as favouring root-and-branch change. Her principal target for change has been government's scope and policies, not its structure or machinery. Her belief in a fairly well-articulated economic theory has not been matched by acceptance of a comparative theory of public administration. An argument can be made that she has had little interest in overturning some strong Whitehall conventions such as the manipulation of ministerial responsibility and the penchant for secrecy. 'The [policy] doctrines are Friedmanite and radical', writes one student of bureaucracy, 'but the practices of office-holding are Keynesian and traditional.'[21] This may relate to

Mrs Thatcher's initial confidence that the ideological and personality strengths of key ministers would be more than sufficient to quell the doubts of higher officials over the strong medicine being applied to the British economy.

One of her first decisions affecting Civil Servants was in fact not unpopular with Civil Service traditionalists. She decided to reduce substantially the number of political and special advisers to ministers, a device for widening the source of ideas available from inside Whitehall used extensively by Wilson, Heath, and Callaghan. In the new Conservative Government the number of full-time special advisers dropped to fewer than ten, three of them in the Treasury. Observers have found it ironical that if ever a new administration needed a group of political advisers working closely with Civil Servants it was Thatcher's, with its emphasis on U-turns from the assumptions and policies of the recent past and its faith that public employees would respond easily to the task of dismantling parts of the government machine.[22] It is doubtful that this symbolic exercise in the art of labour-saving has produced benefits that exceed its less obvious costs.

Mrs Thatcher's first directives on the Civil Service seemed to validate the common view that central institutions can be quite resilient when faced with the prospect of losing staff. On taking office she announced her Government's intention of reducing the size of public sector employment, including the Civil Service, by at least 10 per cent during the lifetime of the 1979 Parliament. In one sense that target is being approached, for after its first two years the Government counted seven per cent fewer Civil Servants (from 731,000 to 679,800). Still, this global figure tends to mask a selective rather than across the board process of shrinkage, as many of the jobs lost were industrial Civil Servants rather than classical bureaucrats, and their departure due more to the running down of British dockyards and loss of foreign orders for weapons than to tough cuts made by ministers.[23] To explain figures this way is not to deny the fact that the trend in public employment has been reversed under the Thatcher Government and that the size of the Civil Service is lower today than at any time in the past fifteen years. It would be lower still if some officials were not essential to the administration of benefits and programs attributable to very high unemployment throughout the United Kingdom. Unlike the general level of unemployment, the change in government employment is seen by the party in power not as a necessary evil but as a genuine accomplishment. It is not surprising that when linked to the

Thatcher administration's stand on Civil Servants' pay, these staff reductions have angered and activated Civil Service unions in ways quite different from under previous Governments.

Two other actions of the Thatcher Government having repercussions across the bureaucracy deserve mention. The first concerns promotions of Civil Servants to senior positions, where politics and administration come together and programs pushed or stymied. While the form is that appointments of Permanent Secretary and Deputy Secretary are made by the Prime Minister, almost invariably they have been done by rubber-stamping the recommendations of the Senior Appointment Selection Committee, itself composed of Permanent Secretaries and chaired by the Head of the Civil Service. Whitehall has been used to setting the course for its own high flyers. Every once in a while the Prime Minister or powerful departmental ministers may blackball a senior nomination, but the Civil Service's top patronage machine is rarely challenged, and almost never on ideological grounds.[24] In the past two years there has been a series of reports that Mrs Thatcher takes a close personal interest in top officials' appointments and has used her own 'channels' to try to ascertain the economic views of candidates, querying ministers and others as to how monetarist the thinking of potential appointees seems to be. There is no concrete evidence of an outright purge of undesirables, but the word is out in village Whitehall that 'any [candidates] with "notoriously Keynesian views" or "wet" personalities would not succeed'.[25] Embryonic as this development may in fact be, it has fed the suspicion that in patronage matters as elsewhere the higher Civil Service may be losing support for its traditional political neutrality.

At this point we can recall another action of the Thatcher Government that probably was meant to 'send a message' to Civil Servants. That was the termination at the end of 1981 of the Fulton-inspired Civil Service Department and the parcelling out of its responsibilities to the Treasury and the Cabinet Office. (The rise and fall of the CSD are described earlier in this paper.) Among other things, the Thatcher Government's action took away the Civil Servants' 'own' department and put decisions about Civil Service matters more directly in the realm of general government policy. The manner in which the CSD was ended (contrary to the recommendations of an official committee of inquiry) appeared to confirm the view that the Prime Minister considered the department a pressure group for the bureaucracy rather than for efficiency or improved management. Undoubtedly it was also part of the fall-out from the Civil Servants' 1981 strike.

V

Whatever their political or ideological beliefs (commonly thought to be less than passionate), by temperament and role senior British Civil Servants dislike sudden and sweeping changes.[26] Their skills in getting and displaying consensus have been objects of pride, notwithstanding the occasional appearance of adversary positions at the beginning of a new Government. At the top the approved model of relationships has been the Oxbridge Senior Common Room rather than the world of British industrial relations. Faced with the Thatcher Government's desire to 'deprivilege' the Civil Servants, officials have reacted uncertainly. Certainly it is much too early to decide whether political leaders' new approaches to the Civil Service have given rise to lasting changes in the behaviour patterns of higher Civil Servants. One could argue that some of them are just waiting for the electorate to remove impediments to the restoration of the *status quo ante* Thatcher. We have some indications, however, that the arrival of a Conservative Government has coincided with the deepening of longer-term changes in the environment in which any future Civil Service must function. A short discussion of these trends will form the backdrop for looking at more recent difficulties.

The concepts are slippery and the basis for generalizing none too systematic, but most observers inside and outside the Civil Service agree that morale and public standing have declined in the past decade, most precipitously of course under Thatcher. This erosion of morale would seem to go beyond the decline in confidence characteristic of the general population and the perennial sense articulated by officials that their public image can never be especially good because of what they have to do. There is a difference in tone between the comment of Lord Bridges (head of the Civil Service in the 1950s) that Civil Servants 'shall continue to be grouped with mothers-in-law and Wigan Pier as one of the recognized objects of ridicule' and the words of Sir Ian Bancroft (last Permanent Secretary of the CSD) deploring 'public vilification of our Civil Servants'.[27] As an élite group, Civil Servants have been accustomed to mass unpopularity; they are much less accustomed to expressions of hostility from the Prime Minister or Cabinet ministers. Hugh Stephenson notes a rapid increase during Mrs Thatcher's first year in office of leaks to the press by Civil Servants and interprets it as indicating a situation where officials were 'deeply unhappy about what was going on and anxious to stop it'.[28]

Less speculative in character have been signs that the Civil Service is moving toward personnel relations of the industrial sort. The most numerous part of the service is still those persons working in manual, clerical and industrial positions and belonging to unions not especially different from those covering their counterparts in private or nationalized corporations. What has changed in the past twenty years has been the expansion of the unions into the middle and higher levels of the bureaucracy to include professionals and experts. The old formula that the higher one goes in the hierarchy, the less one finds trade union attitudes and militancy is still largely true; what has changed is the proportion of higher level Civil Servants joining unions which espouse the values and strategies of industrial unions on the outside. It is revealing that in May 1980 a move to affiliate a large Civil Service union (CPSA), which reaches well into middle grades, with the Labour Party was defeated but with 40 per cent of its members voting for affiliation.

The most overt conflict between the Thatcher Government and Civil Servants has come, predictably, over pay. From the standpoint of the Cabinet, the need to restrain the salaries and benefits of Civil Servants is simply one aspect of its policy of cutting or controlling public sector expenditure to bring down inflation, a policy that it inherited from the preceding Callaghan Labour Government. To many Civil Servants, however, the intention was viewed as more than spreading the sacrifice to just another group in society.

From a financial standpoint, Civil Servants, senior ones especially, had done well out of the new compensation formulas adopted in the early 1970s (a period, incidentally, of Conservative rule). Their pension became indexed (inflation-proof) and their salaries were to be based on the recommendations of semi-independent pay panels utilizing data on comparative 'civilian' jobs. What first demoralized and later activated Civil Servants was not so much the setting of lower cash limits on public personnel expenditure, or of not taking the recommendations of pay panels in times of economic crisis. These steps, along with pay pauses, had been resorted to by previous Government, and had been greeted fairly passively, if not enthusiastically, by most of the Civil Service. What infuriated Civil Servants and their unions was the practice under Thatcher of reaching such decisions unilaterally, without consultation with Whitley Councils, staff associations or unions (such as in the imposition of the six per cent cash limit in 1980) and the Government's refusal to replace the abandoned pay comparability system with any other instrument.[29]

An allied irritant was the determination of the Thatcher administration to apply cash limits more harshly to Civil Servants than to other public employees, especially to those long favoured by Conservative Party politicians. In a period when inflation was running in the 10–12 per cent range, and the Government remained adamant in limiting Civil Servants' salary raises to 6 per cent, police salaries remained index-linked and were increased by 21.3 per cent in 1979, and military personnel were awarded 10.3 per cent raises. Even workers in several nationalized industries, never great favourites of Conservative cabinets, were able to extract between 12.0 and 13.0 per cent in late 1980 and early 1981 – roughly twice the cash limit Civil Servants were being held to.

In the past decade Britons have got used to strikes by miners, railway workers, nurses, and dustmen. The idea of a Civil Service strike, even a selectively targeted one, was more difficult to accept, and the 14-week long confrontation between the Civil Service unions and the Government in early 1981 was an unsettling experience, which in the end did little for either Civil Service morale, mass support for public employees, or government's relations with its officials. The arbitration award that ended the strike gave Civil Servants little more than the Government's original 6 per cent figure. The Prime Minister could hail a victory over inflationary trends and see in it the reward of standing firm against excessive demands from a group that should serve as a model for wage restraint elsewhere.

The longer term consequences of confrontations such as the 1981 strike may turn out to be more important than a temporary triumph of Cabinet tenacity over union militancy. When seen together with the other environmental changes and trends described here, the spectre of increasing adversary relations, industrial norms, and politicization is raised. The effects on recruitment of the replacement of traditional values and relationships by markedly different ones cannot be foretold, in part because there is no substantial evidence that the changes noted here will soon dominate the relationships of political leaders and bureaucrats. That does not mean that they are merely fanciful, however.

VI

The foregoing examination of some aspects of change in recent British administrative life has been selective. It makes no claim to providing a model or a theory or a representative sample. But this brief survey of recent efforts to institutionalize various reforms leads us to conclude that change of some consequence is more likely to originate in shifts in the character of the larger (or external) environment in which a bureaucracy is implanted than in deliberate acts of institution-building which either are not congruent with environmental changes or responses to momentary pressures for some kind of action (usually a cosmetic one). One surmises that the prospects for remaking British central bureaucracy, if that is one's objective, are more likely to hinge on 'events' such as war, long-term economic weakness, European integration, the changing status of women, and the growth or decline of government as a force in society, than by Fulton-style reforms or even Thatcher-style efforts at 'deprivileging'. Whatever the outcome of current efforts to wean or force the Civil Service away from the values and attitudes of the past forty years, one can safely prophesy a period of turbulence ahead for an institution that once epitomized. British stability.

NOTES

1. Henry Parris, *Constitutional Bureaucracy* (London, 1969); Gillian Sutherland, *Studies in the Growth of Nineteenth-Century Government* (London, 1972).
2. The criticisms are summarized in J. B. Christoph, 'High Civil Servants and the Politics of Consensualism in Great Britain', in Mattei Dogan, ed., *The Mandarins of Western Europe* (New York, 1975) pp. 51–5.
3. Samuel H. Beer, *Britain Against Itself* (New York, 1982).
4. Douglas E. Ashford, *Policy and Politics in Britain: The Limits of Consensus* (Philadelphia, 1981) chs 2, 8.
5. For arguments against employing the term 'revolution', see G. K. Fry, *The Administrative 'Revolution' in Whitehall* (London, 1981).
6. The Fulton Report is Cmnd of 1968. See also G. K. Fry, 'Some Weaknesses in the Fulton Report on the British Home Civil Service', *Political Studies* 17 (Dec. 1969) pp. 484–94; Fry, *The Administrative 'Revolution'*; and Anthony H. Birch, 'Westminster and Whitehall', in W. B. Gwyn and Richard Rose (eds), *Britain: Progress and Decline* (New Orleans, 1980) pp. 63–5.
7. Leslie Chapman, *Your Disobedient Servant* (London, 1978) p. 104.
8. For detailed examinations, see Richard A. Chapman and J. R. Greenaway, *The Dynamics of Administrative Reform* (London, 1980), and Peter Kellner and Lord Crowther-Hunt, *The Civil Service: An Inquiry into Britain's Ruling Class* (London, 1980).

9. For a favourable report, see Hugh Heclo and Aaron Wildavsky, *The Private Government of Public Money* (London, 1974); for more critical ones, consult Fry, *The Administrative 'Revolution',* and Ashford, *op. cit.,* ch. 2.
10. Richard A. Chapman, 'Civil Service Recruitment: Bias Against External Candidates', *Public Administration* 60 (Spring 1982) pp. 77–84.
11. Keller and Crowther-Hunt, *The Civil Service*, p. 23. Chapter 5 is entitled 'How Armstrong Defeated Fulton'.
12. 'Administrative Reform in Britain', in Arne F. Leemans, ed., *The Management of Change in Government* (The Hague, 1976) p. 294.
13. Editorial, 'Epitaph for the CSD', *Public Administration* 60 (Spring, 1982) pp. 4–9. This and the next paragraph draw largely from this source.
14. Ibid., p. 6.
15. William B. Gwyn, 'The Ombudsman in Britain: a Qualified Success in Government Reform', paper given at the 1981 annual meeting of the American Political Science Association, New York.
16. Fry, *The Administrative 'Revolution'*, pp. 159–75.
17. Richard Rose, *The Political Status of Higher Civil Servants in Britain* (Strathclyde, 1981) p. 29.
18. A sampling would include Ronald Wraith, *Open Government: The British Experience* (London, 1977); David Leigh, *The Frontiers of Secrecy* (London, 1980); and J. B. Christoph, 'A Comparative View: Administrative Secrecy in Britain', *Public Administration Review* 35 (Jan./Feb., 1975) pp. 23–32.
19. Hugh Stephenson, *Mrs Thatcher's First Year* (London, 1980) p. 29.
20. Michael Lee, 'Whitehall and Retrenchment', in C. Hood and M. Wright, ed., *Big Government in Hard Times* (Oxford, 1981) p. 39.
21. J. M. Lee, 'The Machinery of Government: The Prospect of Redefining the Issues under Mrs Thatcher's Administration', *Parliamentary Affairs*, 33 (Autumn 1980) p. 439.
22. Stephenson, *Mrs Thatcher's First Year*, p. 34.
23. Peter Hennessy, 'Mrs Thatcher takes over the axe', *The Times*, 31 Oct. 1981; *The Economist*, 17 May 1980, pp. 49–50.
24. Jock Bruce-Gardyne and Nigel Lawson, *The Power Game* (London, 1976) pp. 186–7.
25. David Blake and Peter Hennessy, 'Mrs Thatcher Keeps Close Eye on Top Civil Service Postings', *The Times*, 14 Feb. 1980.
26. Richard A. Chapman, *The Higher Civil Service in Britain* (London, 1980); Robert D. Putnam, 'The Political Attitudes of Senior Civil Servants in Britain, Germany, and Italy', in Dogan, ed., *The Mandarins*, pp. 87–127.
27. Anthony Sampson, *Anatomy of Britain Today* (New York, 1965) p. 256; Peter Hennessy, 'Whitehall Concerned Over Public Hostility', *The Times*, 10 Dec. 1980.
28. Stephenson, *Mrs Thatcher's First Year*, pp. 40–1.
29. John Fryer, 'How to create an uncivil service', *The Sunday Times*, 14 June 1981.

4 Virtues Become Vices? The Decline of the Textbook Party System

Kenneth D. Wald*

INTRODUCTION

From time to time, the mailbox disgorges glossy travel brochures which beckon me to sample the cuisine of France, drink beer in Germany, eat cheese in Holland, ride a tram to a Swiss mountain top or find the sun on a Portuguese beach. Understandably enough, travel agents do not similarly entice visitors to the United Kingdom with the promise of a rich cuisine or a moderate climate. Rather, along with shopping on Oxford Street, pub crawls and stage plays, the travel agents promote visits to Parliament, the Tower, Buckingham Palace and Hyde Park Corner as major reasons to schedule a British stop on the grand tour. It is certainly difficult to imagine another country drawing tourists on account of its governmental institutions and political system. What sensible travel folder would suggest that an Italian or Spanish vacation would be incomplete without tours of government buildings or landmarks commemorating great political events? What travel agent fails to tout such activities as highlights of a trip to London? The distinctiveness of Britain's appeal finds eloquent confirmation in the throngs of tourists actually waiting in the rain for tickets to a sitting of Parliament and crowding around the elevated platforms on Speaker's Corner. For many outsiders, even those who are not professional political scientists, the essence of Britain apparently has much to do with its governmental traditions.

Strictly speaking, British political parties are not part of the governmental system. For purposes of nominating candidates to stand for Parliament, staffing the Government and other major functions, the British parties are private organizations. Until 1970, this lack of official recognition even extended to omitting partisan designations from the ballot. The absence of legal regulation, which gives British parties a freedom of manoeuvre denied by statute to their American counterparts, has not disguised the central role of parties in the British system of governance. A distinguished journalist, who once dismissed the Constitution as 'nothing but institutions in unstable equilibrium, which may be overturned in a moment by the verdict of the ballot boxes', thus made it clear that the power of the parties must be acknowledged in any serious discussion of British political life.[1] Ever since the development of a behavioural orientation in political science, the party system, formerly a neglected topic, has been elevated to a central place in the study of the British political structure.

The 1970s were a time of change for many institutions in Britain, the political system not excepted. Few institutions were as thoroughly scrutinized as the party system. A spate of revisionist analysis had the effect of calling into question the primacy which scholars had traditionally assigned to parties in the system of British governance.[2] Some scholars noted the importance of various non-governmental institutions which seemed to pre-empt roles formerly monopolized by the parties. Many questioned just how much parties had really influenced the tenor of political life in Britain. Even those who acknowledged the role of parties in the past began to wonder if their primacy could be maintained under new conditions which seemed to undermine traditional patterns of governance. As a result of this research, the 'classic' British party model of the textbooks now seems as fresh as last month's newspaper.[3]

For parties, like the rest of Britain's political institutions, skepticism has been accompanied by evidence of growing disrepute. There was a time when parties were thought to be the key to the success of the British polity and the operation of the party system provided a standard against which other countries were measured – and usually found wanting.[4] As Britain has declined in world esteem, the party system has clearly lost that intellectual preeminence – within Britain and outside. The British parties are increasingly likely to be cited not as a model for other countries to emulate but as a major factor in promoting British decline. The British themselves now seem disposed to experiment with many devices – referenda, federalism, stronger legislative committees, a bill of rights, proportional representation, primary elections – that would circumvent the party system and probably weaken the capacity of parties to perform traditional roles.[5]

Undeniably, British parties have changed in important respects and the party system has lost considerable prestige. The parties, like Britain after the dissolution of the Empire, seem mired in a perennial search for a new role. Yet precisely because the discussion about new directions is so thoroughly informed by a sense of lost glory, it might be worthwhile to reconsider the changing portrayal of the British party system. After contrasting what used to be said about the party system with more recent commentary, I want to suggest the need for caution lest we overlook important elements of continuity in the operation of the system. Some of the purported 'changes' might be exaggerated. Other developments, thought to be the consequence of actions by the parties, may owe more to forces and factors emanating from outside Britain. Real changes in behaviour may have been accompanied by changes in expectations. As the title suggests, it may be that parties perform much as they used to but that changes in context make those traditional patterns seem less appropriate than once was the case.

THE TEXTBOOK PARTY SYSTEM

To get some sense of the magnitude and dimensions of change in the British party system, it is useful to examine the evolution of 'conventional wisdom' about the nature of the parties. The reference point, the baseline from which change can be measured, is an abstraction labelled the 'textbook' party system'. This refers to a series of generalizations which scholars have traditionally imparted to those students who populate courses in political science.

The major source for these generalizations has been a shelf-full of some of the most widely-utilized textbooks on British governance, mostly volumes published since the late 1950s, and some of the classic articles which frequently turn up in books of readings intended for courses in British and comparative politics. To supplement these standard works, I have also ransacked lecture notes from two survey-level courses on British politics taught at American universities – one course which I attended as an undergraduate, the other which I helped teach as a graduate student. Finally, and this is a confession designed to implicate me with those whom I may seem to be charging with misrepresentation, I have consulted the lecture notes intended for delivery in my own courses. There is bound to be more than a bit of overlap here, with the generalizations of the texts influencing the lectures of my teachers and reappearing, in somewhat diluted form, on my own index cards.

This almost incestuous linkage seems appropriate in light of the remarkably high level of consensus that used to characterize the teaching of British politics. By calling attention to the elements of this consensus, I do not mean to suggest the absence of conflict or disagreement. As the careful reader will note, some of the generalizations verge on inconsistency. The characteristics which I have identified do not appear in all the cited works nor do all the authors mean exactly the same thing when they use a common phrase. Scholars also assigned relatively different weights to the various aspects of the party system. None the less, when compared with many other perennial research areas in political science, most teachers of British politics seemed in broad agreement about the essential features of the party system.

As mentioned above, the starting point for the analysis of British politics was frequently an expression of admiration for the role of parties in the British political system. The inclusion of Britain in survey courses was frequently justified because that country presented such a rare example of stable, open, free, democratic, and representative government, a model of successful political development in a world where success stories were distressingly rare.[6] The analyst in search of the correlates of political stability could do no better than focus on Britain and the secret of its success – or at least a major factor – was the unique role of parties. These organizations, variously described as a 'masterpiece', 'central to the British constitution', 'the backbone of the modern political system', were said to be one of the most important political inventions that Britain had bequeathed to the rest of the world.[7] Symbolic of the importance attributed to it, the party system was frequently covered in the first few chapters of introductory texts, even before many of the more 'dignified' elements of the constitution. There, the student learned that Britain's party system was:

highly-integrated with the government
typically two-party
consensual
devoid of personality cults
highly centralized
disciplined
organizationally complex
class-based[8]

Integration with government

What made the party system so special to many observers was the striking level of integration between parties and the governmental system. Parties were at the heart – if not exactly the heart – of British governmental operations.[9] Ramsay Muir, no uncritical admirer of the party system, conceded its primacy in British governance:

> it is the leadership of a party that gives to the prime minister his enormous power; it is common membership of a party that gives unity of character and aims to a cabinet; it is the existence of an organized supporting party in the House of Commons that enables the cabinet to carry on its work, and (when the party has a majority) endows it with a complete dictatorship over the whole range of government; and this dictatorship is only limited or qualified by the fear of those who wield it lest any grave blunder may weaken the party in the country, and bring downfall at the next election.[10]

Frederick A. Ogg, who had cited these words, emphasized that the party bond alone gave a group of ministers the support needed to retain office and defined the coalition which stood ready to replace the Government at the first opportunity. Ogg found the integration of party with government so thorough that it was difficult to find where one stopped and the other began.[11] Thus the heads of ministries and chief legislators were first and foremost authorities within the party; the normal parliamentary functions of legislation, appropriation and oversight were conducted within a matrix of party considerations. The choice of a Prime Minister was, for all practical purposes, determined by the decisions of a party caucus. Something so basic as control over the legislative agenda rested not with the Honorable Members but with the majority's duly-appointed floor managers. Even the date for a general election was set not according to some fixed and unalterable schedule but, within certain parameters, by the party in power. In sum, according to a French scholar, 'Great Britain is ruled by party government'.[12]

For Americans, many of whom were imbued with an anti-party orientation, such a frank acknowledgement of the primacy of party might have seemed a prelude to denunciation. But in fact, most of the commentators applauded what they saw. The parties were regarded as the elements which made democracy a reality. By simplifying great issues of state and making complex policy options intelligible to the ordinary elector, the parties organized democracy. The identity of the Government was determined by the party balance within Parliament, a balance which rested upon the expression of preference by the mass electorate. By providing the basis of strength for a Cabinet and Prime Minister, the parties were said to reconcile the imperative of democracy with the demands of government. And by also providing an opposition, eager to gain office on the basis of a mass electoral revolt, the party system provided a powerful check on those whom it endowed with seemingly unlimited authority. Parties, more than any other institution, provided a means of harmonizing public opinion and government policy.[13]

If parties contributed to democracy, they were also said to promote efficient government.[14] The tradition of strong party government gave Britain an instrument that could respond quickly and decisively to the problems of the day. Once entrusted with control of the executive through a secure Parliamentary base, the British government could legislate and execute without the many constraints which hindered strong government in the United States – federalism, checks and balances, divided party control, judicial review and so on. The merger of Parliamentary sovereignty with the doctrine of party government permitted a dynamism which American scholars especially admired.[15]

A two-party system

Few texts failed to cite the two-party system as one of the most important features of the British political configuration. Though sometimes a reference to the persistence of progressive and conservative *tendances* in British political development, the concept of the two-party system usually referred to the monopolization of popular votes and seats in Parliament by two and only two political parties. The norm, it was alleged, was for a majority and minority party to dominate political life.

To explain the persistence of bi-partyism, observers have cited a wide range of causes: an inherent dualism in human nature which supposedly reduces complex issues to either/or choices; the impact of history in reinforcing a two-party tradition, the nature of a political system which seems to demand a 'team' approach to government; the absence of severe social cleavages, which permits heterogeneity within 'catchall' parties; and, perhaps most importantly, the structure of the electoral system.[16] By mandating single-member districts and the plurality decision rule, British electoral law was said to narrow the chances of election for third-party candidates and so preserve the two-party monopoly.[17] Supplementing these explanations, Mathiot argued that the preponderance of homogeneous, single-class constituencies gave the two major class-based parties a strong Parliamentary core, leaving relatively few seats where other parties could realistically compete for representation.[18] Mathiot also accepted the more fanciful notions that the two-party system could be attributed to the team-like seating arrangement in the Commons and to a mysterious 'national trait', an Anglo-Saxon genius for reaching compromise on political issues.[19] This fabled instinct for moderation helped to prevent the kind of intra-party splits which had nourished multi-partyism in countries outside the British Isles. According to the literature, then, custom, political structure and national character all worked to preserve the simplicity of a two-party system.

Consensus

Long before the concept was developed systematically, scholars celebrated Britain for its success in developing a consensual political culture, a body of common beliefs which contributed mightily to the perceived legitimacy of the political system. Indeed, this apparent success in achieving such high levels of popular consent on fundamentals was often cited as a major reason for including Britain in a survey course on comparative politics. The party system, characterized by *adversarialism within consensus*, has often been treated as a key factor in promoting such integration. Proceeding from the same fundamental political values, the parties were said to confine their differences to matters of policy on which disagreement would not threaten system maintenance. In restricting disputes to matters of more or less – 'safe' issues that lent readily to compromise – the parties both reflected the public consensus and contributed to its preservation.[20]

Observers were especially inclined to praise the parties for a certain ambiguity in both composition and policy. The wide embrace of the parties meant that groups defined in terms of ancestry, religion, language, tribe, caste and economic status were divided, in greater or lesser degree, between the major parties – blurring what would have been a dangerously close correspondence between social structure and political cleavage.[21] The intensity of partisan debate was also muted by the tendency of new Governments to inherit both the problems and solutions of their predecessors. Though cause for despair to ideologues, the continuity of policy in the face of sharp swings of the electoral pendulum was frequently praised by the texts.

The emphasis on consensus was not meant to mask the existence of genuine differences between the parties. As Ivor Jennings pointed out with some pride, the British parties 'are not mere electioneering organizations, as they tend to be in Canada and the United States, but are truly based upon competing political principles. In preferring one party to another, then, the electorate not only prefers one Government to another but prefers one line of policy to another'.[22] Thanks to the preponderance of centrist elements in the two major parties, these differences were normally subject to negotiation. British Conservatism was portrayed as empirical and proudly non-dogmatic, shunning with equal distaste the extremes of blind reaction and doctrinaire socialism.[23] Suffused with a deep religious tradition and permeated by a commitment to gradualism, the Labour Party was also noted for its moderation and deference.[24] The operation of the British party system seemed to demonstrate to the rest of the world how to keep political conflict from threatening the maintenance of civility and order.

The absence of personality cults

Another prominent feature of the textbook party system, the subordination of personality considerations to issues and parties, was especially attractive to American observers. The penchant for a non-personal style of politics seemed to operate at all levels of the British political system. Thus the main goal of selection committees and conferences in the constituencies was to find a candidate who would pledge fealty to the leadership and work diligently in Parliament to implement the party line. The resources which a potential candidate could bring to a contest – campaign funding, local connections, an attractive spouse, an engaging personality – were thought to be faintly illegitimate or at least secondary grounds for preferring one prospective candidate over another.[25] The same emphasis on policy, rather than personality, influenced relationships between candidate and constituents. Rather than offer voters immediate rewards or stress personal qualities such as competence and initiative, the candidates stood before the electorate as potential representatives of a Government with distinctive policy commitments.[26] According to one frustrated aspirant for Parliament, the electorate's well-documented indifference to the personal views of the contenders made it 'almost impossible for a candidate to obtain the required number of votes if he bases his appeal on his avowed intention of speaking and voting on each issue according to his own opinion and without regard to whether or not it is part of a political programme'.[27] According to Jennings, 'electors vote for parties and not for candidates'.[28]

In the decision calculus of the voter, the personal qualities of the leader and prospective Prime Minister were also minimized; the research suggested that partisanship had greater influence on perceptions of the party leaders than the leaders' image had on the vote.[29] Though not quite as impersonal as these other relationships we have surveyed, the linkage between the parliamentary party and the leadership was also instrumental and largely independent of personal ties.[30] Especially for the Labour Party, contests for the leadership were fought out in the context of policy conflicts rather than personality clashes. The de-emphasis of personality extended even to press coverage of politics; except on rare occasions, the reading public was spared much detail about the life history, life style and idiosyncracies of prominent figures. All in all, this feature of the party system stood in sharp contrast to an American system in which the traits and peculiarities of public officials were the main topics of coverage.

Centralization of authority

Though the growth of extensive party organization outside Parliament was linked to the political incorporation of the newly-enfranchised masses, few observers regarded extra-Parliamentary institutions as testaments to the prevalence of inner-party democracy. To the contrary, an impressive collection of observers, stretching at least from Ostrogorski to McKenzie, maintained that the highly-developed structure of the parties contributed to a pronounced centralization of authority. This theme, the lack of popular control over party life, has become another bit of conventional wiscom about the party system.[31]

As evidence for the hierarchical nature of authority, one could point to any number of 'unbalanced' relationships between the various components of the party. The apparent independence of candidates and constituency associations in general elections was in reality tightly circumscribed by the concentration of money, organs of publicity, advertising and policy-setting at party headquarters in London. The central apparatus also held the ultimate sanctions of certification over candidates and of outright disaffiliation over recalcitrant constituency organizations. Though these options were seldom exercised, their existence none the less underlined the location of final authority at the centre.

The subordination of peripheral bodies to central control held for even the most democratic of institutions in the party most strongly committed to the principle of inner-party democracy. At the annual Conference of the Labour Party, the fate of resolutions depended largely on the bloc votes cast by the secretaries of the major trade unions. Once Conference had adjourned, the decisions about including resolutions in the manifesto and putting them on the Parliamentary agenda were left to discretion of the leadership of the parliamentary party in consultation with the National Executive Committee. Given these limits on democracy at the Labour Conference and the absence of any attempt by the Conservatives to utilize the annual gathering as a mechanism for popular control, one of my instructors once dismissed the Conferences as little more than 'pep rallies'. Several texts seemed to agree with this assessment, assigning to Conference the function of providing symbolic gratification to maintain the allegiance of activitsts.

Discipline

The centralization of authority had its counterpart at the Parliamentary level in the form of strong party discipline. Though the term was not often used, at least in the sources I consulted, the typical backbencher was portrayed as little more than 'lobby fodder', a loyal supporter of his leadership who had little room for initiative or discretion. The pressures for conformity to the line came both from below, in the form of constituency activists who saw their role as supporting the national leadership, and from the Parliamentary leadership itself.[32] Because the maintenance of office required reliable support in the Commons, MPs were given few opportunities to challenge the party line. Aside from the opportunity to compete for the privilege of introducing a Private Member's Bill or to confront the leadership in a meeting of the parliamentary party, the MP had little chance to guide the direction of government policy. The norm was solidarity.[33] The member who strayed too often from this norm endangered his or her chances of political advancement and risked the ultimate sanction of expulsion from the party and an unwelcome sojourn in the political wilderness.

Organizational complexity

Whatever the reality of authority behind the democratic facade, the parties were portrayed as complex organizations marked by high levels of formal articulation.[34] This characteristic was most often mentioned in connection with the parties' impressive capacity for electoral mobilization through an integrated network of activists, canvassers and paid agents.[35] The impression one gets from many accounts is of a pair of potent war machines poised to strike at the short notice of dissolution, a military analogy that recurred with some frequency in several influential textbooks. What also impressed observers, beyond the 'armies' of campaign workers, was the high level of party activity directed to purposes other than immediate electoral success. According to Herman Finer,

> British parties are always actively present, everywhere present, and vocally present. They research, issue literature, hold meetings, conduct week-end and summer schools, organize local (district and ward) effort, participate in local-government elections and membership recruitment, and, above all, keep everyday contact with the members of the Commons and directly with the Cabinet.[36]

This extensive listing of tasks implied a complex structure with fully developed organizations at the constituency, regional and central levels. Such structural differentiation was evident in the complex diagrams which usually accompanied discussions about the multifunctional character of British parties. In their capacity to undertake all the activities described by Finer, it seemed that the British parties were performing nearly all the 'functions' essential to the maintenance of the political system – making them comparatively less specialized than appropriate for a nation with such an advanced political system.

The high level of organizational development also extended to party delegations within Parliament (and many local authorities as well). The texts routinely emphasized the hierarchical organization of the majority contingent into a leader, Cabinet, Government and supporting backbenchers. These components were connected by formalized channels of access and communication. Though the names may have differed, the Opposition usually mimicked the structural arrangements of the majority.[37] Even the factions within parliamentary parties exhibited many of the trappings of organization – committee structure, publications, regularized channels of contact with constituency supporters and the like. Depicted as comprehensive, interlocking, organizational networks that touched practically the entire society, the British parties almost seemed closer to the model of totalitarian parties than to the ad hoc electoral alliances of other Western nations.[38]

Structuring the vote

At the electoral level, British parties were especially noteworthy for their class-based character, a trait easily enough explained by the paramount role of class distinctions in British social structure. The centrality of class to party competition could be seen clearly in the agenda of political controversy and the social basis of party support.

The issues which divided the parties most cleanly, at the level of popular support, electoral manifestos and divisions within the Commons, centred on questions about class or with class implications: the level of social welfare benefits, trade union rights and privileges, the claims of state-aided education, the priority to be given public housing, choices among systems of taxation, the desirability of incomes policies, etc. Though not the only issues on the public agenda, these matters were the stuff of consistent debate and disagreement between the parties. If the concept of an agenda is broadened to include party images and themes, then the point about class divisions still holds. Though it never adopted an exclusive definition of the term, the Labour Party always claimed to represent the working class, seeking votes on the grounds that it alone could achieve a judicious mix of equity and competence in the management of British affairs. Befitting a party faced with a mass electorate mostly engaged in manual labor, the Conservatives laboured to transcend 'narrow' class interest by stressing 'national' themes of financial stability, tradition, patriotism and religion.[39] Though not fixated by class war and able on occasion to find a middle ground, the parties (so the texts indicated) never forgot that they envisioned different forms of social organization.

Pulzer's famous assertion, 'Class is the basis of British party politics; all else is embellishment and detail', was often cited in discussions about the social composition of the parties.[40] At the mass level, it was clear from the earliest post-war election studies that social class, usually measured by occupational status, was the primary dividing line in political behaviour.[41] The class cleavage obscured the development of cleavages along the lines of nationality, religion and region.[42] The 'fit' between social and political cleavage was not exact but close enough that the exceptions to it – the working-class Tories – were classified as deviant cases and made the subject of special inquiry.[43]

The link between class and party was especially clear in the case of Labour. Unions representing a preponderance of the work-force were formally integrated in the party, supplying the bulk of individual members, most tangible campaign resources and the party's most reliable voting strength. Though the Conservatives had no formalized equivalent in corporate support, the texts usually emphasized the central role of business enterprises in party finance and suggested that the Conservatives followed a corporate model in party operations (e.g., heavy use of market research and advertising) and organization (the emphasis on hierarchy). At the élite level, the parties also exhibited ties with distinctive occupational communities. The major parties each had recognizable social profiles, the Conservatives finding their 'centre of gravity' in the aristocracy and business élite, Labour recruiting most heavily from the children of manual workers.[44] The relative simplicity of the British social structure thus left its mark on British politics by imprinting the parties with clear class identities.

THE NEW CONSENSUS

What has just been described may well sound like ancient history to persons who now follow developments in British politics. According to the current political commentary., the party system no longer conforms to the classic British party model. This commentary, laced with metaphors of war and violence, speaks not of consensus and harmony but of catastrophe, disaster, the breaking of moulds – hardly the terminology appropriate to the land of the civic culture. The party system is breaking up 'not slowly and gradually, but with Mount St. Helen's force'.[45] We are witnessing, in the hopeful words of one participant, 'a change in the British political system as profound as we have seen this century'.[46] Much of the prognostication has focused on Labour, a party said to be 'destroying itself as the main party of reform and progressive change'.[47] Even though journalists speak most frequently of Labour's wilful 'disintegration' and 'political self-destruction', the Conservatives have not escaped altogether from the prophecies of doom. In a party that venerates unity almost above all other values, a former leader has publicly excoriated his successor, incited the faithful to revolt and flirted openly with the idea of a cross-party coalition.[48] An ousted Cabinet minister, foreseeing 'disastrous' election results, has charged that the ship of state is being steered straight for the rocks.[49] The spectacle of Tory disharmony prompted a newspaper famous for its level-headedness to suggest that

> Never in recent experience has a Leader been so publicly on trial and exposed, so openly doubted by many of her colleagues in Cabinet and outside, so repeatedly dive-bombed by her immediate predecessor, so heavily rejected in every opinion poll.[50].

As Labour resists a 'siege' from a 'horde' of ultrademocrats, the Conservatives go 'in search of a miracle' to restore credibility to party policy.[51]

Noticing this unprecedented turmoil, political scientists have had to revise their notions about the operation of the party system.[52] As a symbol of this evolving awareness, consider the changing tone in the commentary of Samuel Beer, a scholar regarded as one of the most perceptive observers of British affairs. In *British Politics in the Collectivist Age*, published in 1969, Beer searched for the factors which contributed to the success of British politics and he accorded the party system a place of honour. The book ended with the prediction that 'the old party dualism would seem likely to have a long, vigorous and useful future'.[53] Contrast the admiring tone of this conclusion with the sequel, subtitled *The Political Contradictions of Collectivism*, which speaks of 'pluralistic stagnation' and 'paralysis of public choice' in modern Britain.[54] The blame for this descent can be apportioned liberally but the parties earn a major share. Like Beer, other authorities on British politics have redefined their mission from locating the correlates of stability to hunting for the sources of pathology.[55]

Nearly every one of the adumbrated features of the party system seems to have been called into question by a series of developments:

(1) *Decline of party supremacy*. The supremacy of parties in the political system, once buttressed by constitution and convention, seems to be giving way under the onslaught of several forces. In part, the power of the parties has been challenged by the same factors that have circumscribed the authority of Parliament. Two of the major constitutional issues of recent years – devolution of governing

authority in Scotland and Wales and Britain's continued membership in the European Economic Community – were decided not by a vote in Parliament but by the results of popular referenda. Of course, Parliament was not bound to follow the results of the 'advisory' polls but a Government would find it most difficult to ignore the voice of the people – and those decisions were sustained.[56] If the arguments of the anti-Marketeers prove prophetic, then Parliament will also find its sovereignty under challenge from the claims of the EEC legislative assembly. Even if Parliament reasserts its familiar role, it is not clear that the parties will be in a condition to direct British affairs with their traditional vigour. It remains to be seen how the power of the parties can withstand the introduction of permanent subject committees in the Commons – a potential independent base of power for MPs – or the possibility of some kind of proportional representation. In the Labour Party, the choice of the leader, formerly the exclusive preserve of the parliamentary party, has been given over to an electoral college in which MPs hold a minority of votes. The well-documented decline in party cohesion within Parliament also poses major challenges to the parties as effective agents of governance.[57]

Perhaps in response to these trends, it seems clear that the parties no longer have sole authority in matters of recruitment of personnel or political initiative. A host of extra-parliamentary armies now march under banners as disparate as the National Front, the Anti-Nazi League, and, in milder form, the 'community politics' bandwagon so popular with Liberals and Nationalists. Conflicts are increasingly settled in the courts and the streets – arenas where the writ of party runs less effectively.[58] Though it is too soon to start fitting the British body politic for a pluralist jacket, the fit seems closer than it used to be.

(2) *'Anti-democratic' trends*. Once regarded as the major expressions of democracy, parties are now portrayed as major threats to that value. The problem of democracy stems in large part from the apparent 'capture' of the party apparatus by extremist elements. These groups, differing dramatically from the party's core electorate, have asserted their voice in constituency organizations, Conference and the national executive, seeking to impose their will, in place of the electorate's, on the party's legislative agenda.[59] Though this charge may sound applicable only to Labour, a milder version of the same process has been sighted in the Conservative Party.[60] As McKenzie argued years ago, British democracy rests on the principle that legislators may be held accountable to the electorate but not to the wishes of any extra-Parliamentary organization.[61] The trends within the parties seem to threaten that norm.

(3) *The decline of efficiency*. A similar fate has befallen the parties with regard to the value of efficiency. As noted above, declines in party cohesion make it more and more difficult for the Government to react swiftly to crisis and or to map out coherent policies to deal with long-range problems. When parties do act decisively, it has been charged, they tend to complicate matters unduly by rashly undoing the work of the previous Government. For S. E. Finer, the 'adversary politics' motif has been a major factor in undercutting economic growth.[62] Changes in macroeconomic policy which accompany swings of the electoral pendulum destroy the long-range planning necessary for recovery. In a striking change of perception, scholars of Britain now seem to be calling for a greater degree of inertia in policy or at least for ways to insulate policy planning from capricious partisan-inspired U-turns.[63]

(4) *Two-partyism*. The stability of the two-party system was called into serious question by the general elections of 1974. The two major parties, who had averaged more than 90 per cent of the popular vote and virtually all the Parliamentary seats in the previous eight elections, were reduced to claiming just 75 per cent of the vote and less than 95 per cent of the seats in the Parliament elected in February. The most striking decline in major party support was evident in the Celtic fringe (Ireland excluded) where parties of communal nationalism obtained 14 seats in October 1974.[64] The decline of duopoly would have been even more evident had the electoral system rewarded the Liberals with a number of seats commensurate with their nearly 20 per cent of the popular vote.[65] The quite limited restoration of two-party dominance in 1979 was quickly overshadowed by the emergence of a new party, the Social Democrats, largely composed at the élite level of Labour moderates. Fighting in alliance with the Liberals, the new party has scored dramatic by-election victories in marginal seats and constituencies formerly regarded as 'safe' for the major parties. Though commentators have cautioned against the assumption that these by-election results will be replicated under the conditions of a general election, there is clearly a sense that something big is happening.[66]

(5) *Polarization*. The obituaries of Lord Butler, the first postwar Conservative Chancellor of the Exheqeur, have noted the coincidence of his death with the rejection of 'Butskellism', a term signifying the consensus economic policies of post-war Labour and Conservative governments. 'Conviction politics', to use the only concept held in esteem by both Margaret Thatcher and Anthony Wedgewood Benn, has replaced 'consensus politics'. In a political

system where theory has traditionally been denigrated in preference to brute empiricism, both parties have begun to enact policies on the basis of more systematic theoretical substructures. In the search for a standard of consistency, the parties have moved further out from the centre of the political spectrum, reversing normal evolutionary processes by changing from broad churches into sects. As the activists of the two parties move further apart, each camp becoming less representative of the parties' core electorate, the rhetoric of contemporary politics seems angrier, more likely to threaten the maintenance of political order. The conflicts within parties have also grown sharper and more divisive.

(6) *Personalism*. Fewer and fewer electors seem disposed to vote for the proverbial pig just because it wears the proper rosette.[67] Whether or not the individual candidate now counts for more than a hundred votes, the candidates are acting as if their personal qualities made a difference. The Liberals and Nationalists have pioneered this localistic approach by paying a great deal of attention to the nuances of constituency casework. With this reliance upon a 'getting the dead cat out of the alley' style of politics, their campaigns seemed more American than British.

Reform of the Labour Party has also resulted in greater attention to the qualities of candidates and Members of Parliament. Mandating that sitting MPs go through a process of renomination has accentuated the courting of constituency parties by elected officials.[68] Even before mandatory reselection. Labour MPs have been finding it more and more difficult to satisfy the often conflicting demands of constituency activists and the predominantly centrist leadership in the Parliamentary Party.[69] The emergence of Tory 'wets' may well call forth similar conflict in Conservative associations.

The surprising success of the Labour dissidents may well accelerate this trend toward a 'personal' style in politics. Even though it was widely thought that dissidents were doomed because they lacked a party label, two Labour MPs who ran as Independents because of conflicts with their constituency parties regained the seats in February, 1974 (though failing to hold them in October).[70] More spectacular yet was the success of two of the SDP founders, Shirley Williams and Roy Jenkins, in returning to Westminster at least partly on the strength of their personal appeal.

(7) *Organizational decay*. The once vaunted party machines seem to suffer from progressive atrophy. In terms of finance, individual membership and capacity to employ full-time agents, Labour has

decayed very rapidly. The thinning of Labour ranks has made it much easier for Bennites and other left-wingers to capture control of the nominating apparatus of local parties. Individual membership in the Conservative associations has also declined.[71] The vibrant grass-roots enthusiasm for movements like the Liberal/SDP Alliance and the Campaign for Nuclear Disarmament, developments which belie Britain's reputation for phlegmatism, underscore the relative decline of established parties as effective agents of mobilization.

(8) *Dealignment*. The frozen cleavage structure has been another apparent casualty of recent political development. Politics is no longer just about class. Britain, like other advanced industrial societies, has begun to confront new kinds of issues – race relations, communal nationalism, European integration – that do not cleave to the social structure.[72] The complexity of these cross-cutting issues has unleashed startling levels of electoral volatility.[73] Political behaviour is less accurately predicted from individual social characteristics.[74] The polls suggest that among what should be its core constituency, the skilled working class, Labour could manage no better than a dead heat with the Conservatives in 1979.[75] Conversely, the Conservative grip on the middle class electorate appears to be diminishing.[76] The success of the SDP/Liberal alliance, based upon the capacity of the new movement to amount an effective cross-class appeal, also seems to belie conventional wisdom.[77]

SO WHAT ELSE IS NEW?

Even so general an inventory as this makes it clear that the textbook party system has faller on hard times. Each one of the developments just cited warrants far more complete analysis than time or space permit here. Taken together, they constitute the basis for a new consensus about British parties, leading to quite non-traditional conclusions about the nature of political life in the United Kingdom.

But before we throw away the old textbooks and compose new model answers for old essay questions, let me suggest some cautions. I think we need to ask ourselves some questions about the nature of political change in Britain: how much has really changed in Britain? Have some of these apparent 'changes' represented corrections to earlier generalizations that failed to capture the dynamic properties of the party system? Have we seen new patterns of political life or merely a return to normality after a generation of atypical experience? Conversely, have we invested momentary departures from stable patterns with a permanence they do not deserve? To what extent are the observed changes due to peculiar events in Britain or a function of world-wide trends which have manifested themselves elsewhere? Has Britain's economic decline caused us to focus disproportionate attention upon insitutions that could not bear similar scrutiny in more 'successful' nations? Are the parties being charged with sins for which they do not bear responsibility? Finally, is the performance of the party system relatively constant but our expectation different – so that we judge the parties more harshly for doing what they have always done? All these questions suggest limits to the new revisionism of which three will receive attention here:

(1) the degree to which things have really changed;
(2) the degree to which those changes which are "real" can be attributed to developments within Britain; and
(3) the extent to which parties have been stable but our expectations have changed.

To begin with, some of the developments which are being described as 'changes' may not deserve that title either because they are not new or because they mark departures from norms that were not particularly well established. Take, for example, the suggestion that parties have lost much of the trust and affection they used to elicit from informed observers. But have the parties customarily enjoyed praise and approbation? Though Americans have tended to see British parties as a model worthy of emulation, the vision has not always been so benign on the other side of the Atlantic. Ostrogorski's famous analysis of mid-Victorian Liberalism was a warning that the development of mass parties posed a grave peril to the democratic process:

> Every attempt at asserting the freedom and independence of political thought was now repressed; for every difference of opinion was a blow struck at the unity of the party of which the Caucus had constituted itself the permanent guardian. The agressive ardour of the Radical enthusiasts coincided with the middle-class selfishness of the wire-pullers in stifling opposition and the spirit of criticism in the Associations, and they became in English society a great school of fanaticism, of intolerance, of contempt for other people's opinions, and of suspicion, which impugns the honesty and sincerity of opponents beforehand. Political language, platform eloquence, naturally grew all the more passionate and violent and full of personalities. Even when devoid of violence the jealous and irritable belief fostered by the Caucus produced an impatience of discussion which more and more infected political life.[78]

These charges were echoed by other observers in Britain.[79] Nor is there anything particularly new in Professor Finer's charge that the parties have sacrificed the public interest in their pursuit of electoral power.[80] From at least the late nineteenth century on, disgruntled political figures have charged that elections degenerate into bidding wars for the support of electors, making 'sound' economics impossible and thus destroying Britain's productive capacity. To judge by the severity of the criticisms, parties were perceived not as the crowning glory but the Achilles' heel of the British political system.

The assertion that Britain usually has a two-party system with a single party commanding a parliamentary majority may be another 'norm' that rests upon a misunderstanding of British political development. This characterization simply falsifies much of the experience of modern Britain. There have been twenty-seven general elections since 1885, when the electoral system is generally reckoned to have achieved modernity by the enfranchisement of a majority of adult males. In ten of these elections (1885, 1886, 1892, 1900, January and December 1910, 1918, 1923, 1929, and 1974 – February), no single party obtained a majority of seats in Parliament.[81] Though the term 'coalition' may be too strong to describe the governments which emerged from these ten elections, in each case the largest party was forced to rely upon formal or tacit alliances with small parties to retain control of Parliament. Besides these cases of 'minority' government, five other elections produced governments with precarious single-party majorities of ten seats or fewer.[82] Measured by the standard of party representation in Parliament, the two-party model seem less 'normal' than is often suggested.

If the two-party model is descriptively questionable, as I have just asserted, its 'logic' is also open to attack. In Britain, like the United States, the strength of the two major parties in national politics has rested on the prevalence of one-party politics throughout large sections of the country. During the golden age of party duopoly from 1945 through 1970, most constituencies were 'safe' seats for one of the parties. Labour could rely for its core parliamentary strength upon Scotland, Wales, and the heavy industrial areas of England. The phalanx of Labour MPs confronted an equally secure bloc of Tory representatives from the agricultural areas, business seats and southeast. The number of units with genuine two-party competition – the marginals – was relatively low. In an important sense, then, the two-party norm has always been something of an illustion.

The tendency to over-generalize from limited data may also account for the suggestion that political parties have been permanently eclipsed by the rise of extra-Parliamentary pressure groups committed to 'direct action'. On the Labour side, the rise of these groups was fuelled in large part by the disappointment of many socialists with the perceived 'betrayal' of the 1964–70 Wilson Government. Though some of the populist groups continue to function and a few even flourish, many leftists have now abandoned the extra-parliamentary route to rejoin the Labour Party and some of the individuals who gained prominence through their role as leaders of pressure groups – Frank Field (Child Poverty Action Group), Jack Straw (National Union of Students), Peter Hain (various direct action campaigns) – now sit as Labour MPs or stand as prospective Parliamentary candidates. More broadly, the current debate within the Labour Party about the infiltration of extreme leftists is an oblique testimony to the growing sentiment among activists that control of the party really does matter.[83] To a more limited degree, the Conservatives experienced a similar cycle. In response to their disappointments with Edward Heath's Government of 1970–74, disgruntled activists formed a variety of pressure groups designed to press for the defence of 'middle class' interests. These groups soon dwindled as the post-Heath Conservative leadership espoused a much more aggressive version of class politics in public debate.[84] For both parties, the defections to 'direct action' groups proved ephemeral historical episodes, temporary aberrations from the norm of party dominance. Scholars, like the activists, seem to have given up too quickly on the parties as mechanisms for change.

Though it is hard to gauge the magnitude of change without precise quantitative indicators, there can also be some doubt about the degree to which party unity and internal harmony have declined. In writing about current troubles, commentators seem to portray the decade or so after World War II as a golden age, when the parties were moderate and unified, MPs obeyed the whips and the extra-Parliamentary organizations knew their place and kept it. This portrait clashes with reality at several points. The unity of the parties has always been fragile and has occasionally given way to bitter internal conflict. For the Tories, the Suez affair demonstrated that MPs were willing to break ranks and that the supposedly inert constituency associations were not unwilling to apply the screws to dissident MPs.[85] The Profumo scandal, which also ignited some backbench Tory rebellion, suggested that dissidence did not invariably lead to the application of sanctions.[86] In the case of Labour, the years of opposition after 1951 were marked by Conference battles, attempts at intimidation, public protest, the withdrawal of the whip, resignations from the Shadow Cabinet and similar disturbances.[87] Throughout the period, several observers noted that MPs from both parties were not so hobbled as commonly asserted and did have opportunities to influence events through several avenues.[88] Jackson anticipated much recent writing when he demonstrated the limits to party discipline and the possibilities of effective dissidence.[89]

If the golden age seems less burnished upon closer inspection, so the contemporary period is less leaden than frequently portrayed. The charges of increasing party extremism require especially careful scrutiny. In and of themselves, the reforms Labour has recently adopted can be interpreted as modest structural reforms that will bring British practices in line with other democratic societies.[90] 'Mandatory reselection' means only that sitting MPs cannot count on automatic renomination and have instead to face a selection conference before regaining party support. That sounds suspiciously like a variant of the primary election process whereby incumbents in the United States are held accountable for their actions. The attempt at securing accountability in Britian has been criticized on the grounds that selection conferences may not accurately represent the electors and citizens whom the MP is supposed to serve.[91] But American experience with primary elections suggests that opening up the nominating process to all registered electors will not necessarily guarantee participation by a representative sample of the electorate.[92] In any case, the charges about the unrepresentative character of selection conferences applies just as well to the original process by which sitting MPs first earned party support. Furthermore, would there be any better guarantee of a close fit between constituency opinion and MP if the selection were made at central headquarters? Regardless of the answer, reselection would probably strike residents of many democratic countries as an essential element of the electoral process. The involvement of extra-parliamentary organs in the choice of a leader has been the norm in other parties committed to democratic socialism and has been carried one step further by the rival SDP, which elects both its parliamentary and non-parliamentary leadership by a postal ballot of the entire membership.[93] Similarly, the attempt to construct electoral manifestos directly by conference, which the Labour Party has so far resisted, resembles the process of mass consultation utilized by parties in the United States.

The substance of the reforms does not seem particularly extreme nor is it clear that the proponents see them as weapons to be used in remaking the party according to some kind of Bolshevik model. Rather, according to the Kogans, the success of the reforms was occasioned by loyal party members who felt betrayed by the actions of recent Labour governments and saw the need for changes which would keep future governments mindful of commitments made during a campaign.[94] The campaign on behalf of the new policies was scrupulously democratic, its success due not to manipulation or intimidation but to the superior organizing skills demonstrated by the reformers. One may justifiably quarrel with the wisdom of the changes, proposed and enacted, without suggesting that they constitute part of a revolutionary strategy designed to undermine the Constitution. Perhaps American scholars, with their history of pressing for more 'responsible' party systems, can appreciate the context of these reforms better than their British colleagues.

To reiterate, it may be that parties have departed less from textbook standards than recent commentary would suggest. Some of the alleged 'changes' are less dramatic than they seem, some may be only short-term deviations from norms and others may be developments that are more 'normal' than the conditions they are said to undermine.

Even if we momentarily grant that the party system has been changing radically, how much of this change can be attributed to developments within Britain? If similar trends have been evident in other countries, then the British parties probably deserve less blame for initiating the contemporary crisis. In fact, according to Kevin Phillips, Britain is not the only country where the bloom is off the two-party rose: 'From Canada and Britain to Belgium and Germany, fragmentation is taking place. In a postindustrial time the minor parties are feeding on the breakdown and increasing irrelevance of old party loyalties fashioned during the era of industrialization. And the process seems to be gathering force as the ideologies of the left and right prove unable to solve contemporary economic difficulties'.[95] The rise of a new centre party in Britain has counterparts in the emergence of the New Democratic Party in Canada and the 'National Unity Campaign' of John Anderson in the United States. In the smaller European democracies, small 'broker' parties are increasingly playing a pivotal role in the allocation of power. The resurgence of ethnic nationalism, regarded as an important sign of party destabilization is Britain, has also marked political life in many countries outside the United Kingdom.[96] Similarly, Britain has not been alone in watching the emergence of competitors to parties in the form of strong interest groups, increasingly politicized courts and other newly-emergent political actors.[97]

Like the decay of the two-party system, the *mechanism* responsible for mass political dealignment in Britain is tied to social and economic developments common to most advanced societies. The rise of electoral volatility throughout the 1970s coincided with the entry into the electorate of a large cohort of persons born after the second World War.[98] Though precise statistics are hard to come by, it appears that the 1974 British electorate contained more than 3.5 million first-time voters, more than 10 per cent of total participants.[99] This new cohort, characterized by a 'post-industrial' value system and highly susceptible to short-term electoral forces, has accounted for some of the dramatic shifts in aggregate vote patterns detected in the last three British general elections.[100] This cohort proved to be a destabilizing influence in several countries which had, like Britain, lowered the voting age and experienced a demographic 'bulge' due to the immediate post-war baby boom.[101]

Another important aspect of dealignment, the decline of classvoting, is also at least partially a function of trends in social development throughout the West. Though knowledge of an individual's occupation now proves less reliable in predicting the vote, recent research provices evidence of a corresponding increase in the predictive power of the individual's residential environment.[102] This research is consistent with a model of 'post-industrial' social development in which a number of factors – the decline of traditional industry, the rise of light industry and a burgeoning service sector, marked occupational diversification, increased geographical mobility and some equalization of consumption patterns – all contribute to a divorce between work place and home place. As a consequence of these new conditions, the immediate 'occupational community' loses influence in the shaping of individual perspective and, for the manual workers in particular, class solidarity recedes in the face of increasing concern about the quality of home life and the prospect of individual or family mobility.[103] The new voting patterns then reflect the more instrumental orientation of increasingly 'privatized' electors. Social characteristics are not divorced from the vote; rather, they take new forms and patterns as a consequence of worldwide changes in the nature of social stratification.

I have suggested that some changes in the party system are illusory and that others can better be explained by worldwide trends rather than 'internal' factors. The final caution about the new model of party life is reflected in the title for this chapter and has been referred to obliquely throughout the text. Simply put, much of the current dissatisfaction seems to stem not from changes in the traditional behaviour of the parties but instead from a disenchantment with certain features that once were cited as the virtues of the party system. When American scholars looked at the British party system, they perceived a system in which the parties provided the electors with clear and unambiguous plans of action; those plans became the basis for government legislation and were eventually enacted; and the party which had lost the election spent its time in opposition formulating the alternative strategy which it would present to the populace at the next election. From at least the time of Woodrow Wilson, this image has been so appealing that it became the standard which guided many of the academic reformers in their attempts to refurbish the American party system.[104] The most systematic of such efforts, the work of the Committee on Political Parties of the American Political Science Association, was strongly influenced by scholars who 'saw the British parties and party system as empirical referents . . . [and hoped to see] American parties become like British parties . . . '.[105] What these observers wanted most of all was a party system which would offer the electors clear choices on policy questions and deliver on the promises made in a campaign – as the British parties were thought to do. As that last clause was meant to suggest, the descriptive accuracy of the APSA report has long been suspect but the document none the less shows why the British party system seemed to be such a powerful model.

Ironically, the same features which attracted American observers are now thought to be responsible for Britain's current troubles. In Finer's analysis, Britain is afflicted with 'adversary politics', a condition of virtual elective dictatorship, because the electoral system converts modest electoral victory into unlimited power. The consequence is a series of wild swings in policy because the victorious party immediately dismantles the work of its predecessor and enacts a brand new set of policies from its manifesto. However accurate this description, it nicely illustrates the role of changing perceptions. There was a time when 'adversary politics' was thought to be responsible for Britain's political success. Parties were praised for their willingness to commit to specific policy goals and the governmental system was endorsed because it enabled the victor to make good on its promises. American observers wanted to remake their party system in that image, to generate 'internal sovereignty', to recover the dynamism of government that had died with Franklin Roosevelt. But to observers on both sides of the Atlantic, it now seems that responsible party government – the explicit statement of party objectives, the maintenance of party discipline, the enactment of party pledges upon election, the high degree of responsiveness – is the very source of Britain's current troubles. To quote Richard Rose, 'British government is party government – but that does not ensure that it is good government'.[106] It might not have occurred to earlier observers that there could be a difference.

What I have tried to suggest in these pages is the need to place the development of the British party system in a broader perspective which considers history, international trends and the role of changing expectations. When these factors are taken into account in assessing changing patterns of party politics, I suggest that there may be less there than meets the eye. Perhaps those old textbooks deserve a reprieve or at least a second look.

NOTES

*I would like to thank the editors for their support and suggestions and H. Pierre Secher for never getting rid of his old textbooks. I also owe a major debt to Professors Raphael Zariski of the University of Nebraska and Merle Kling of Washington University. Though neither would claim to be a 'British expert', they both stimulated my interest in British politics and have influenced my own teaching on the subject.

1. J. L. Garvin, 'Imperial and Foreign Affairs', *Fortnightly Review*, 1 Oct. 1909, p. 568.
2. The range of this revisionist literature is demonstrated by the following works: Richard H. S. Crossman, *The Myths of Cabinet Government* (Cambridge, Mass.: Harvard University Press, 1972); 'Blowing Up a Tyranny', *The Economist*, 5 Nov. 1977, 11-16; Anthony King, 'Political Parties in Western Democracies', *Polity*, 2 (Winter 1969) 111–41.
3. Bruce E. Cain, 'Challenges and Response in British Party Politics', *Comparative Politics*, 12 (Apr. 1980) 335–48. Jeffrey B. Freyman, 'The Labour Party and Partisan Change in Britain', paper delivered to the Annual Meeting of the Midwest Political Science Association, Cincinnati, Ohio, 1981; Dennis Kavanagh, 'New Bottles for New Wines: Changing Assumptions About British Politics', *Parliamentary Affairs*, 31 (Winter 1978) 6–21; Kavanagh, 'Party Politics in Question', ch. 9 in *New Trends in British Politics: Issues for Research*, ed. Dennis Kavanagh and Richard Rose (London: Sage Publications, 1977) 191–220. There would have been less need for such sharp reappraisal if more attention had been paid to a series of important articles: David Butler, 'American

Myths About British Parties', *Virginia Quarterly Review*, 31 (1955) 46–56; Dennis Kavanagh, 'An American Science of British Politics', *Political Studies*, 22 (Sept. 1974) 251–70; Jorgen Rasmussen, 'Party Responsibility in Britain and the United States', *Journal of American Studies*, 1 (1967) 233–56.

4. Leon Epstein, 'What Happened to the British Party Model', *American Political Science Review*, 74 (Mar. 1980) 9–22; James K. Pollock, 'A Comparison of the American and British Party Systems', *Journal of the Royal Institute of International Affairs*, 9 (Mar. 1930) 207–21.
5. Representative works of advocacy include J. C. Banks, *Federal Britain*? (London: George G. Harrap, 1971); Vernon Bogdanor, *Devolution* (Oxford University Press, 1979) and *The People and the Party System: The Referendum and Electoral Reform in British Politics* (Cambridge University Press, 1981); Peter Paterson, *The Selectorate: The Case for Primary Elections in Britain* (London: MacGibbon and Kee, 1967); Woodrow Wyatt, *Turn Again Westminster* (London: Andre Deutsch, 1973); Michael Zander, *A Bill of Rights* (Chichester, Sussex: Barry Rose, 1975).
6. A. Lawrence Lowell, *The Government of England* (New York: Macmillan, 1920; repr. of 1912 edn) I, p.v. Richard Rose, *Politics in England*, 2nd edn (Boston: Little, Brown, 1974) pp. 1–8.
7. In order, these phrases come from Andre Mathiot, *The British Political System*, trans. Jennifer S. Hines (Stanford University Press, 1958; trans. of 1955 French edn); W. Ivor Jennings, *The British Constitution*, 4th edn (Cambridge University Press, 1962) p. 29; R. M. Punnett, *British Government and Politics*, 2nd edn (New York: W. W. Norton, 1971) p. 100.
8. To make the narrative sound less barbaric, I have omitted phrases like 'it has been argued' and 'so it is said'. The reader should understand that I am reconstructing arguments made by other scholars rather than describing my own understanding of the party system.
9. Sydney D. Bailey, *British Parliamentary Democracy*, 2nd edn (Boston: Houghton, Mifflin, 1962) p. 8; Ivor Bulmer-Thomas, *The Growth of the British Party System* (London: John Baker, 1965) I, p. v.; Mathiot, *British Political System*, p. 81; William Sharp McKechnie, *The New Democracy and the Constitution* (Port Washington, NY: Kennikat Press, 1971; report. of 1912 edn) pp. 67–8; Frank Stacey, *The Government of Modern Britain* (Oxford University Press, 1968) p. 281.
10. Cited in Frederic A. Ogg, *English Government and Politics*, 2nd edn (New York: Macmillan, 1947) p. 480.
11. Ibid., pp. 481–2.
12. Mathiot, *British Political System,* p. 81.
13. Cecil S. Emden, *The People and the Constitution*, 2nd edn (London: Oxford University Press, 1956) p. 101, 166; J. Harvey and L. Bather, *The British Constitution* (London: Macmillan, 1964) p. 83; Jennings, *British Constitution*, p. 188.
14. For a notable dissent from this position, see Kenneth Waltz, *Foreign Policy and Democratic Politics* (Boston: Little, Brown, 1967).

15. 'Toward a More Responsible Two-Party System: Report of the Committee on Political Parties, American Political Science Association', *American Political Science Review*, 44 (Sept. 1950) supplement. See also Butler, 'American Myths', and Kavanagh, 'American Science'.
16. Bailey, *British Parliamentary Democracy*, p. 141; Bailey, ed., *Political Parties and the Party System in Britain* (New York: Frederick A. Praeger, 1952) pp. 38–9; Emden, *People and Constitution*, pp. 115–16; Harvey and Bather, *British Constitution*, 87ff., pp. 111–12; Jennings, *British Constitution*, pp. 57–9; Ogg, *English Government*, pp. 482–3.
17. Punnett, *British Government*, p. 101.
18. Mathiot, *British Political System*, p. 71. See also Jorgen Rasmussen, 'The Implication of Safe Seats for British Democracy', *Western Political Quarterly*, 19 (Sept. 1966) 516–29.
19. Ibid., 88ff.
20. James Christoph, 'Consensus and Cleavage in British Political Ideology', *American Political Science Reivew*, 59 (Sept. 1965) 629–42; Harvey and Bather, *British Constitution*, pp. 83–4; Jennings, *British Constitution*, pp. 30–1, 188; Mathiot, *British Political System*, pp. 15–16, 31–2, 63, 87–8, 109ff.; Punnett, *British Government*, pp. 23–8.
21. Jennings, *British Constitution*, pp. 30–2.
22. Jennings, *British Constitution*, p. 188.
23. Ian Gilmour, *Inside Right: a Study of Conservatism* (London: Quartet Books, 1978); Trevor Russel, *The Tory Party* (Harmondsworth, Middlesex: Penguin, 1978).
24. Egon Wertheimer, *Portrait of the Labour Party* (London: G. P. Putnam, 1929).
25. Austin Ranney, *Pathways to Parliament* (Madison: University of Wisconsin Press, 1965); Michael Rush, *The Selection of Parliamentary Candidates* (London: Nelson, 1969).
26. Bailey, *Political Parties and Party System*, pp. ix–x; Dennis Kavanagh, *Constituency Electioneering in Britain* (London: Longmans, Green, 1970).
27. Stephen King-Hall, 'The Independent in Politics', in Bailey, *Political Parties and Party System*, pp. 111–12.
28. Ivor Jennings, *Party Politics* (London: Cambridge University Press, 1961) I, pp. 260–1.
29. David Butler and Donald Stokes, *Political Change in Britain* (New York: St. Martin's, 1969) 383–8.
30. Harvey and Bather, *British Constitution*, p. 92.
31. A. H. Birch, *The British System of Government* (New York: Frederick A. Praeger, 1967) p. 115; Leon Epstein, 'British Mass Parties in Comparison with American Parties', *Political Science Quarterly*, 71 (Mar. 1956) 97–125; Robert McKenzie, *British Political Parties*, 2nd edn (London: Mercury Books, 1963); Geoffrey K. Roberts, *Political Parties and Pressure Groups in Britain* (London: Weidenfeld & Nicholson, 1970) p. 77.
32. Harvey and Bather, *British Constitution*, pp. 95–6.
33. Emden, *People and Constitution*, p. 135.
34. Ibid., p. 143; Harvey and Bather, *British Constitution*, pp. 95–101.

35. Jean Blondel, *Voters, Parties and Leaders: The Social Fabric of British Politics* (Harmondsworth, Middlesex: Penguin, 1967) p. 88.
36. Herman Finer, *The Major Governments of Modern Europe* (Evanston, Ill.: Row, Peterson and Co., 1960) p. 74.
37. R. M. Punnett, *Front Bench Opposition: the Role of the Leader of the Opposition, the Shadow Cabinet and Shadow Government in British Politics* (London: Heinemann, 1973); D. R. Turner, *The Shadow Cabinet in British Politics* (London: Routledge & Kegan Paul, 1969).
38. For suggestive comparisons in this vein, see Jerome Gilison, *British and Soviet Politics* (Baltimore: Johns Hopkins University Press, 1972).
39. Robert McKenzie and Allan Silver, *Angels in Marble: Working Class Conservatives in Urban England* (University of Chicago Press, 1968) pp. 18–36.
40. Peter G. J. Pulzer, *Political Representation and Elections: Parties and Voting in Great Britain* (New York: Frederick A. Praeger, 1967).
41. Bailey, *Political Parties and Party System*, pp. 168–76; Jennings, *British Constitution*, pp. 65, 191–2.
42. Richard Rose, 'Class and Party Divisions: Britain as a Test Case', *Sociology*, 2 (May, 1968) 129–62.
43. McKenzie and Silver, *Angels in Marble*; Eric A. Nordlinger, *The Working Class Tories* (London: MacGibbon and Kee, 1967).
44. W. L. Guttsman, *The British Political Elite* (London: MacGibbon and Kee, 1968) chs 9–10.
45. Anthony King, 'Whatever is Happening to the British Party System', *PS*, 15 (Winter 1982) p. 10.
46. Roger Pincham, Liberal Party chairman, cited in Geoffrey Godsell, 'British Labour Party Puts Its Future on the Line', *Christian Science Monitor*, 28 Sept. 1981, p. 1.
47. Ibid., p. 1.
48. See 'Heath Ready to Play Role in Coalition', *Manchester Guardian Weekly*, 6 Dec. 1981, p. 3; Julian Haviland, 'Impassioned Plea by Heath Gets Short Shrift from Tories', *The Times*, 15 Oct. 1981, p. 1.
49. Michael White, 'Thatcher Completes Rout of "Wets"', *Manchester Guardian Weekly*, 20 Sept. 1981, p. 3. See also Ian Gilmour, 'Drake and the Dole', *Manchester Guardian Weekly*, 13 Dec. 1981, p. 4. Some Conservative peers have also joined in the fray: 'Peers Criticize Unemployment "Inaction"', *Guardian*, 16 June 1982, p.5.
50. 'The Conservatives in Search of a Miracle', *Manchester Guardian Weekly*, 18 Oct. 1981, p. 10. For an example of the Prime Minister's inability to persuade a natural ally, see 'Setting the People Free – a Wee Bit', *The Economist*, 27 Feb. 1982, 33ff. Six months later, in the aftermath of the successful recapture of the Falklands, the same Prime Minister was said (*Guardian*, 16 June 1982, p. 1) to have 'secured the greatest personal political triumph from her parliamentary colleagues since the end of the second world war'. As I will argue below, writing on the party system has frequently tended to over-generalize from the moment.
51. Bernard Crick, 'Too Much Preaching, Not Enough Planning', *Manchester Guardian Weekly*, 20 Sept. 1981, p. 21; Peter Jenkins, 'The Siege of Labour Goes On', Ibid., 4 Oct. 1981, p. 4.

52. Epstein, 'What Happened to of the British Party Model'.
53. Samuel H. Beer, *British Politics in the Collectivist Age* (New York: Vintage, 1969; reprint of 1965 British edn) p. 434.
54. Samuel H. Beer, *Britain Against Itself* (New York: W. W. Norton, 1982).
55. See the introductory chapter in this volume.
56. The Scottish referendum actually passed by a narrow margin but devolution was dropped because the measure failed to gain the required majority of the registered electorate.
57. Philip Norton, *Dissension in the House of Commons, 1974-1979* (Oxford University Press, 1980); Norton, *Conservative Dissidents: Dissent within the Parliamentary Conservative Party* (London: Temple Smith, 1978); John E. Schwarz, 'Exploring a New Role in Policy Making: The British House of Commons in the 1970s', *American Political Science Review*, 74 (Mar. 1980) 23–37.
58. On the increasing political role of the courts, see John Griffith, 'A Law Unto Themselves', *New Socialist*, Mar./Apr. 1982, 22–5; Nicholas de Jongh, 'Romans Ruling Could Threaten Plays', and 'A New Form of Censorship', both in *Manchester Guardian Weekly*, 28 Mar. 1982, p. 4; Richard Evans, 'Defeated Labour Candidate may go to Court', *Times*, 20 July 1982, p. 3. For the civil servants, see Peter Kellner and Lord Crowther-Hunt, *The Civil Servants: An Inquiry into Britain's Ruling Class* (London: MacDonald & Janes, 1982).
59. Michael Foot, 'The Labour Party and Parliament', *Manchester Guardian Weekly*, 20 Sept. 1981, p. 5; Dianne Hayter, 'Democracy at Stake', *New Socialist*, Mar./Apr. 1982, 13–14; and Paul McCormick, *Enemies of Democracy* (London: Temple Smith, 1979).
60. 'Undermining Mr. Whitelaw', *The Economist*, 20 Mar. 1982, 14–15.
61. McKenzie, *British Political Parties*, pp. 644–7.
62. S. E. Finer, ed., *Adversary Politics and Electoral Reform* (London: Anthony Wigram, 1975) and *The Changing British Party System, 1945–1979* (Washington, DC: American Enterprise Institute, 1980); Michael Stewart, *The Jekyll and Hyde Years* (London: J.M. Dent, 1977).
63. See Ian Aitken, 'Old Bill and New Force', *Manchester Guardian Weekly*, 4 Apr. 1982, p. 5.
64. The development of communal nationalism is discussed in William L. Miller, *The End of British Politics: Scots and English Political Behaviour in the Seventies* (Oxford University Press, 1981).
65. F.W.S. Craig, *British Electoral Facts, 1885–1975* (London: Macmillan, 1976).
66. Ian Bradley, *Breaking the Mould? The Birth and Prospects of the Social Democratic Party* (London: Martin Robertson, 1981); H.M. Drucker, ed., *Multi-Party Britain* (New York: Praeger Special Studies, 1979); John Grigg, 'Change and Continuity in British Party Politics', *The Round Table*, 281 (Jan., 1981) 33–9; Peter Jenkins, 'Iron Nerve of an Astute Political Gambler', *Manchester Guardian Weekly*, 4 Apr. 1982, p. 4; 'The Roads Beyond Hillhead', *Manchester Guardian Weekly*, 4 Apr. 1982, p. 10; King, 'Whatever Is Happening'. Even the astrologers have confirmed the trend; Michael Parkin, 'Thatcher Gets Advice from Old Moore', *Guardian*, 20 July 1982, p. 3.

67. Ivor Crewe, Bo Sarlvik and James Alt, 'Partisan Dealignment in Britain, 1964–1974', *British Journal of Political Science*, 7 (Apr. 1977) 129–90; Ivor Crewe, 'Prospects for Party Realignment: an Anglo-American Comparison', *Comparative Politics*, 10 (July 1980) 379–400.
68. 'Back to the Barricades', *The Economist*, 13 Mar. 1982, p. 38.
69. John E. Turner, 'The Labour Party: Riding the Two Horses', *International Studies Quarterly*, 25 (Sept. 1981) 385–437.
70. Dick Taverne (Lincoln) and E.J. Milne (Blyth) won election as independent Labour MPs in February, 1974. Both were defeated by official Labour candidates in October of that year.
71. Dick Leonard, *Paying for Party Politics: The Case for Public Subsidies*, 'PEP Broadsheet No. 555' (London: Political and Economic Planning, 1974).
72. Crewe, 'Prospects for Realignment', pp. 382–3.
73. Hilde T. Himmelweit *et. al., How Voters Decide: a Longitudinal Study of Political Attitudes and Voting Extending Over Fifteen Years* (London: Acacemic Press, 1981).
74. Richard Rose, 'Class Does Not Equal Party: the Decline of a Model of British Voting', *Studies in Public Policy*, no. 84 (Glasgow: University of Strathclyde, Centre for the Study of Public Policy, 1980).
75. Ivor Crewe, 'Why the Conservatives Won', in *Britain at the Polls, 1979*, ed. Howard R. Penniman (Washington: American Enterprise Institute, 1981) p. 280.
76. According to Gallup Poll data, the level of Conservative support among the upper-middle class electors declined from a high of 90% in 1951 to only 62% in October, 1974. There was a drop-off from 76% (in 1959) to 47% (October, 1974) for voters classified as middle to lower-middle class. These data appear in 'Voting Behaviour in Britain, 1945–1974', in *Studies in British Politics*, ed. Richard Rose, 3rd edn (New York: Macmillan, 1976) pp. 204–15. According to Ivor Crewe ('Why the Conservatives Won', p. 281) the recovery was quite limited in 1979. For an analysis of the causes of this phenomenon, see David Jary, 'A New Significance for the Middle Class Left? – Some Hypotheses and an Appraisal of the Evidence of Electoral Sociology', ch. 7 in *The Middle Class in Politics*, ed. John Garrard *et. al.* (Farnborough, Hants.: Saxon House, 1978) 133–82.
77. Jorgen Rasmussen, 'Another Look at Those Recent By–Elections', *British Politics Group Newsletter*, no. 27 (Winter 1982) 2–4.
78. M. Ostrogorski, *Democracy and the Organization of Political Parties* (Garden City, New York: Anchor Books, 1964 [1902]) I, pp. 294–5.
79. The party system is treated as something exceptional and a little discreditable. Men may be willing to die for party but they seldom praise it. For two centuries Englishmen, while throwing an incredible amount of ardour and energy into their great faction fight, have systematically condemned it. . . . From the time of the great Duke of Marlborough ...to the present day, there has been an unbroken stream of theoretical condemnation. No sentiment is more likely to elicit applause at a public meeting than the statement that 'this, Mr. Chairman, is not a party question, and I do not propose to treat it from a party standpoint'.

    Sidney Low, *The Governance of England* (London: T. Fisher Unwin,

1914) p. 195. For examples, see Hillaire Belloc and Cecil Chesterton, *The Party System* (London: Howard Latimer, 1913).

80. For an interesting precursor to the 'adversary politics' school, see McKechnie, *New Democracy*, pp. 113, 125–6, 158–60.
81. This classification includes 1918, when the Conservatives needed the support of the 127 'Coalition' Liberals for their parliamentary majority.
82. The data are obtained from Craig, *Electoral Facts*.
83. Peter Hain and Simon Hebditch, *Radicals and Socialism* (Nottingham: Institute of Workers Control, 1978); Martin Shaw, 'Moving In and Moving On', *Labour Leader*, Jan. 1980, 3.
84. Ian Bradley, *The English Middle Classes Are Alive and Kicking* (London: Collins, 1982) esp. chs 10–11; Roger King and Neill Nugent, eds., *Respectable Rebels: Middle Class Campaigns in Britain in the 1970s* (London: Hodder & Stoughton, 1979).
85. Leon D. Epstein, 'British M.P.s and their Local Parties: The Suez Case', *American Political Science Review*, 54 (June, 1960) 374–90.
86. Jorgen Rasmussen, *The Relation of the Profumo Rebels with Their Local Parties* (Tucson: University of Arizona Press, 1966).
87. Compare Ian Mikardo, 'The Fateful, Hateful Fifties', *New Socialist*, Mar./Apr. 1982, 45–7, with Stephen Haseler, *The Tragedy of Labour* (Oxford: Basil Blackwell, 1980).
88. Peter G. Richards, *The Backbenchers* (London: Faber & Faber, 1972).
89. Robert J. Jackson, *Rebels and Whips* (London: Macmillan, 1968).
90. This argument was first made to me by Ivor Crewe at a panel sponsored by the British Politics Group during the 1980 meeting of the American Political Science Association in Washington, DC.
91. For a historical precedent with uncanny parallels to the present controversy over 'reselection', see Ostrogorski, *Democracy*, I, pp. 95–9.
92. James I. Lengle, 'Demographic Representation in California's 1972 and 1968 Democratic Presidential Primaries', in *Presidential Politics: Readings on Nominations and Elections*, eds James I. Lengle and Byron E. Shafer (New York: St. Martin's 1980) 201–39.
93. Ken Coates, *Democracy in the Labour Party* (Nottingham: Spokesman, 1977) pp. 54–75.
94. David Kogan and Maurice Kogan, *The Battle for the Labour Party* (London: Fontana, 1982).
95. Kevin Phillips, 'Post-Conservative America', *New York Review of Books*, 13 May 1982, pp. 30–1.
96. Uri Ra'anan, *Ethnic Resurgence in Modern Democratic States* (London: Pergamon, 1980).
97. At the 1982 conference of the Council on European Studies, Kay Lawson chaired a panel entitled 'When Parties Fail'. Britain was not represented.
98. Ronald Inglehart, *The Silent Revolution: Changing Values and Political Styles Among Western Publics* (Princeton University Press, 1977).
99. Allan Zuckerman and Mark Irving Lichbach, 'Stability and Change in European Electorates', *World Politics*, 29 (July 1977) p. 548.
100. Ibid., pp. 547–9. See also John W. Books and JoAnn B. Reynolds, 'A Note on Class Voting in Great Britain and the United States', *Com-*

parative Political Studies, 8 (Oct. 1975) 360–76; and Crewe, 'Why the Corservatives Won', pp. 276–82.

101. For American data, see Norman H. Nie, Sidney Verba and John R. Petrocik, *The Changing American Voter,* 2nd edn (Cambridge, MA: Harvard University Press, 1979) esp. pp. 350–2.
102. W. L. Miller, 'Social Class and Party Choice in England: A New Analysis', *British Journal of Political Science*, 8 (July 1978) 257–84 and 'Class, Region and Strata at the British General Election of 1979', *Parliamentary Affairs*, 32 (Autumn 1979) 376–82. For data showing the persistence of environmental social influences in an American setting, see Thomas G. Guterbock, 'Social Class and Voting Choice in Middletown', *Social Forces*, 58 (June 1980) 1044–56. For evidence that the decay of (individual-level) class-voting in Britain was election-specific rather than an inexorable secular trend, see the interesting analysis by Douglas A. Hibbs, Jr., with Nicholas Vasilatos, 'Economic Outcomes and Political Support for British Governments Among Occupational Classes: A Dynamic Analysis', *American Political Science Review*, 76 (June 1982) 259–79.
103. Patrick Dunleavy, 'The Political Implications of Sectoral Cleavages and the Growth of State Employment', *Political Studies*, 28 (Sept. 1980) 364–83; Mark N. Franklin and Anthony Mughan, 'The Decline of Class Voting in Britain: Problems of Analysis and Interpretation', *American Political Science Review*, 72 (June 1978) 523–34; John H. Goldthorpe *et. al., The Affluent Worker: Political Attitudes and Behaviour* (Cambridge: Cambridge University Press, 1968) ch. 5.
104. See Austin Ranney, *The Doctrine of Responsible Party Government* (Urbana: University of Illinois Press, 1954), for evidence on the power of the British model.
105. Evron M. Kirkpatrick, 'Toward a More Responsible Two-Party System: Political Science, Policy Science or Pseudo-Science', *American Political Science Review*, 65 (Dec. 1971) p. 974.
106. Richard Rose, *Do Parties Make a Difference*? (Chatham, NJ: Chatham House, 1980) p. 1.

5 At the Pleasure of Parliament: the Politics of Local Reform in Britain

Douglas E. Ashford

For more than a century local government has been at the heart of major controversies over institutional reform in Great Britain, and for over a century British politics has always managed to procrastinate making a decision. Even the Local Government Act of 1972, the product of nearly three decades of debate (with no major action), is little more than a compromise forced on central government by the immense inefficiencies and inadequacies of a local government system that had remained essentially unchanged since 1888. In this respect, the issues and outcomes surrounding local reform efforts in Britain are perhaps the best illustration of the inability of modern British politics to adapt its venerable tradition of democratic governance to the needs of the advanced industrial state.

Institutional reform is never an easy problem because it involves tinkering with well-established political traditions and constitutional principles. For this reason, it is probably more desirable to make institutional adjustments gradually and over long periods of time. The most serious error of refashioning the institutional fabric of British local government is undoubtedly that delay caused the government to attempt a global solution. As we shall see, the intricate relationships between central and local politics defied such summary treatment and as a result reform gave way to those interests, most often those advanced by central government itself, that could dominate the decisionmaking process. In the broad sense of institutional change, that is, searching for a new balance of political forces that imply some fundamental change in power relationships in the society, British local government has not been reformed at all despite the fact that it has dominated much political debate since Richard Crossman announced his intention of making basic structural changes more than fifteen years ago.

Institutions are an intricate array of organizations to aggregate and to disaggregate authoritative decisionmaking in society. As such they are subject to an evolving set of external forces, social, economic and political. The politics of institutional change is essentially how a society chooses to reach the compromises and to make the adjustments that any set of institutions must endure. In democracies, this is a particularly delicate process because democratic governance operates around numerous principles that may inhibit change such as protecting individual rights, preserving minority interests, and intentionally fostering a political opposition. For these reasons, institutional reforms of many kinds are possibly the best test of the viability of democratic government because it assumes that democratic governance can simultaneously pursue what in any non-democratic system would be considered contradictory goals: partisan political forces are asked to change the rules of the game while also maintaining democratic values. In short, institutional reform means changing the baseline for judging the acceptability or legitimacy of government itself.

Authoritarian government avoids this dilemma simply by denying political legitimacy to the opposition and thereby excluding partisan politics. With these conditions in mind, we can begin to see the enormous problems of local reform in Britain and in many other realms of decisionmaking as well.[1] There are certainly numerous ways in which partisan interests penetrate decisions throughout British society, but the institutionalization of partisan politics, and therefore the opportunity to engage in radical institutional change, is very narrowly defined in British politics. The British constitution itself evolved by institutionalizing the role of the opposition (significantly, always written as the Opposition in British commentaries) *within* Parliament. Unlike nearly every other democracy of the Western world, the role of partisan politics *outside* what is both formally and constitutionally a very restricted institutional foundation has never been defined very clearly and any effort to do so is extremely threatening to the British concept of democratic governance.

In no other country are the ambiguities of constitutional authority so concentrated in a single institution. Both partisan political interests and policymaking are almost exclusively the prerogative of the House of Commons. The ease of exclusion of extra-parliamentary political forces is almost unmatched among democratic governments. The constitutional constraints placed on normal decisionmaking,[2] not to mention on decisions involving several levels of government or cutting across functional lines of government, are, therefore, extremely rigid. Political self-interest itself suggests that politicians enjoying such a well-guarded institutional monopoly of power would not be likely to weaken their institutional power-base except under the most extraordinary circumstances. As in every other democratic political system in the world, local politicians are the most obvious contenders in sharing central authority. But in Britain, they are virtually cut off from either political or institutional channels that might bring their political resources to bear on central decisions.

The institutional crux of the problem of sharing power with localities arises from the critical importance of the Opposition within the House of Commons. Though the House of Lords still influences legislation, and, perhaps more importantly for policymaking, also influences parliamentary scheduling and the legislative workload, the Commons is the only arena where central–local conflicts can be reconciled. While there has been a cross-party group of MPs primarily concerned with local government, they seldom cross party lines when crucial votes are taken. The bureaucracy at both the central and local levels no doubt plays an important role in regulating daily differences though very little systematic study has been done of this extra-parliamentary device. The effect on policymaking, however, is much the same as the effective exclusion of local interests within the House of Commons because the privileged consideration given local government associations and large cities cannot become the focus of major political conflict. The result is that many of the daily problems that might be politicized in other democracies are removed from the political arena by the special status given high Civil Servants, which itself rests on the power of Parliament.

Local reform implies a fundamental realignment of partisan politics within a country's political institutions. If Britain has been regularly disappointed with the results of its reform and reorganization efforts at the local level, it is, as I have argued in much more detail elsewhere,[3] because British political institutions, in the broad sense outlined above, place such an enormous constitutional and political responsibility on such a narrow institutional base. Unable or unwilling to engage in a fundamental restructuring of partisan forces as they are or might be involved in central-local politics, the system never really deals with the most fundamental question of local reform itself. British reformers have repeatedly tried to deal with one of the basic kinds of institutional change without ever accepting that the political roots of existing institutions must also change. Approaching such an intricate problem with such an inadequate notion of what is implied is almost certain to lead to disaster. Perhaps the best demonstration of my argument is that British local government today is no less satisfactory to either central or local politicians that it was several decades ago. After an extended and in many ways thorough examination of the options for change and the needs of local government, both the left and the right are not content with the results of what was undoubtedly one of the most ambitious reform efforts over the 1970s. Ever since the major reform attempted by the 1972 Local Government Act, both Labour and the Conservatives, as well as the so easily ignored subjects of the law at the local level, have tinkered with the new system. Their behaviour in many ways only confirms the historic British tradition of ignoring the problems of local government except as they impinge directly on the immediate partisan interests of central governments.

The result is that institutional change at the local level experiences only the worst possible effects of partisan politics. As I shall discuss in more detail, local government remains vulnerable to whatever short-term goals the party in power may wish to impose while seldom seeing changes that address many of the fundamental problems of local government itself. Partisan intervention can be exercised at remarkably little political risk to central politicians and therefore also risks being ill-conceived and ill-designed. Central policymakers can readily procrastinate over those questions that seem too complex and, more importantly, those questions that might threaten the powers of Westminster and Whitehall. There is no more dramatic illustration than the bitter controversy surrounding the Local Government, Planning and Land Act of 1980 under Michael Heseltine, Mrs Thatcher's Secretary of State for the Environment, but the same behaviour can be readily observed in the proposals of his predecessor, Peter Shore, under the Callaghan Government.

Localities are at the whim and fancy of changing Governments, but they never see change designed to meet their needs or preferences. Put differently, the nature of institutional power within the British system places virtually unqualified power in the hands of central politicians.

They are free to pursue their partisan interests at almost no political cost and, in the eyes of political observers from any other democracy, with an almost suicidal determination to extract partisan advantages without putting forth new answers to the terribly difficult problems confronting local government in every democracy. Whatever the answers to the financial, technical and legal problems of local government might be, the British system seems the least likely to discover them. But the much greater loss to British democracy, to which I shall return in the conclusion, is that British politics is deprived of the vitality and diversity that a strong system of local democracy provides. The real tragedy of the British spectacle of local reform is that a potential source of strength and innovation has been made a source of weakness and contention. In the most pessimistic terms, the failure to deal with local reform in Britain saps the vitality of British democracy itself, breeds doubt over Britain's ability to solve her own problems and undermines confidence in democratic governance.

PARLIAMENTARY SOVEREIGNTY GONE WILD?

The pattern of partisan manipulation of British local government can be traced from the development of mass democracy in the early nineteenth century. The first major reform, the Municipal Corporations Act of 1835, was little more than a necessary sequel to the Parliamentary Reform Act of 1832. Under the impulse of Whig radical reformers, Parliament could do no less than make minor concessions in the direction of local democracy. Like many reforms of the period, the Royal Commission leading to the proposal was heavily influenced by the utilitarians, for whom local democracy was an unfortunate complication in pursuing the greatest good for the greatest number.[4] Then, as in future years, it seemed to rest with the conservative forces in Parliament to impose severe restrictions on reform. The Municipal Reform Bill proposed elected councils for 285 larger towns and cities, but this was reduced to 178, while the shires remained the preserve of the Justice of the Peace and the rural aristocracy who controlled county government. To reassure the aristocracy in Parliament that the elected councils would not make excessive or too radical demands on Parliament, it was agreed that a quarter of the members of the elected councils, the aldermen, would be elected for six years (the Tories actually wanted them elected for life).

Of course, in the 1830s the intricacy of contemporary local

government problems was barely anticipated. None the less, many restrictions were imposed that continue to hamstring local government to the present. The aldermen provided an inertial force on localities and their assured seniority meant that they came to dominate local council committees. Although abolished in the 1972 Act, aldermanic seniority enabled them to manipulate the committee system and inhibited reform from within. Their conservative practices also contributed to local inefficiencies that so easily dominated the debate once a global reform was attempted in 1972.[5] More important in building barriers between central and local government, the Treasury acquired the right to review all loans and property sales, the origins of a loan 'sanctioning' control that has now been expanded by Heseltine and his predecessors to curtail local financial powers in many ways. In the early version of Heseltine's 1980 law, localities were even deprived of the right to use income from their own capital investment and sales without Whitehall's approval.

Because tax and budgetary powers have figured so strongly in the debate of the recent decades, it is important to note that even at the early moment in the development of local government partisan intervention to serve short-term interests was easily imposed on the nascent local government system. The system of local taxation (rating) developed over the 1840s in response to poor relief responsibilities imposed by the Poor Law Amendment Act of 1834. But the tension between the threat of increased local taxation to meet social needs and fears of greater central taxation always seemed to work to the disadvantage of the localities. At the same time, ministers were not hesitant in using their central fiscal powers to push other proposals through Parliament. In 1846, for example, Sir Robert Peel, much against his own better judgement, used money from the Treasury's Contingency Fund to subsidize local taxes in order to persuade his aristocratic supporters in Parliament that the unforeseen effects of Corn Law repeal would not rebound with increased local taxation, most of which would fall on local landowners.[6]

The intricate and often opportunistic system of transfers to local government as a reward for accepting new tasks was also set in motion. Early education grants were made in 1833, and during the wave of reform under the Whigs, localities were soon receiving subsidies for prisons, asylums, judicial administration and police. The rule of thumb was that those functions that were essentially 'national' in character should be paid for by central government. The unfortunate precedent was that Parliament developed a handy instrument and an irresistible incentive to enlarge local responsibilities as it saw fit, while local defences or bargaining powers on accepting such responsibilities, and their often unforeseen additional costs, were eroded. In 1830 grants to localities were only £100 000, but even in the early stages of enlarging government's social role in the mid-nineteenth century grants quickly multiplied to over a million pounds by 1870. Already the capacity of localities to keep pace with the costs of a modern state were in doubt. Local taxation actually doubled from 1830 to 1870 (from 8 to 16 million pounds), but subsidies grew with abandon and became the precedent for defining the future development of the transfer system in terms that suited Parliament while making minimal concessions to the fiscal constraints on local decisions.[7]

Much as we admire British democracy as the pathfinder for democratic systems throughout the world, its failure to read many of the unmistakable signals of the changing relationship between central and local government is an early sign of the growing gap between central and local political interests. Disraeli found it convenient to disburse central government surpluses to the benefit of local landowning classes and Gladstone could not be distracted from his desire to reduce central income taxes in order to consider the growing disparities within the local tax structure. With relatively little concern for the growing urban problems of Britain, both parties found it convenient not only to ignore the plight of localities but to use central resources to minimize the possibilities of decisive local political intervention. By the time of Sir Edwin Goschen's 1871 report on the inability of the burgeoning towns and cities to meet their needs, it was clear that unless more resources were made available to Britain's urban population that the problems of urban misery and urban decay would multiply.[8] But it was in no one's political interest at the central level to raise such perplexing questions, although Goschen made a second attempt to redress the growing inequalities and insufficiencies of local resources when the 1888 Local Government Act was passed. Many Victorian officials were aware of the inequities of local taxation. A third attempt at increasing local taxes for the cities was made by Henry Fowler, President of the Local Government Board, as supporting legislation for the 1888 Act, but to no avail.

As Fowler noted, in 1817 land was providing two-thirds of local revenues and, in 1891, 15 per cent. Indeed, long before the Layfield Committee recommended in 1976 that a local income tax was the best option to preserve an independent role for local government, Goschen suggested in 1868 that income tax be shared with localities. This was only the first of numerous occasions when the progressive government of the day chose to reduce the political viability of local government rather than confront its declining role in British politics and its growing institutional isolation. A further blow came in 1894 when districts were created in the counties. Following the precedent of the early nineteenth century, agricultural land was derated (reduced in value) by half for local tax purposes in order to assure that Parliament, still in the hands of landed aristocrats, would accept more pressing Conservative reforms for central inheritance taxes. A local tax relief of £2 million was needed to massage central politicians into accepting a reform of higher political priority.[9]

The Local Government Act of 1888 is correctly regarded as the nineteenth century milestone in local government reform, but like the reforms to follow, it was more concerned with catching up with the past than preparing for the future. At last counties were relieved of the judicial rule under the Justices of the Peace and elected councils were established throughout the system, a generation or more later than local electoral forces took hold of the local government systems of much of Europe and North America. True, democracy made steady progress at the national level, but few realize how retarded was the march of competitive politics at the local level in Britain. Even so, the Conservatives managed to impose extraordinary anomalies on local government, many of which lived on to plague local reform in 1972. No friend of mass democracy, even the *Economist* was moved to write, 'the continuity of traditional areas triumphed over any thought that they might be reshaped for the work in hand'.[10]

The most detrimental effect was to institutionalize the 'town versus country' dichotomy in the local government system. The two-tiered counties were to help preserve rural influence on the system, and the unified boroughs or urban governments were to help contain the dangerous and unpredictable political forces gathering in Britain's miserable urban slums. In fact, the initial Bill planned to have boroughs of 150 000 persons, but the Act decreased the number to 50 000 with the effect of even further entrenching urban and rural interests. Though it is not clear that the results were intended, there was perhaps no better way to assure that local political forces would exhaust themselves in internecine warfare rather than mobilize in order to demand an effective political voice in Westminster; better to have the threatening political interests at the local level engaged in perpetual warfare against each other than against Westminster. The self-defeating response of the local authorities to the 1972 Bill and the defeat of the localities in 1980 are mute testimony to the political acumen of central politicians a century ago who saw or perhaps only sensed a way to insulate Parliament against the diverse and distracting demands of local politics.

In their classic study of nineteenth century local government, Redlich and Hirst pinpoint how central political reform was played off against local reform in order to neutralize the partisan potential of local politics at higher levels of government. In their words, the rural voter remained a passive subject of conservative politics even though '1834 rescued his morale (poor relief), 1846 gave him bread (Corn Law repeal), 1884 gave him the vote, (and) 1894 (district councils) gave him a local council'.[11] Conservative political interests dictated institutionalizing the 'town versus country' dichotomy in British politics, and the same national partisan interests continued to define the parameters of choice for Peter Shore in the late 1970s and for Michael Heseltine in the early 1980s. Of course, the same social cleavages can be found in other local government systems, but the crucial institutional difference is that where rural inertia was exploited to protect political interests elsewhere it was the product of an explicit bargain between levels of government which enabled localities to extract additional privileges and benefits from central government. The social difference is not unique to Britain or even to democratic systems, but the particular way in which central politicians managed to harness these differences to protect central government against the political mobilization of local interests is.

In many respects, the potential clash of central and local partisan interests has only been replayed at a different tempo ever since the turn of the century. The Royal Commission on Local Taxation of 1901 foreshadows the Layfield Committee of 1976. Acknowledging the fiscal dependence of localities on the Treasury, the 1901 Commission reviews many options, including the often discussed local income tax, only to conclude by suggesting a new payment to localities to relieve the burden of growing local taxes.[12] From the debate over the 1920s emerges the Local Government Act of 1929 and its related legislation. Again, the political costs of obtaining parliamentary consent were high. To placate rural interests, agricultural land was totally exempted from local taxation and industrial property derated by half.[13] A large unconditional grant (then 30 per cent of local revenues) consoled localities, but also made the giant transfer the focal point of local concerns in dealing with central government in the future. Although local interests were not bought off in quite as crass a way as happened in other democracies, they were indeed given fiscal support in ways that minimized the chances of ever resurrecting local partisan interests that might threaten Westminster. Fifty years later Parliament was still debating the same problem.

BIPARTISAN SUBJECTION OF LOCAL GOVERNMENT

Exploring the nature of partisan politics as it relates to the development of local government is very different from considering the effects of partisan intervention. The reason for this is particularly important in British politics because the institutionalized role of the Opposition is so fundamental to British politics, and, in turn, serves to insulate central government from local partisan change, demands and preferences. In effect, the nature of partisan politics excludes localities although the effects of partisan decisionmaking have rigid statutory meaning at the local level. The extraordinary political rhetoric that Parliament's exalted position encourages is, of course, often remote from the real concerns and problems of local government. The overall result is a disjointed and sometimes irrelevant debate that may serve central partisan interests without providing policy solutions. Put differently, there is no clear institutional link between levels of government that, on the one hand, keeps central politicians honest and, on the other hand, enables local politicians to influence decision-making at higher levels.

For understandable reasons, the local government debate in Britain is carried on in the disjointed political context in which local government finds itself. As I have outlined, the foundations for this curiously disconnected spectacle were laid in the nineteenth century as various measures sought to protect basically Conservative dominated localities from central level party realignment. This may have worked satisfactorily in an earlier century when the role of government was more modest, but in the era of the welfare state it works very poorly. Local government cannot protect itself from the adversarial excesses of central politics, but central government is in no way *politically* accountable for whatever unreasonable and capricious demands it places on local government. Central politicians may go on about the 'accountability' of local government, but in a political sense the problem is just the reverse.

Seen in this political framework, much of the legal, technical and organizational confusions surrounding the development of the British local government system over the past 30 years are only the natural consequences of a system whose institutionalized capacity for sensing needs, evaluating options and innovating at the local level is treated sporadically and inconsistently by central leaders, if not simply neglected. The setting itself became an obstacle to sensible reform and reorganization appropriate to the growing interdependence of central and local government in the advanced welfare state. In fact, the truncated nature of the central-local relationship was barely noticed in the development of British local government since 1945. Local government was assumed to be the willing handmaiden of central policy. Subsequent problems and difficulties in meeting central objectives were readily dismissed as the petulant and backward habits of stuffy local councils. For a generation, this attitude has barely changed.

The post-war Labour Government was understandably heavily engaged in compensating for the neglect of domestic needs over nearly a decade of wartime pressures, and in getting its own heavy burden of central reforms through Parliament. Many of these, of course, radically changed the functions of local government, in particular the formation of the National Health Service which removed nearly 2000 hospitals from local control at one sweep. As in the prewar period, the Ministry of Health remained the central department most concerned with local problems. There was no ministry that even acknowledged the existence of local government until the Conservatives created the Ministry of Housing and Local Government in 1951, mainly to press their winning electoral proposal of providing more housing. Following in the venerable footsteps of Peel, the Conservatives reorganized the machinery for local transfers in 1957 by introducing a General Grant involving a measure of need.

In its overall effects, the partisan treatment of local problems within the British system is probably not greater than in most modern democracies, but there are serious dislocations between the expression of partisan interest at the central level and reaching effective policy solutions. The massive grant (rate support grant) to local governments is a typical example. The system has been successively amended ever since 1948, when Labour opted for a grant formula based on resources and therefore directed towards equalization. A few years later the Conservative Government again reorganized the system in rural areas as well as urban areas. Over the 1970s both the Labour and Conservative parties continued to make direct changes in the system in order to favour their constituencies. While this behaviour is not surprising, it has been almost totally a function of central calculations of political advantage and has not led to a workable solution to the problems of local government. In this respect, the most recent efforts of Heseltine to impose new restrictions and to completely reformulate the basis for the grant is an old chapter in British local government history. The problem is that the obligations and difficulties of local government are constantly increasing while central government seems unable to direct its partisan concerns about the grant in a way that will lead to the long-term solution.

Another well-known example was the debate over the reorganization of London in 1963. The London reorganization itself was long delayed because of partisan deadlock and in many ways set the pattern for subsequent reforms of local government throughout the country. Because of Labour's victory in the local elections, the Conservative proposal for forming a metropolitan authority took on symbolic importance. In his account of the debate, Smallwood observes that Labour opposition to the London reorganization bill soon became a 'phalanx hardened into a monolithic mass that was unable to offer anything in the way of creative originality as an opposition force'.[14] Although the Inner London Education Authority was conceded by the Conservatives in order to keep Labour's educational accomplishment intact in central London, Labour's opposition was so transfixed on this issue that very few constructive proposals were forthcoming. Again, the point is not that partisan adjustments are not made in the policy process, but that complex issues are often so simplified that the solutions are either of very little duration or the complexities are often left to be resolved by bureaucrats.

Because the economic problems of the 1970s worked to make the grant transfer to local government (about 40 per cent of their total revenues) the focal point of the most recent controversies over local reform, some note should also be made of the 1966 Local Government Act, which established the form it would take until the 1980 Local Government, Planning and Land Act. Intent on undoing the Conservative rejection of a resource-based or equalization element in calculating the grant, Labour created the Rate Support Grant (RGS). The goal was admirable, to reduce the local tax burden, but the result was to impose an intricate regression formula for calculating needs and an overall standard for calculating resource deficiencies (inadequate local tax base). Though Heseltine's new law imposes a procedure that is no less obscure and in many ways much more arbitrary, the effect was to shroud the transfer with so many statistical manipulations that none but the carefully tutored have any idea what the transfer means. The political effect was to encourage tinkering with the variables, procedures, and formulae to achieve immediate benefits for local supporters on the left or right without addressing the more fundamental issue of the inadequate local revenues. From Westminster's perspective, the result was ideal. Ministers could exploit the grant system in obscure ways, but local governments were unable to raise the basic issue because they were being provided with funds. So long as the economy could stand the drain, there would be no problem. In microcosmic form, the RGS symbolized the political opportunism and disjunctions of the entire British local government system.

Given the institutional setting, the result was predictable. Labour fiddled the grant to help urban areas and the Conservatives fiddled the grant to help their rural bastions. Inadvertently, the archaic dichotomy of 'town versus country' was reinforced which, in turn, helped neutralize local government for a more sensible system. In the meantime, an impetuous minister, Richard Crossman, decided that the entire structure had to be reorganized. He already had a committee at work on management problems of local government and simply extended its mission to consider global reform after suitable changes in the group.[15] The mighty labours of this Royal Commission have been extensively analysed elsewhere,[16] but the issue of immediate importance was that partisan decisionmaking again demonstrated its capacity simply to reverse the intent of extensive inquiry and planning to no apparent dismay of the major political interests.

The debate over the 1972 Local Government Act corresponded to the pattern of 1963 London debate. Political boundaries are easily reduced to immediate partisan interests in any democracy, but in Britain both Labour and Conservatives dwelt on new boundaries at the expense of full consideration of equally important problems such as the new functions of local government. The initial intent of the Royal Commission on local government was to create unitary authorities with more concentrated powers, centered on more populated urban areas, and Labour's proposal followed this design. The Conservative Heath Government simply turned Labour's proposal on its head. Concentrated powers were now given to the more rural countryside local authorities while urban local authorities had greater division of powers and were therefore further handicapped in meeting urban needs. With the possible exception of Sweden, no major democratic system has been able to consolidate local government as much or around such clearly partisan aims. After more than five years of political debate, all the political parties seemed exhausted, and the final version of the 1972 Act was not seriously contested.[17]

Perhaps the most serious indictment against the 1972 Act was that only two years after the law came into force in 1974, central politicians launched new proposals and expressed dissatisfaction. Given the enormous effort that had been made, there was good reason to be dissatisfied. The virtues of rationality and simplicity, which so often misled governments over the 1960s, had produced not one, but five different local government structures: London, metropolitan counties and districts, non-metropolitan counties and districts, and separate systems for Scotland and Northern Ireland. Few Members of Parliament seemed embarrassed that their Herculean efforts had spawned a monster. By 1974 the conditioned response to local problems was so ingrained that none even seemed aware that they had devised a system that reinforced most of the political disjunctions of the old system. Why they thought that any parliamentary body would be able to reorganize an intricate system of local government in a single law is, of course, the true exposure of "dogmatism" in British local reform.[18]

TINKERING OR SMASHING?

Labour's reactions to the 1972 law after it came into effect in 1974 is an essential prelude to Heseltine's most recent attack on the system. The two episodes reveal more clearly than any previous events how local government may become simply a pawn in the hands of central politicians, a pawn which is easily sacrificed to the manoeuvres of more powerful players. Although Labour did not come to office in 1974 with any clear plans to revive the local government debate, the ease with which their Secretary of State for the Environment, Peter Shore, could fish in troubled waters tells us much about the excesses of adversarial politics as well as the defenceless state to which local government had been reduced.

Like the Heseltine proposals and laws from 1979 to 1981, Shore's proposals reveal the extent to which local government reform has been reduced to a convenient instrument of central partisan interests. Shore's basic idea was to restore powers to those districts that had lost powers to the upper tier of local government in the non-metropolitan or 'shire' areas. Many of these towns were old unified authorities (boroughs) that were generally under Labour control. After the 1972 Act they found themselves subordinated to predominantly rural county government which, as we noted above, had stronger powers than the districts, especially over education. The concept, if it can be favourably labelled, was simply to restore powers to those districts whose powers were partially limited by their location in non-metropolitan areas. Shore first revealed his strategy in response to a parliamentary question (probably planted) in August 1974,[19] though it was known even then that his Labour colleagues in charge of major social service ministries (primarily education and health) were loath to subject local government to another round of reorganization barely months after the 1972 Act had come into effect.

Shore called his plan 'organic change' though its disruptive and disconnected effects make it hard to see why it was in any sense 'organic'. Actually, there were two strategies at work, one to make immediate changes in the distribution of functions that would favour offended Labour Party towns, and another that would totally restructure the system once again. The first issue could only be decided in an arbitrary way and produced a good deal of confusion. For example, Cardiff appeared on early lists of favourably inclined towns, but later disappeared because it felt secure in a historically Labour-controlled county and change would bring additional complications under special rules governing Welsh local government. In later versions, the 'big nine' districts (over 200 000 persons) were included, but this would also include Bristol, a city of over 400 000, whose loss to the county of Avon would make the county totally unviable.[20]

A second, longer-term, strategy was also underway. In September 1975 the Party circulated a discussion document on devolution and in June 1977 the National Executive Committee published their 1977 report, *Regional Authorities and Local Government Reform*. The report was consistent with Shore's short-term strategy of enhancing the powers of districts, but also envisaged the long-term objective of converting the new system (then barely three years old) into 200 multi-purpose councils organized around 12 elected regional councils. 'Organic change' was only the nose of the camel in the tent. As had happened so often in the past, the proposals left the local government associations completely divided; the Conservative-controlled Association of County Councils fiercely attacked 'reform by stealth' and the Association of Metropolitan Authorities found the redistribution of powers attractive. Heseltine, then the Opposition spokesman for local matters, called it 'midsummer madness'.[21] But the effective resistance actually came on two fronts: the Labour local councillors were aghast at the prospect of undergoing another major change within a few months of adjusting to the 1972 Act and the Labour ministers most affected in the cabinet were in no mood to concede more power to local authorities. One must also recall that at the time, the Prime Minister, Callaghan, was trying to avoid splitting the Parliamentary Labour party over devolution and was undoubtedly unwilling to launch another divisive debate in Parliament on the eve of a general election.

But like any ambitious young minister, Peter Shore was not easily discouraged. The austerity measures of the late 1970s left few ways he could make his mark because the major policies under the Department of the Environment, housing and transportation, were expensive and easily cut back. Even if not prepared to go all the way with him, his cabinet colleagues naturally wanted to do anything possible to restore Labour's power in local government. Perhaps the 1979 White Paper was intended more as political ammunition than as serious policy, but it did announce the Government's intention of redirecting education powers to the lower tier for the nine big towns and cities enveloped in rural counties and the devolution of social service powers on an even larger scale.[22] Shore's determination to proceed launched a new round of frantic objections as well as some considered skepticism from local government experts, of which the most important was probably the tightly knit rejection by Steward, Leach and Skelcher showing how many of the same conflicts and confrontations that Shore claimed to avoid could easily occur under the the new system. As they concluded, 'Flexibility of response to problems is not necessarily the same as flexibility in division of functions between authorities. Indeed, it could be the latter makes the former more difficult'.[23]

The second and more feasible change advanced under Labour was to reform the RGS. Space forbids outlining all the problems of the British transfer system,[24] but it has never been a politically neutral policy instrument. There had always been the problem that high property value in London necessitated a special 'claw-back' to compensate for its high resources. The formula for the needs component was easily fiddled. As Diane Dawson made clear to the Layfield Committee, there is no objective rationale at all for the preparation of grant based on needs and resources, and as W. Godley outlined, the resources element in the grant only worked to increase the spending of localities with low property values, but did not help in bringing down spending in localities with high property values.[25] What seemed to the uninitiated to be a highly sophisticated device acquired its reputation more for its obscurity than for its reasonableness or flexibility. It had never been difficult to use the RGS to pursue political aims. For example, under Labour between 1975 and 1980 the percentage of the RGS allocated to the more conservative non-metropolitan counties decreased from 57.3 per cent to 53.6 per cent, while London's share increased from 13.3 per cent to nearly 17 per cent. If one is considering a grant of roughly £10 billion, these marginal adjustments involve millions.[26]

The institutionalized inability of central partisan forces to help regulate central-local negotiations of this kind is in many ways more evident in the manipulation of the grant than in the more obvious partisan motives of Shore's 'organic change'. The effects are concealed from the public and beyond any organized influence by local governments. True, the creation of a National Council on Local Finance in 1974 offered some hope of closer collaboration, but the ground rules and economic assumptions for their consultation are all decided by ministers, most importantly the Treasury itself, whose estimates cannot be questioned. The grant is an important insight into the role of partisan politics because it reveals the impotence of partisan influence when confronted with many of the intricate and unpredictable issues of the modern welfare state. Shore himself was supportive of proposals for a 'unitary grant' that would abolish the two elements, and the mandarins of the Department of the Environment made their favoured solution perfectly clear before the Layfield Committee. Indeed, for all the ideological differences between Labour under Callaghan and the Conservatives under Thatcher, the solution to the grant problem proposed in 1980 is almost identical to the DOE proposals of 1976. This would, of course, not be the first time that high Civil Servants had managed to persuade ministers of opposed parties that they should pursue the same policies.

While it is not the primary focus of this essay, it can be noted that one effect of the partisan simplification of the grant problem has often been to place even more power in the hands of Whitehall. Whatever the ideological and partisan differences between Callaghan and Thatcher, the reformulated grant in 1980 was almost identical to the proposals of 1976. It had already been recognized by the Callaghan Government that the high rate of increase in the grant must end and the fundamental principles of the new grant system were actually devised under his Government. The necessity to heighten the partisan intensity of these issues has in effect often meant that the mandarins simply rewrite their ideas from the previous Government with a new rhetorical flourish that suits the new Government. Naturally, Labour did not want to be reminded of this because Heseltine's exaggeration of the abuse of local spending powers provided ample partisan ammunition. Again, one would not be surprised to find similar partisan bias in any democratic system, but the highly accentuated partisan treatment in Parliament helps top administrators to pursue the same basic objectives while a largely irrelevant debate goes on in the House of Commons.

Amid the polemics of party politics, we often forget the remarkable similarity of both the personal and policy problems confronting Shore and Heseltine. As Wilson's protegé and a product of the Labour Research Office, Shore lacked the usual credentials of a Labour militant. Heseltine may superficially appear closer to the Conservative stereotype, but as a self-made millionaire he was in many ways no closer to the Conservative tradition than his own Prime Minister. In terms of policy options, they were both young, ambitious ministers trying to move up in ministerial circles with very few resources, perhaps unintentionally under Shore and the economies imposed by the world oil crisis, while intentionally under Heseltine and the proclaimed monetarist principles of the Prime Minister. Both situations worked to the same effect, and help explain why both Shore and Heseltine have pursued such similar policies. Of no small concern to those hoping to restore the vitality of local government in Britain, both were able to brush aside the political interests of their own supporters at the local level in order to create a favourable image at the central level. Heseltine would treat the localities no more sympathetically than Shore, even though they were heavily controlled by Conservatives in the early years of the Thatcher Government.

The Thatcher Government found new justification for its proposals, but the idea of a single grant wholly under central control was by no means new. The fact that Heseltine's reform of the grant had only a marginal bearing on the mysterious economic policies of the new government seemed to make little difference. It is, first, doubtful whether local spending actually affects the borrowing requirement of central government if increased spending is raised by taxation. There is an indirect connection insofar as high public sector wage settlements do rebound to raise salaries throughout government. However, local Civil Service wages were already rigidly controlled through the 'cash limits' budgeting practices applied to local grants. Cash limits means that the Treasury can set the allowable percentage increase in public wages for the coming year, an estimate that applies to roughly two-thirds of local spending. The wisdom and the justice of making local government responsible for wage policies that national government itself appeared unable or unwilling to achieve itself is, of course, questionable.[27]

The second and irrefutable objection to Heseltine's proposals to curb local spending is that the evidence simply does not bear out his charges. Were local government indeed as profligate as Heseltine argued, then one might justify new controls as a means of subduing inflation. But localities had a better record at meeting self-imposed limits than did central government. Putting aside the 5.4 per cent overspent in 1974–75 when localities were absorbing all the costs of implementing the 1972 Act (one local government found its newly built city hall in another area), between 1975 and 1980 local government had overspent by less than one percent in two fiscal years and actually *underspent* by one and even two percent in three years.[28] Even taking into account that Labour had been generous in providing grants, the behaviour of local government in the recent past hardly justified Heseltine's attack. A better argument might be made that overspending was caused by the Conservatives themselves, in part by cutting grants and in part by plunging Britain into a depression that placed larger burdens on localities. They overspent by 2.9 per cent in 1980–81 and by an estimated 5.9 per cent in 1981–82. Even so local government spending had undergone a real loss of 18 per cent since 1975–76.

A more objective assessment of Heseltine's problem may be that he was trying to use a very clumsy policy instrument to achieve very vague policy objectives. His 1979 version of the Bill would have placed arbitrary limits on both spending and taxation. The device to do this is largely a product of several decades of mindlessly relying on the RGS to finance local government. As most local authorities argued, he already had control of the needs element of the grant because this estimate was made by central government. The open-ended aspect of the old grant was the resources element because it could only be used to provide more grant for localities with low resources, but it could not prevent high spending localities with high resources from spending more. The second loop-hole could only be plugged by taking away the localities, right to determine their own level of taxation. Under the new Bill, in calculating the new Block Grant, central government would set both the approved level of need and also impose an approved level of taxation (standard poundage). As local governments exceeded the approved level of spending, a completely undefined coefficient (the 'multiplier') would be introduced to determine the point at which the grant would be reduced.[29]

His eagerness to impose this triple threat to local budgets caused Heseltine to make a number of blunders and he acquired the nickname of the 'ayatollah' of the Department of the Environment. Under the pressure of a proverbially overloaded parliamentary agenda, the first Bill of 246 complex clauses was scheduled for initial debate in the House of Lords, enabling an outraged Labour Opposition to protest on procedural grounds that any bill with financial implications must first pass through the House of Commons. A new and shortened (149 clauses) Local Government Bill was introduced the next month and received Royal Assent in November 1980, keeping the main provisions for the new Block Grant, but eliminating many detailed planning controls and a section placing new limits on how local governments might invest their own capital receipts.

Were the implications for local budgets not so serious, the early exercises in Heseltine's forced economies would have made the new 1980 Act appear ludicrous. In September, 1980, for example, he tried to impose penalties on 13 Labour Party local councils, only to withdraw his threats when new Block Grant arithmetic gave different results. Although his most bitter venom was directed at the London Labour boroughs (who could generally afford to raise local taxes and thereby escape his net), his strategy was equally severe on Conservative councils. An estimate of possible penalties in 1981 included 25 of the 39 counties, although by then Heseltine's attack plus the performance of the Thatcher Government had restored Labour control in about half the rural areas.[30] The Department of the Environment revealed the capriciousness of the new system by admitting that there were in fact two ways of assessing overspending, each of which produced different results.[31] All the local government associations were outraged, although the Association of County Councils deferred to the conditions of the 1980 Act, hoping (incorrectly) that Heseltine's fury might subdue as new restrictions were proposed. The Labour Party Conference voted to repeal the 1980 Act in their fall 1981 conference.

Because the 1980 Act did not give Heseltine the power to limit local taxes, an even more controversial Local Government Finance Bill was introduced in 1981. The Bill threatened a revolt among moderate Conservatives in the Commons, thirteen of whom abstained on the first reading.[32] By then, Heseltine had given up his hope of unilaterally imposing limits on local taxes and had opted for a local referendum on any supplementary rates (additional taxes later in the year). But he was warned by the influential 1922 Committee that his Bill might still be defeated, and the second reading was delayed. Finally, for the second time Heseltine was forced to withdraw a major bill. The second Local Government Finance Bill was finally accepted because it contains an escape clause permitting the localities to borrow if their initial tax levy proves inadequate.[33]

The dogmatic determination of Heseltine probably exceeds that of any of his predecessors though, as we have seen, the underlying instruments and principles have been long established in the British local government system. Heseltine was prepared to reject the advice of Conservative and Labour local councils alike, even forcing the steadfastly loyal Association of County Councils into a crisis. Buckinghamshire, one of the counties with heavy new burdens that would be penalized, resigned from the ACC in protest over their weak resistance to the new legislation. Several others threatened to follow. The Secretary of State also heaped coals on the heads of backbenchers, already in despair over the future of the Conservative Party. To provide a climax to his unrelenting campaign to reduce local spending, the courts reversed his decision to impose penalties on six London boroughs.[34] Thus, the most curious of all the problems created by Heseltine is that British institutions enabled him to carry on the spectacle despite near universal condemnation from all interested parties and from both sides of the House.

THE ROOTS OF INSTITUTIONAL DECLINE

Writing about developing countries some years ago, Huntington hypothesized that when a country's institutional framework could not manage existing levels of political mobilization, the country was in a state of institutional decay.[35] Perhaps this heavy judgement on the Third World could be profitably applied to advanced industrial countries. Indeed, one might argue that in Britain the issue of local reform and reorganization compounds the problems Huntington saw. Not only are central institutions unable to aggregate demands effectively, but ministers have repeatedly exploited the plight of local government to meet their immediate partisan objectives. Localities are excluded from political decision-making machinery at the central level, and many, if not most, of the decisions made over the past two decades have aggravated rather than relieved the conflicts among levels of government. Heseltine is only the most recent chapter in what seems a suicidal intent by the House of Commons and the cabinet to destroy the fabric of local democracy and to subject localities to an array of arbitrary controls that even ministers themselves cannot explain.

In a complex world of issues and policies, British institutions remain a narrowly defined and exclusively operated structure of aggregating demands and integrating decisions. Neither central nor local governments have simple problems with simple solutions. Institutions are the mediating structures of modern democracies, but if they are neither sensitive to the limits of their powers nor to the inadequacies of their decisions, democratic governance is jeopardized. In no other democracy of Europe or North America could one imagine so few persons assuming such total control over local decisions. And in no other democracy could we imagine ministers surviving unscathed from producing so many partial, inadequate solutions to pressing problems. If any of the major changes of the past two decades had worked reasonably well, one might overlook the aggrandizement of authority in the name of parliamentary sovereignty. It is possible that statesmen know answers that may not have occurred to others, but what we have seen is an endless series of improvisations and patchwork policies that leave local government worse off than before.

The institutional origins of this failure are, in my view, much more important than even the plight of British local government. The immense service of British localities to the state simply can be ignored. The political interests that are harnessed to diffuse authority in other countries are permitted to strike capriciously at the daily workings of the system. Mutual dependence has been turned into mutual hostility and suspicion. The roots of the problem are deep in the British political tradition and protected by constitutional assumptions found in the origins of British democracy itself. Law was once the bastion of a beleaguered Parliament against an absolutist monarch. In dealing with local government over the past generation, law has become a whimsical instrument of partisan interests to be used at will against local councils.

NOTES

1. The difficulties in bringing highly adversarial politics to bear on complex policy decisions is the theme of my book *Politics and Policy in Britain: The Limit of Consensus* (Philadelphia: Temple University Press, 1981). The same basic criticism can also be found from both the left and right. For a view of socialist frustrations see Evan Luard, *Socialism Without the*

State (London: Macmillan, 1979). A less partisan account of how difficult territorial decisionmaking has been in Britain is Anthony H. Birch, *Political Integration and Disintegration in the British Isles* (London and Boston: Allen & Unwin, 1977).
2. The nature of the constitutional constraints is fully discussed in Nevil Johnson, *In Search of the Constitution* (Oxford: Pergamon, 1977).
3. See Douglas E. Ashford, *British Dogmatism and French Pragmatism: Central-Local Policy Making in the Welfare State*, (London and Boston: Allen & Unwin, 1982).
4. See Bryan Keith-Lucas, *The English Local Government Franchise* (Oxford: Blackwell's 1952).
5. The limitations of space make it difficult to fully explain how British political behaviour contributes to the power of bureaucracy. For a good description critique of the administrative reform efforts at the local level see John Dearlove, *The Reorganization of British Local Government* (Cambridge University Press, 1979). The flagrant manipulation of the grant throughout Victorian England far exceeds the excesses of the 20th century.
6. See my essay, 'A Victorian Drama: the Fiscal Subordination of Local Government', in Douglas E. Ashford, ed., *Financing Urban Government in the Welfare State* (London: Croom Helm, 1980) pp. 97–118.
7. Ibid., pp. 97–118.
8. See the Goschen Report, *Reports and Speeches on Local Taxation* (London: Macmillan, 1872) pp. 2–51. The Late Victorian Report which is very similar is the Fowler Report, *House of Commons Papers*, vol. 27, 1893, pp. 1–111.
9. Ashford, 'A Victorian Drama: the Fiscal Subordination of Local Government'.
10. *The Economist*, 16 June 1888.
11. Josef Redlich and Francis W. Hirst, *Local Government in England*, vol. 2 (London: Macmillan, 1901) p. 446.
12. Ashford, 'A Victorian Drama: the Fiscal Subordination of Local Government'.
13. For a good history see Bryan Keith-Lucas and Peter G. Richards, *Local Government in the 20th Century* (London and Boston: Allen & Unwin, 1978). The best detailed history of financial and budgetary bargaining in the interwar period is by Gerald Rhodes, 'Local Government Finance 1918–1966', Appendix 6 in Layfield Report, *Local Government Finance* (London: HMSO, 1976) pp. 102–73.
14. Frank Smallwood, *Greater London: The Politics of Metropolitan Reform* (New York: Bobbs-Merrill, 1965) p. 306.
15. The first report is *Management of Local Government* (Royal Commission on Local Government in England, London: HMSO, 1967) and the later proposals are *Report*, (Royal Commission on Local Government in England, cmnd 4040, London: HMSO, July 1969).
16. For a variety of assessments of the Commission see H. Victor Wiseman, 'The Royal Commission on Local Government in England', in H. Victor Wiseman, ed., *Local Government in England 1958–69* (London: Routledge & Kegan Paul, 1970) pp. 96–144; R.A.W. Rhodes, 'Local

Government Reform – Three Questions', *Social and Economic Administration*; 8 (Spring 1974) 6–21; Douglas E. Ashford, 'Reorganizing British Local Government: a Policy Problem', *Local Government Studies*, 2 (Oct. 1977) 1–8; Stephen Bristow, 'The Criteria for Local Government Reorganization and Local Authority Autonomy', *Policy and Politics*, I (1972) 143–62.

17. For a complete discussion of the debate and its contents see Bruce Wood, *The Process of Local Government Reform* (London and Boston: Allen & Unwin, 1976).
18. Ashford, *British Dogmatism and French Pragmatism*.
19. The response to the question is discussed in the *Guardian*, 4 Aug. 1974.
20. After the confusions that had already been introduced during the local government debate from 1969 to 1972, few people noticed that Shore's proposal would also completely reverse the existing pattern of functional responsibility. In effect, in more rural areas (non-metropolitan counties or shires) the districts would regain powers similar to those of the districts in the more urban areas (metropolitan counties). The proposal and selected districts are discussed in *The London Times*, 18 Aug. 1978.
21. *Guardian*, 8 Sept. 1977.
22. Department of the Environment, *Organic Change in Local Government*, cmnd 7457 (London: HMSO, 1979).
23. J. D. Stewart, S. Leach and K. C. Skelcher, *Organic Change: A Report on Constitutional Management and Financial Problems* (Birmingham: Institute of Local Government Studies, 1978) p. 55.
24. See C. D. Foster, R. Jackman, and M. Perlman, *Local Government Finance in a Unitary State* (London and Boston: Allen & Unwin, 1980).
25. W.A.H. Godley, 'Reflections on the Control of Local Expenditure and its Financing', Appendix 7 in Layfield Report, *Local Government Finance* (London: HMSO, 1976) pp. 54–73. The complexities of reconciling local government spending with the much larger issue of control of public sector wages is one of the many ramifications of local government policy that was never debated.
26. Ashford, *British Dogmatism and French Pragmatism*.
27. For discussion of this facet of the problem see Gwyen Bevan, Keith Sisson and Philip Way, 'Cash Limits in the Public Pay Sector', *Public Administration* (UK) 59 (Winter 1981) 379–98.
28. The full analysis appears in the *County Council's Gazette*, Oct. 1981, p. 202.
29. For details on the new grant see Victor Moore and Louise Catchpoole, *The Local Government Planning and Land Act 1980* (London: Sweet & Maxwell, 1980) and Glen Bramley and Andrew Evans, 'Block Grant: Some Unresolved Issues', *Policy and Politics*, 9 (1981) 173–204.
30. *The Times*, 3 June 1981.
31. *The Economist*, 30 May 1981.
32. *The Times*, 14 Nov. 1981.
33. *The Times*, 17 Dec. 1981.
34. *The Times*, 22 Oct. 1981.
35. Samuel Huntington, *Political Order and Political Decay* (New Haven: Yale University Press, 1967).

6 Devolution and Identity in Scotland and Wales

Norman Furniss

In this chapter I will review the political history of devolution in Britain from the introduction of the Scotland and Wales Bills in the House of Commons in 1977 through the Hillhead by-election in March 1982. In the course of the discussion and in a separate section I will propose an explanation of why after the 'technical' defeat of the provisions of the Scotland Bill and the overwhelming rejection of the Wales Bill in respective referenda there remains a political history to review. Despite commonalities imposed by the form of the Scotland and Wales Bills, to see that this political history is fundamentally different is to begin to understand the nature of possible future developments.

My conclusion, which I hope to make persuasive as the discussion proceeds, is that the problems of devolution for Scotland and Wales will continue to be a feature of British political life. For Scotland the issue is how to extract the maximum (some in England would say 'disproportionate') economic and political benefits from union while keeping administration as independent and as flexible as possible. This aim to be realized requires a strong political party to be the 'carrier' of Scottish interests. In the 1970s this party was the Scottish National Party; in the 1980s it could be either the Labour Party in Scotland or the Social Democratic–Liberal Party Alliance. For Wales the aim is cultural defense broadly defined, which makes at least the threat of party representation in the House of Commons less important but which increases the need for effective spokesmen and nonpolitical action ('effective' both in relation to the relevant Welsh constituencies and to British nonparliamentary decision-makers). It follows that 'pressure group activity' is less extensive but could become militant much more easily in Wales than in Scotland.

I

The key transition in the British government's regional policy came when concern shifted from whether regions were 'depressed' and if so what could be done for them, to how regions could further national economic goals. This shift occurred during the first Labour Government of Harold Wilson, 1964–70. As I have described elsewhere, the explicit goal of the Government was to mobilize Scottish and Welsh producer groups to raise 'activity rates', to lessen inflationary pressures at the centre, in brief to forge a partnership for economic renewal. To meet this goal a more elaborate institutional structure – the Welsh Office, the 'Scotland Plan' – was established, and existing institutions were given new mandates.[1] Thus, in the words of a 1977 memorandum to the Select Committee on Scottish Affairs:

> The Secretary of State for Scotland's increasing involvement in problems of economic development . . . led in 1964 to his being assigned more explicit responsibilities in the comprehensive machinery for economic planning.

The destabilizing elements in this program were, first, that the results, measured in economic performance, were extremely meagre when compared to professed governmental expectations and, second, that the impact on regional producer groups was underestimated. In my previous research I found that most Scottish producer groups did not see themselves as 'Scottish' at all until told that they were. At this point it became unclear, particularly in light of the perceived failure of national economic policy, why their mandate should not be the articulation of Scottish grievances and why the central government itself was not somehow responsible for regional ills.[2] The response from the centre to this new pressure to 'do more' for Scotland (or Wales) was to increase public investment in the regions and to establish a number of what came to be called 'quangos' to deal with particular identified problems. There are now by my current count ninety-six related to Scotland, ranging from the Scottish Development Agency, to the North of Scotland Hydro Electric Board, to the Scottish Tourism Consultative Council, to the Scottish Central Committee on Technical Education. This list does not include the over two hundred *ad hoc* bodies established by the Scottish Office.

What was missing in the new pattern of centre–regional interaction was any explicit political component, or, to put the point another way, accountability. As Keating and Bleinam relate in their useful historical overview of *Labour and Scottish Nationalism*, there was no interest in the Labour Government or among most Labour MP's for political devolution.[3] For this a political challenge was needed, and it emerged in the form of the Scottish National Party (SNP), which in a by-election in November 1967 captured what had been the safest Labour seat in Scotland and became ten years later the major challenge to Labour political domination in Scotland. The rise of the SNP from, in the words of one of its supporters in the 1930s, a movement that 'has attracted some of the most generous spirits in Scotland – and some of the greatest cranks in Christendom' to a serious political force had not been foreseen.[4] It owed much to the transformation of British industrial structure which led to the articulation of regional planning in the first place and to the reorientation of producer groups as (mostly dissatisfied) spokesmen for Scottish interests. In the new political climate every SNP victory seemed to produce a flurry of white papers and public expenditures. The minds of Labour Party leaders were particularly concentrated on the threat – the party historically had relied on large majorities from the 'Celtic fringe' to win national elections. In the February 1974 election Labour would have been defeated without the addition of Welsh and Scottish seats; after the October 1974 election the SNP was the main challenger in every Labour marginal but one. That attention was justified was further underlined by opinion poll findings of a strong correlation between increased support for the SNP and decreased prospects that the Labour Government would fulfill its pledge in its UK election manifesto to 'create elected Assemblies in Scotland and Wales'.[5]

This mention of manifesto pledges raises the final element leading to the introduction and successful passage of the Scotland and Wales Acts in 1978. Generations of radical British politicians had promised a form of self-government to Scotland and Wales. Self-government had been part of official Labour Party policy since Keir Hardie until 1945 and had produced some ringing promises, as this from the Secretary to the party, Arthur Henderson, in 1918: 'The Labour Party is pledged to the widest and most generous measure of home rule that can be devised . . . we regard the claims to self-government on these lines as strictly analogous to those of Ireland.' Now, to be sure, in power the Labour Government tended quickly to lose its zeal for Home Rule. Still the tradition of support was important for three reasons. First, the Callaghan Government was able to present the Bills as the fulfillment of a long-term commitment, not as the panicky reaction to SNP gains. Second, left wing Labour MPs opposed to the idea of devolution (for example, Eric Heffer) were sympathetic to the argument that manifesto pledges ought to be carried out. After all, the whole thrust of the Labour left, at least until Tony Benn, has been to get appropriate language into manifestoes and then to pressure the Government to 'live up to' the terms. Third, to cast devolution as the culmination of almost a century of struggle for Home Rule meant the introduction of Bills that could apply to *Scotland and Wales alone*. The reader may have noticed a dearth of reference to Wales; the reason is that developments in Wales played an insignificant role in the new political orientation. To offer an Assembly only to Scotland, however, would seem too cynical; 'Home Rule all round' was the basis of the radical devolution tradition. At the same time the difficult and politically unrewarding task of deciding what to do about devolution for *England* could be shelved. The Home Rule legacy permitted the introduction of devolution for Scotland and Wales first, and, one is sure most politicians in both parties hoped, last.

PASSAGE OF THE SCOTLAND AND WALES BILLS

The considerations mentioned above do not add up to a ringing affirmation of the value of devolution, a point to keep in mind when we describe such details as the '40% rule'. The Government was slow to introduce any legislation, and when finally proposed, even the promise of a referendum in each nation did not prevent enough Labour defections to avoid defeat of the necessary guillotine motion. ('Guillotine' – or timetable – motions limit the time spent on amendments and thus prevent the bills from being 'talked out'.) Only after further SNP municipal gains in 1977 – including the capture of Glasgow – did Callaghan make passage of the guillotine motions a matter of confidence. This time the motions carried, and the Bills started the process of becoming Acts.

What these Bills actually meant then became the major contention in debate. The ambiguity was apparent in the four principles laid down by Callaghan during the Second Reading of the Scotland Bill: recognition of 'diversity and distinctive tradition of Scotland and Wales'; conservation of the economic and political union of the United Kingdom; preservation of the 'continuing and unimpaired sovereignty of Parliament'; assurance of fairness to all.[6] Strictly interpreted, the third point reduces the first to insignificance, while the fourth would seem to require that no English region be adversely affected by anything the Scottish or Welsh Assemblies might do. Within this framework, none the less, the Bills were to find their place. Each took the same form. Each began with the disclaimer (thrown out during debate) that the Act would not affect 'the supreme authority of Parliament to make laws for the UK or any part of it'; each established a national Assembly with enumerated powers; each concluded with the referendum question, 'Do you want the Provisions of the Scotland/ Wales Act of (1978) to be Put into Effect?'' Beneath the similarity of form, however, lay major differences in potential power. The Welsh Assembly was given no new devolved powers at all; rather a narrow range of (already delegated) functions was gathered in one place. These were identified in Sections 11 and 12 as 'cultural manifestations' (museums, art galleries, libraries, the Welsh language, crafts, sports), services to the war handicapped, and 'public passenger transport undertakings'. The Assembly (Section 13) even lacked direct access to the Secretary of State for Wales. The Scottish Assembly in contrast was given wide discretion over the spending, albeit not the gathering, of money. It was the primary check on the activities of the Scottish Office; it was responsible for overseeing economic development. There was the potential for debate on major substantive issues.[7]

That the level of debate in either Assembly might have risen above that in the House of Commons would not have been a difficult feat. Both parties were handicapped. Most Labour MPs outside Scotland and Wales were at best indifferent about the Bills; some in England, Scotland and Wales supported them on the grounds that they might then be defeated. As Donald Anderson (Swansea, East) explained, 'there has to be an end to the spectre of devolution, and the only way properly in which to exercise [sic] it is by a referendum'.[8] And no one in the cabinet professed to want anything akin to 'federalism', which in the words of Michael Foot would 'undermine the supremacy of this House, which, I believe, is the most important precious possession of the British people'.[9] The Conservative Party was able to take but limited advantage of this situation during the debates because of its own internal divisions. Instead of a ringing affirmation that what is right, the chief Conservative spokesman, Francis Pym, was obliged to declare that the status quo was unsatisfactory and that what was needed instead of the Bills were 'All-Party Talks' of such an ephemeral nature that Labour MPs could take time out from their bickering to ridicule the official alternative. This idea of 'All-Party Talks' was adopted as an uneasy compromise between those who felt the status quo was indeed perfectly satisfactory (for example Maurice Macmillan), those 'Tartan Tories', associated with Sir Alec Douglas Home who wanted something special for Scotland although they were not sure what, and a few converts to the value of devolution basically along the lines proposed by the Labour Government. These converts included notably Edward Heath, who used the occasion to point once again to what he saw as the basic negativism of Margaret Thatcher's policies without committing himself to anything specific – for example, as *The Economist* noted, Heath was 'conveniently abroad' at the time of the Guillotine Motions.

Dreary debate was the consequence, less dreary than might have been expected on the Wales Bill, more dreary on the Scotland Bill. To take the high points of the Wales debate first, the President of the Plaid Cymru – Welsh National Party – Gwynfor Evans, gave a long and persuasive account of the Assembly as a movement toward fulfillment of official Labour and Liberal Party goals. He welcomed the Bill as a 'step in the right direction' and attempted to link the desire for self-government for Wales both to the 'much wider movement among submerged nations in Europe' and to the beneficial effects of decentralization for any state, be it Germany or Britain.[10] There was also an exchange over whether true socialists should support national movements as an attack on 'capitalism at its softest spot' or dismiss them as 'regressive ethnocentricity'. Marx, Lenin, Sartre, even Tom Nairn, were cited.

The Scotland Bill debate was a much sorrier affair. Rhetorical flights, of course, were in evidence, especially among opponents. Francis Pym was led to announce that one cannot have 'a quasi-federal part of a country which was a unitary state, such as ours. . . . It was on this very point that we lost Ireland. If this Bill goes into effect, it is on this very point that we might lose Scotland'. This remarkable summary of Irish history and ignorance of what 'federalism' means was apparently not thought serious enough to challenge. In general, opponents tended to mix catastrophic consequences with trivial causes, as here by Iain Sprout: 'I detest the Bill. If passed, it will lead to the breakup of the UK. . . . If, for example, *The Daily Record* and *The Scotsman* and possibly the BBC, were to shut up for 12 months, the whole issue [of devolution] would go away.' Turning to the SNP, its parliamentary leader, Donald Stewart, stuck doggedly to the position that the only thing that interested the party was independence: 'The thought that a free Scotland might be a socialist Scotland does not frighten me. The fact that it might not be a socialist Scotland does not frighten me.' Among professed 'socialists' references to Marxism and Sartre were dropped to be replaced by calls for public ownership. 'Socialism, not nationalism, is the answer.'[11] And no account could be complete without mentioning the lengthy and repetitious interventions of Tam Dalyell on what came to be called the 'West Lothian question': 'how can I, representing West Lothian, vote in Westminster on issues affecting England when representatives from England cannot vote in Edinburgh on issues affecting Scotland?' This not irresolvable conundrum Dalyell also managed to expand to fill a book titled *Devolution: the End of Britain*.[12] From this morass two thoughtful interventions stood out. Enoch Powell gave a persuasive account of how an Assembly established with great expectations and given miniscule financial responsibility would inevitably be frustrated in its activities. Better then to drop the experiment. For the supporters, John Mackintosh, while admitting the Bill was not perfect – mainly because of Conservative opposition to any financial powers –, tried to portray it as a useful measure toward general constitutional reform, 'a stepping stone to a form of greater internal democracy which we, as a drastically overcentralized country, badly need.[13]

While the debate proceeded at what, despite the Guillotine, must have seemed interminable length, the Government was able to shepherd the Bills through relatively intact, with two exceptions. The first occurred when, primarily as a result of parliamentary mismanagement, the Government was unable to prevent the offering of an amendment that established a 40 per cent threshold clause in the upcoming referenda. At least 40 per cent of the electorate had to vote yes. The second occurred the same night when the House adopted an Amendment proposed by Jo Grimond that stated that if a majority of persons in the Orkney Isles area or the Shetland Isles area voted negatively in the referendum, the Act would not apply to them regardless of what happened in the rest of Scotland.

REFERENDA AND THE 1979 GENERAL ELECTION

The government was able later to deflect Grimond's Amendment; the 40 per cent threshold remained. The stipulation was relatively severe. In the Referendum on European Community membership, for example, the turnout in Scotland was 61.7 per cent; 58.4 per cent of the voters approved, making the percentage of the electorate voting yes

35.75. For another example, in the 1979 General Election the Conservative Party would win the support of 33 per cent of the British electorate. None the less, this clause was not expected to be decisive. Polls showed a majority of Welsh opposed to the Act, while in Scotland the majority in favour exceeded the barrier. What happened during the referenda campaigns was a steady decline in support for the Act. When the vote occurred, 52 per cent of Scottish voters approved, 33 per cent of the electorate. In Wales the referendum showed 243 048 in favour and 956 330 opposed. In a recent study Miller describes the reasons for the Scottish result. He found first that while the idea of devolution continued to have roughly the same level of support, opponents of the Act managed to turn the referendum into a party test. (In this the statement by Sir Alec Douglas Home that he would vote 'no' on the prospect of getting a better form of devolution later probably helped.) This switch was all the more successful because the referenda campaigns coincided with a period of rapidly escalating Labour unpopularity.[14] Finally, mention should be made of the level of campaign debate in which the old arguments in the House of Commons were trotted out once again – and by the same people; Tam Dalyell was ubiquitous. The Labour Party as a body was never able to mount an adequate defense. 'Do you want the Provisions of the Scotland Act of 1978 to be put into effect?' itself is no rallying cry. As with the 1969 French referendum on regional reform, few voters knew what the provisions were. What was needed was a force or position to mobilize devolution sentiment. But John Mackintosh had died; the Labour Party in Scotland was divided and unwilling to associate with the SNP or Liberals; the idea of putting up numerous pictures of Jim Callaghan with the caption 'vote yes' said nothing about devolution and moreover could be effective only should Callaghan personally remain popular, which was decreasingly the case.

After the referenda results, Callaghan realized that enabling legislation to establish a Scottish Assembly (the Welsh was no longer an issue) would not pass. His plan was to put the bill aside until a revival of Labour's fortunes would make a general election opportune. Then, a strengthened Labour plurality might have the votes to establish the Assembly. (During the campaign it was a fair anticipation that devolution sentiment in Scotland might be mobilized to Labour's benefit.) This idea was thwarted by the changed position of the SNP. After months of supporting the Government, the SNP Members of Parliament signed a no confidence motion on the grounds that the Government was not putting into operation what, after all, still was the majority expression in Scotland. This proved (barely) to be the first successful such motion since 1924.

The ensuing General Election was thus fought at almost the worst possible time for Labour. The monthly Gallup question, 'Do you approve of the government's record to date?' reported in the *Daily Telegraph*, was showing a gap of around 40 per cent negative to positive; six months earlier opinion had been roughly divided. In the event, Labour's showing was not as disastrous as might have been predicted. The Conservative Party did, however, win a clear majority of seats, 339, with 43.9 per cent of the vote. Labour finished with 268 seats and 36.9 per cent, the Liberal Party with 11 seats and 13.8 per cent. Part of the reason for Labour's relatively good showing was its continued strength in the 'Celtic fringe'. In Wales the party received 49.1 per cent of the vote (49.5 per cent in October, 1974) and 22 seats (23 in October, 1974). In Scotland the party received 41.5 per cent of the vote (36.3 per cent in October, 1974) and 44 seats (41 seats in October, 1974). Most of the 1979 gains were at the expense of the SNP, which fell from 30.4 per cent of the vote in October, 1974 to 17.3 per cent in 1979 and from eleven to two seats in the House of Commons.[15]

After the General Election the Scotland and Wales Acts were duly repealed on 21 June and 26 June, 1979 respectively. The Labour Party did not contest the repeal of the latter. And while the Secretary of State for Scotland continued to broach his idea of All-Party Talks, he made it clear, as Michael Foot remarked, that the option approved by a majority of Scottish voters would not be discussed: 'The Government's view is that anything remotely similar to the Scottish Assembly could hardly be devised and put through without there being another referendum' (which Pym opposed). Instead, the aim was for 'improvement of parliamentary procedures for handling of Scottish business'. No wonder opponents of devolution like Julian Amery brushed this idea aside: 'Together we converted the Conservative leadership from rather lukewarm support of devolution to wholehearted opposition.'[16]

Indeed, with the Tories in effective opposition and the threat of SNP to Labour's position in Scotland greatly reduced, prospects for devolution seemed bleak. This opinion was widespread in Parliament – we have seen the 'annihilation of any hope of devolution for Scotland for years to come'; in the press – 'Scotland's "noes" may reduce nationalism to a myth'; and in academic commentary – 'in the absence of a clear-cut result which might have settled the issue, the referendum decided it in favour of those who sought to diffuse it, as against those who might have sought to keep it alive . . . the result of the referendum has moved devolution away from the centre of the political stage. . . .'[17] Yet in a few short months devolution, if not back at centre stage, was at least making noises from the wings. In the next section I will describe how; in the final section I will argue why.

II

The first revival of devolution ferment was in Wales. The issue, as might be expected from the referendum result, was not political *per se* but cultural. In their election manifesto, the Conservative Party, for reasons hard to relate directly to their general policy line, had undertaken to establish in Wales a fourth television channel in the Welsh language. The plan was to start broadcasting twenty-two hours a week of Welsh language programming in September 1982. After the election the Government began to have second thoughts. The estimated cost of providing the service for an anticipated peak viewing audience of 70 000 (a figure later found to be too low) had risen to £35 million per year. This cost was to be divided roughly between the fifteen independent television companies, all but one of which were vehemently opposed to the added burden, and the BBC, which was being subjected to very unpopular spending cuts. The sensible move seemed to be to defer the idea to a more financially happy time.

Unexpectedly for the Government this decision brought outraged cries of betrayal from a wide sector of Welsh opinion and culminated in the announcement by Gwynfor Evans that he would fast 'until death' unless the Government reversed its decision. Now this threat itself is indicative of the distinctive basis and expression of Welsh national feeling. No one would have expected Donald Stewart or Willy Wolfe (the President of the SNP) – or for that matter James Callaghan, Margaret Thatcher, Edward Heath, Tony Benn *et al* – to fast over any issue. And had they stated they were to do so, the reaction most likely would have been derision, not sympathy. The threat by Evans, however, was taken seriously, and pressure mounted on the Government to reverse its position once again. In the event, the Home Secretary announced that after all plans for the Welsh channel would go forward, a decision with major implications not only for the survival of the Welsh language but also more immediately for university graduates who happened to be fluent in Welsh. In general, the increasing mandated use of Welsh in administration, broadcasting, and the judicial process is making fluency in the language a useful skill for the first time since at least the 17th century.

The revival of devolution movements – it would be inaccurate to say 'opinion' – in Scotland was more politically traditional and displayed the usual complex features associated with political revivals. I shall distinguish four. First, the Labour Party in Scotland brought the whole devolution issue back into prominence through a series of progressively expansive declarations on the need for a Scottish Assembly. In its latest form outlined in the March, 1982 Conference at Perth, the Assembly would have the ability to vary the UK level of income tax. This financial power, it was – finally – made clear, meant that the Assembly would 'not have to accept the judgment of the UK government about the level of devolved services'. Accompanying the presentation of an Assembly scheme far more radical than that proposed in the Scotland Bill was a sharp attack on the other parties. The Conservative protestation that they had really wanted a form of devolution was termed a 'straight forward lie'. The SNP were dismissed as 'separatist cavemen'. As for the SDP (about which more below), they were accused of 'trickery'. 'They are in favour of devolution the same way as people are in favour of summer sunshine.'[18]

This latter part of the Labour Party's message showed that mobilization of prodevolution opinion continues to be seen as a good political strategy. The former reveals a new appreciation of the potentialities of an Assembly under a Conservative rather than a Labour national government. This appreciation is well described by George Galloway, then the (very left) chairman of the Labour Party in Scotland in an interview with the *Scottish Marxist*:[19]

> The first point I'd like to make is addressed to those particularly inside our own movement whose efforts effectively destroyed the chances of devolution last time. . . . Had we had an assembly which would in fact have been controlled by the LP there would have been no council sales in Scotland, because that was a devolved issue. . . . The Criminal Justice (Scotland) Act . . . had there been an assembly, this act would not have been passed . . . and the current situation about cuts and the attack on local government would have been of an entirely different character.

> Perhaps more generally, a Scottish Assembly, speaking for the whole of the Scottish people, would have been a powerful voice with which to attack the Tories, and limit their ability to wreak the kind of destruction which they are doing to Scottish society.

One now sees again why the Conservative Party quietly buried their idea of 'All-Party Talks' on devolution.

The second factor leading to renewed possibilities for devolution was the rise of the Social Democratic Party as a potential competitor to Labour for devolution opinion. (The Liberal Party has long been a proponent of devolution, and both David Steel and Jo Grimond represent Scottish constituencies. The electoral appeal of the party, however, has been too geographically isolated to pose a challenge to Labour domination in Scotland.) Among the converts to the party is Iain MacCormick, son of the founder of the SNP and himself a former Scottish National Party MP for Argyll. In his new position of Scottish press officer for the SDP, he portrayed his party as the best hope for a 'sensible and workable system of devolution'. What the system would be was presented in somewhat negative terms at the SDP Conference by Robert Maclennan, MP for Caithness and Sutherland and the party's constitution maker. He pledged the establishment of a Scottish Assembly at the 'earliest possible date' without making 'the mistakes of those whose temporary commitment to an assembly was motivated by political expedience, the mistake which led the Labour Government to set up an assembly without adequate or indeed any financial powers of raising revenue'.[20]

The third factor refocusing political attention on devolution has been a series of opinion poll findings that respondents are increasingly dissatisfied with the present form of Scottish governance and favour some devolutionary change. We should emphasize that this desire does not spring unprompted from many lips. When asked, for example, in a MORI (Market and Opinion Research International) survey commissioned by *The Scotsman* 'Which are the two or three most important problems facing Scotland at the moment', 'devolution' came in eighth, well behind unemployment, strikes (industrial relations), and inflation, and marginally behind general economic conditions, economic growth, housing, and vandalism. Still, the Labour Party and the SNP have shown the issue can be turned to electoral advantage, and its popularity has grown steadily since the referendum:

TABLE 6.1 *The most desirable form of government is Scotland (in %)*

	March 1979	*November 1980*	*November 1981*	*March 1982*
Completely independent Scottish Assembly, separate from England	14	19	22	23
A Scottish Assembly as part of Britain but with substantial powers	42	44	47	53
No change from the present system	35	29	26	19
No not know	9	9	5	5

SOURCE [MORI Poll. In *The Scotsman*, 5 Mar. 1982]

The final factor was fortuitous: the successful effort of Roy Jenkins to win the Hillhead by-election held in March 1982. We call the factor 'fortuitous' because Glasgow Hillhead was hardly the constituency and Scotland was hardly the area an anglicized, 'urbane' (to use the invariable journalist's adjective) Welshman with a south of England accent would choose to contest. Its significance for us was three-fold. First, to be considered for leadership of the Social Democratic Party, Jenkins had to win a seat in the House of Commons soon. His previous loss of a by-election increased the pressure to demonstrate his appeal to voters, not just to the London 'media'. Second, in the process of the campaign the SDP became identified as a credible 'carrier' of devolution sentiment, the implications of which we will elaborate in the next section of this chapter. Third, the campaign nicely illustrated the contemporary state of British parties as well as the potentials and limitations of the devolution issue in Scottish politics. It warrants, then, a brief review.

The Hillhead constituency, which included but was not restricted to the only middle class residential area in Glasgow, had been held by the Conservative Party for over sixty years. The Tories had chosen a candidate, Gerald Malone, who had mastered his party's brief and who promised to represent the constituency well. Moreover the Conservative Government was unusually anxious that the seat be held, primarily because Roy Jenkins was contesting it. Leaders visited the constituency; money was found suddenly for public works; the tax on whisky was raised by much less than had been anticipated. The Tories could be expected not to lose voters unnecessarily; the only possible handicap, unmeasured, was Malone's Catholic religion.

The Labour candidate, David Wiseman, began with more apparent difficulties. A Londoner reputed to be a 'Bennite', Wiseman, it was felt by Labour Party managers, would have trouble projecting the requisite 'moderate' image. Under these circumstances Labour's strategy was to keep Wiseman as shielded as possible from the press and indeed from the voters. Wiseman was allowed to talk at most a couple of minutes at the end of 'his' press conferences. The hope was that if Wiseman could avoid saying anything that could be construed as inflammatory (which he did), and if Labour could hold its traditional support, a SDP–Tory division of the remainder might give the party a victory.

Electoral uncertainties were further increased by the candidacy of the SNP candidate, George Leslie. To be sure, the SNP had no realistic hope of capturing the seat; even in its best days its support in Hillhead had been low. In Leslie, however, the party had selected an energetic, left-wing candidate who had, moreover, the assistance of the largest number of volunteers. A share of the vote significantly in excess of 10 per cent would revive SNP spirits and affect the outcome in unpredictable ways. The closeness of the ensuing contest was borne out well in the polls. At the outset of the final week of campaigning, a poll conducted by William Miller showed only 1.5 percentage points separating the three major candidates. During the final week at least one of the national polls showed each of the candidates in the lead.

Faced with these challenges, Roy Jenkins quickly abandoned the original SDP strategy of capturing the constituency by storm – with the slogan 'Vote for a Prime Minister from Glasgow' and so on – and settled down to intensive campaigning. Much effort was devoted to delivering lengthy speeches and answering questions devoted to the complexities of Scottish education, local government reform . . . and devolution. The point surely was not to sweep the audience off its feet but to project the image of a sober, thoughtful and *safe* candidate who would not lead the country toward the extremes of Thatcherism, Bennism or separatism. There is some impressionistic evidence that in the last days of the campaign this appeal was decisive. 'Our own soundings suggest that it was fear which cast the votes. . . . People were less frightened of Jenkins.'[21] In any event, Jenkins won the seat decisively with a 'swing' (if the term means anything in a multi-party race) of 16.7 per cent Conservative to SDP:

TABLE 6.2 *Results of the Hillhead by-election (25 Mar. 1982)*

	Vote	*%*
Jenkins (SDP/LIB)	10 106	33
Malone (Conservative)	8 086	27
Wiseman (Labour)	7 846	26
Leslie (SNP)	3 416	11
Others	853	3

In the process, as mentioned above, Jenkins raised anew the question of devolution. His opening idea was that the question should be considered as part of a program for constitutional reform in the United Kingdom as a whole that would spread the blessings of decentralization, more accountable government, throughout the land. Nevertheless, and this was the important point, the Scottish situation was so different that devolved powers had to be greater in scope, and it was so pressing that the establishment of an Assembly could *precede* general reform. This Assembly would have legislative control over Scottish private and criminal law, the administration of justice, health, housing, roads, agriculture, tourism, and town and country planning. It would have jurisdiction over various agencies designed to promote economic growth including the Highlands and Islands Development Board and the Scottish Development Agency. With these powers was to go significant financial responsibility. 'The Assembly should have substantial revenue-raising power of its own. A substantial proportion of UK income tax should go to the Assembly from the day it is set up.'[22] Finally, Jenkins raised, as other proponents of devolution had been loath to do, implications of this sort of Assembly for general institutional governance. To reduce overlap and needless bureaucracy one tier of Scottish local government should be eliminated. The House of Lords could usefully be replaced by a second chamber more on the lines (here I speculate; the accounts are not clear) of the German Bundesrat. A system of judicial review would be required. In sum, during the campaign Jenkins was led to articulate a devolution program far more extensive than that presented in the Scotland Bill and in its economic and constitutional features more radical than the current Labour Party position.

Now, it is quite correct that enthusiasm for a Scottish Assembly had not previously been a major component of Jenkins' political philosophy. As Michael Foot remarked, during their long association Jenkins' commitment to devolution had 'somewhat escaped me'. And

Foot was equally correct in noting that a number of SDP parliamentary leaders (most obviously Shirley Williams) had shown great hostility to the Scotland Bill when they were Labour MPs. Jenkins' interest in devolution clearly arose during a hard-fought campaign in which his political survival could have depended on his ability to project a commitment to Hillhead in particular (thus his undertaking not to move to a safer constituency) and a concern with Scottish problems in general. His ideas on devolution were accompanied by position papers on regional policy, on what to do about Clydeside, on local housing reform.

After the by-election the question naturally arose as to whether all this was now official SDP policy. Jenkins' reply was that 'I know of no major issue on which any of the policies I have put forward would be overturned by the party membership.'[23] This statement, even without a Falklands crisis, would hardly propel devolution back into the centre of British politics. But together with the renewed interest of the Labour Party in a Scottish Assembly, the possibility that Labour and the SDP would battle for the bulk of Scottish seats, leaving some rural and Eastern seats to the Tories (on the basis of the Hillhead results the Conservatives would be lucky to win two seats in urban Scotland), and the overwhelming public support for devolution (with fewer than one-fifth of respondents favouring the status quo), there is again the prospect that in Scotland after the next General Election devolution will be back on the political agenda. In the next section I will suggest reasons why in quite different ways devolution continues to be a major issue in Welsh and Scottish political life.

III

In a rather brief paper, we can touch only on a few of the major particularities of the Scottish and Welsh nations and state why they are politically significant.[24] We begin with Wales as an entity. Under the Act of Union between Wales and England in 1536 English dominance was officially confirmed. Unity was to be complete; there were to be no administrative or legislative distinctions between the two nations. We see here a relationship that could be termed 'internal colonialism': The Welsh élite was coopted, anglicized; no national institutions remained that could be vehicles for élite or class mobility.[25] Those on the 'periphery' were isolated and denied effective utilization of their cultural heritage. This heritage was primarily religious and linguistic, both of which were ignored in the Declaration of Supremacy which established an English national church with services in English, that is in a language which was virtually unintelligible to most Welsh. The Welsh language was further proscribed as the areas in which it could be used became matters of state concern. Thus, when the British government in the mid-nineteenth century finally took seriously the education of the population, English was substituted for Welsh as the language of instruction.

To this institutional conformity was added the internal migration generated by the Industrial Revolution. There was a massive movement to industrial Southern and Eastern Wales both from rural areas in the North and from England. English 'immigrants', as might be expected, occupied at first most of the supervisory positions and formed the core of Conservative Party political domination until the Reform Act of 1885. One consequence of this population shift has been that the historical area 'Wales' has boundaries that can only be termed artificial. They are at their least meaningful, moreover, precisely where the population is greatest. To cite one indicator: In the 1971 census the mean percentage of inhabitants in Welsh border counties born in England was thirty. The low was 21 per cent English; the high was 38 per cent.

That in Wales there remains a national identity to pursue politically, that Wales, for example, did not follow a path similar to Brittany, can be attributed in part to the linkage between religious nonconformity and the Welsh language forged during the nineteenth century. The religious component too often is neglected by scholars, but its presence was essential.[26] 'Nineteenth-century non-conformity in Wales was in a unique position. It was the dominant form of worship; it was in a position of educational, religious and social leadership in the communities.'[27] The local character and democratic organization of the chapels reinforced the isolation of the largely Anglican Welsh aristocracy and contributed to the efforts to preserve or revive Welsh cultural traditions. 'Preachers and ministers became the authors, poets, collectors of songs, grammarians, historians and so on, even stranger, they took over the organizing of thoroughly secular institutions like the Eisteddfod.'[28] And all activities were conducted in *Welsh*; after the institution of national education in 1870 the chapels became the primary source of Welsh language instruction. The language was disseminated further through religious periodicals which by 1866 had a circulation of around 120 000.[29]

Welsh culture and language had thus been grounded in contemporary social institutions. Its political expression was made possible by the Reform Act of 1885, which enfranchised the rural voters who contributed to the Liberal landslide in the same year. Elected in 1885 were twenty-two non-conformists, over half Welsh speaking. Their cause continued to be disestablishment of the Anglican church, which reached another climax in 1902 with the Balfour Bill's stipulation that county taxes must be used equally to support all schools. (That is, the non-conformist population would underwrite Anglican schools.) Lloyd George led the opposition with the slogan 'no control, no cash'. Counties refused to turn over the taxes; the chapels filled; and finally in 1914 the long sought Disestablishment Bill was passed.

In retrospect, this triumph can be said to have left an ambiguous legacy. The outrage removed, the chapels settled back to respectability. Trade unions offered a powerful alternative social and socializing function. Cultural activities of the chapels were no longer so vital to local communities. At the same time the local chapel orientation discouraged national organizations and encouraged splits among Baptists, Methodists, etc. Finally, of course, the salience of religion in general has declined. This is not to deny the tremendous influence of non-conformity on Welsh trade unionism or on the Plaid Cymru; the latter we will discuss further. But it does increase the identity between what is distinctly Welsh and the Welsh language, a language understood by a distinct minority of the population in an age when its viability always must be thought to be in question. And it impedes the effective utilization of the new pattern of centre–regional relations for national benefit that I now will describe in the case of Scotland.

The Scottish case can be presented usefully in contrast to the Welsh. We begin with geographical position and population mix. The distance between the major population centres of England and Scotland has helped reduce the movement of population south to north. Even the border areas are remarkably differentiated. The highest percentage of English-born residents in a Scottish county is ten (Dumfries); the highest percentage of Scottish-born residents in an English county (Berwick upon Tweed) is nine. In general, of all the British 'regions' Scotland in the early 1970s had the largest percentage of people who have lived there all their lives (82 per cent) and for the last ten years (97 per cent).[30] Turning to institutions, the 1707 union between England and Scotland was in theory an agreement negotiated and approved willingly by the parliaments in both nations. Under its provisions, only political institutions were merged; Scotland retained, and retains, her separate and divergent legal system, educational structure and national church.

Nor should this loss of parliament be seen as a major blow to the effective expression of Scottish opinion – one must not equate the position of early eighteenth and mid-twentieth century parliaments. At least up to the great 'Disruption' of 1843 that split the church, and the large immigration of Irish Catholics to Western Scotland beginning at around the same time, the General Assembly of the Church of Scotland provided an effective forum for the presentation of Scottish opinion. The result was that, unlike the case in Wales, the Scottish élite (middle class, professionals, whatever word one wants to use) remained integrated within the nation. Indeed, the union can be said to have confirmed their position both through the guaranteed continuation of separate legal, church and educational systems and through their new ability to call upon the centre, London, to deal with the very real threats of disruption from the Scottish periphery, the 'Highlands'. This is why the model of 'internal colonialism' does not apply to Scotland.[31] Contemporary observers saw yet another advantage in the abolition of a separate parliament brought on by the union: As the *Caledonian Mercury* argued in 1783, the attention of Scots was freed from the 'nonsense and distraction of politics' to concentrate on 'trade, industry and improvement of the soil'.[32]

Given this background, the question arises as to why within Scotland national political expression has now become useful, not nonsense and a distraction. The answer, which I develop in 'Political Component of Scottish Nationality', is found in the intersection between two factors: The decline in the benefits brought by union, and the new pattern of advanced industrial economic development that fosters a type of centre-region power relationship that makes political expression a rational strategy for Scottish groups and voters to pursue. The first consideration, of course, pertains not to material benefits relative to other British regions but to material benefits relative to what the Scottish élite and other politically relevant actors argue could reasonably be expected were Scotland not part of the United Kingdom. The second consideration we discussed at the beginning of this chapter from the perspective of Westminster. We can now present, though hardly 'prove', the argument in a more general form: The broad pattern of economic policy and administration in advanced industrial states leads to at least a verbal commitment to regional planning, decentralization, federalism – the precise form varies from state to state. From the standpoint of the centre, this orientation has the negative unanticipated consequence of reviving or legitimating expressions of national identity in 'regions' where this identity has social, cultural or linguistic grounding.

For Wales we find this effect as well. The budget of the Welsh Office rose in ten years from £48 000 to over £1 100 000; significant development aid was channeled to Wales; the Welsh Trades Union Congress became a champion of devolution; the 1979 General Election manifesto of the Plaid Cymru devoted twenty-two of its twenty-four pages to socioeconomic issues. These manifestations are limited, however, by the grounding of Welsh identity in what is now a culture and language appreciated by a minority. There has been no electoral threat to Labour domination from political expressions of Welsh nationality; thus while the Plaid may devote its time to socioeconomic issues, it is seen by the electorate as the party of the Welsh language.[33]

In Scotland the situation is quite different. The sense of nationality is sufficiently widespread to permit producer groups to become effective champions of Scottish interests. Pro-devolution opinion is sufficiently pervasive to pose a challenge to and an opportunity for the Labour Party in Scotland. In short, from the standpoint of the region, national identity can be used to increase the benefits of union. For Scotland the benefits have been greater than for any other region in Britain; the need for benefits is similarly large. The latter as well as the former is shown in the following table on taxes and subsidies taken from the *1980 Report* of the Scottish Trades Union Congress:

TABLE 6.3 *Scottish and UK taxes on expenditure and subsidies (1976)*

	Taxes (£m)	*Subsidies* (£m)
UK	16 549	3 472
Scotland	1 583	554
Scotland as % of UK	9.6	16.0

NOTE (Consumption method of computation)

We see in Table 6.3 both the effectiveness of the new pattern of centre-region power relations to channel benefits and the limitations imposed by this relationship. *Separatism* would end the game to the detriment of the regional partner.

FUTURE POSSIBILITIES

The account given in this paper is intended as a general explanation of the difference between the movements toward devolution in Scotland and Wales. When we come to a discussion of future possibilities, however, we must be careful not to flirt with structural determinism. The key point to remember is that movements toward devolution or toward any other social change must have concrete political carriers. Structural features may permit but they do not produce particular kinds of political action. Devolution movements in particular are susceptible to the kinds of tensions that impede realization of potentialities. I will now attempt to make these somewhat lofty comments more concrete.

To take the case of Scotland first, periodically during the 1970s the SNP was able to take advantage of the political dealignment in Britain to mobilize voters concerned with the devolution issue. The divisions within the party and perhaps the very inarticulateness of its leadership allowed it both to be a reasonable carrier of Scottish grievances and to represent something more radical should these grievances not be addressed. Thus we see the growth of support for the party independent of any expressed attitudes toward self-rule. And thus we see the significance of Miller's finding that at the time of the 1974 general elections 76 per cent of Scottish respondents – including 70 per cent of those voting Labour and 69 per cent of those voting Conservative – stated that SNP victories were 'good for Scotland'.[34]

This upsurge in SNP fortunes, however, always has been tenuous. The party has been subject to a continuous tension between the excitement of 'independence' that brings in money and volunteers and the realization that, particularly under the British electoral system, the party would have to broaden its appeal to avoid poor performances at the polls. Thus the party has no automatic claim even on pro-separatist opinion. In late 1982, for example, pro-separatist opinion exceeded SNP standing in the polls. The lack of any minimal basis of support is underscored by the absence of any cultural revival (signs of which the SNP leadership tends to disparage) or linguistic differentiation to succor the party through hard times.[35] As I stated earlier, 'a credible threat of separatism remains the missing component in the political expression of Scottish nationality'.[36] The debacle of the Scottish referendum and the no confidence vote seems to have marked the beginning of the fall, whether permanent or not one cannot say. The party is now dominated by what we could call the 'fundamentalist faction' whose position is typified by the 1980 Conference slogan 'Independence, Nothing Less' (and, it is fair to add, 'Nothing Else'). Reaction to devolution schemes has been of a similar nature – 'Labour's devolution costs money. Independence is free.'[37] This intransigent front cannot conceal a myriad of factional and personal disputes. The status of the 79 Group is particularly controversial. The Group has managed to push through a few conference resolutions making 'Civil Disobedience' for the first time part of official policy, committing an independent Scotland to leaving NATO, and so on;[38] one can assume that the acquiescence of others in the party has been tactical. Certainly the party's image with the electorate has not been improved. The disappointing showing of George Leslie at Hillhead has been confirmed at the 1982 regional elections where the SNP won only 13 per cent of the vote (as opposed to 20 per cent in 1978) and ceased even to be the second party in all regions except the Central. Representatives of the left faction fared particularly badly in the regional elections.

The mistake of some commentators has been to equate the decline of fortunes of the SNP with lessening prospects for devolution. As I have tried to show, this conclusion overlooks the stake the Labour Party in Scotland has in the establishment of a Scottish Assembly and in the devolution issue generally. In normal times, and lacking a system of proportional representation, the party could be expected to dominate any Scottish Assembly. Devolution continues to be a promising electoral issue. And it would be inaccurate to portray support for devolution within the Labour Party in Scotland as a matter only of electoral advantage or jobs for the boys. As two studies suggest, even many Labour MPs tend to think of themselves as Scottish oriented and to act accordingly. With an admittedly incomplete sample, Mishler and Mughan found that roughly half of their respondents saw themselves as 'Scottish' and 'always' perceived national conflict in British politics. When asked whether they would prefer to stay at Westminster if a Scottish assembly were established, a bare majority (53 per cent) said yes. The remainder stated they would stand for the Assembly or were undecided in their plans. (Among Scottish Conservative respondents 82 per cent stated they would not leave the House of Commons.)[39] Keating found these opinions paralleled in parliamentary behaviour. As opposed to their English colleagues, Scottish MPs of all parties were less likely to sponsor bills affecting the whole of Britain, spent less time in general parliamentary debate, were less likely to be participant in committees (e.g., Defence) not related directly to Scotland. In short, 'most Scottish MPs concentrate on securing benefits for Scotland'.[40] Moreover, apart from party considerations, the stake of producer groups in Scotland in securing benefits through an assertion of separate Scottish identity should not be forgotten. An Assembly could regularize this centre–regional interaction.

Finally, lest the Labour Party feel further exertions could be postponed, the decline in the SNP has been accompanied by the rise of the SDP as a challenge to Labour Party dominance. That the potential of the party is large is seen in the following MORI polls (Table 6.4) on voting intentions and second preferences:

TABLE 6.4 *Scottish voting intentions*

May 1979 Election		*May 1981*	*March 1982*
Conservative	31.4	23	18
Labour	41.5	42	39
Lib/SDP	9.0(Libs)	20	29
SNP	17.3	15	14
Other	0.8	—	—

Second preferences

First preference	*Second preference*					
	Con	*Lab*	*Lib/ SDP*	*SNP*	*Not vote/ other*	*DK*
Conservative	1	2	45	7	25	20
Labour	2	—	30	24	27	17
Lib/SDP	15	25	24	9	11	16
SNP	5	20	34	—	27	14

SOURCE (*The Scotsman*, 3, Mar. 1982)

And, as we have seen, the SDP through Roy Jenkins has adopted a strong pro-devolution stand. Once again, however, it is necessary to interject some complexities. While potential support for the SDP is high, so is the prospect of rapid decline. To outline only two major considerations: first, there is the tension between the leadership of mostly 'moderate' former Labour MPs and the active membership consisting, in the words of the *New Statesman*, of the 'white, educated, nervous and confused middle class'. These members have shown 'a clear reluctance to embark on radical policies on taxation, public schools or devolution. About the only new measures for which there [is] any enthusiasm concerns union bashing'.[41] These members could be claimed or reclaimed by the Tories. The second tension is between the English and Scottish sections of the party. The Scottish, both membership and – thanks to the conversion of Roy Jenkins – leadership, are on record as strongly favouring devolution. So, of course, does David Steel. The English, both membership and leadership, have expressed no such commitment. The ability of the SDP to present itself as an effective carrier of Scottish interests remains open.

The Welsh case again can be contrasted to the Scottish, and it can be presented more briefly. Because of the significant language differences the role of party as carrier of national interests is less central. The role is shared, often uneasily, with extra-parliamentary organizations whose orientation usually is more militant. For Wales the most important group is the Welsh Language Society (the Cymdeithas yr Iaith Gymraeg) which has a strict policy of nonviolence (another chapel legacy) but which does advocate civil disobedience defined to include the destruction of television and radio broadcasting equipment. Although ties with the Plaid Cymru are close (the leadership of the Society, for example Meinir Evans, often consists of children of Plaid leaders), the traditional political process is rejected as being too uncertain and too slow.

The Plaid itself is divided in similar ways as the SNP. Philip Rawkins has identified four types of activists: 'fortress nationalists' (unconcerned with policies other than the protection of Welsh culture); 'cultural militants' (with the same aim but advocating disobedience, often members of the Welsh Language Society); 'party loyalists' (pragmatic and gradualist concerned with persuading English opinion); 'modernists' (described as 'devolutionists rather than fervent nationalists', advocating economic reorganization and greater social justice).[42] It is this last group that was responsible for most of the 1979 Election Manifesto on economic and social change.[43] The division between this group and the third is seen in the leadership dispute between Gwynfor Evans and Dafydll Elis Thomas. Evans, who has led the Plaid for over thirty years, is a lay minister and chairman of the Union of Welsh Independents, the Congregational denomination in Wales. He adheres strongly to a nonviolent, constitutional program. As he describes in *Nonviolent Nationalism*, 'The morality of the use of violence derives for me from what I understand of Christ's life, teaching and death. . . . Means and ends are structurally inseparable.'[44]

We have described his successful campaign for a Welsh language television station. The difference in tone as well as program is seen in the statement of Thomas after his election as vice president of the Plaid. Thomas declared himself 'in favour of militant action over housing and unemployment, in favour of an alliance of the left in Wales to resist and bring down the government'.[45]

The difficulty with both party and extra-party activity, of course, is that what is distinctively Welsh pertains only to a minority of the population of Wales, restricted indigenously to rural areas in the North and West but bolstered by the identification of a number of middle class professionals. That is why calls for a 'union of the left' have failed. We have noted that the Welsh public sees the Plaid as a language protection, not a 'left', party. The Labour Party has no incentive to lead the public to think otherwise – the Plaid simply is not electorally strong enough to be either a threat or a useful ally. There is no broad pro-devolution sentiment to mobilize, as the Welsh referendum confirmed. Producer groups likewise are handicapped in their ability to get 'more for Wales'. While the activities and the money spent by the Welsh Office may increase, these are better seen as examples not of 'devolution' but of what I have termed 'administrative/spatial decentralization'. The new pattern of centre–regional relations makes bodies like the Welsh Office useful forums for greater *central control*.[46] In the power relationship centre–region, the latter gains only in very particular circumstances. These I have argued are present in Scotland; they are not in Wales.

These considerations lead to a projection that some form of Scottish Assembly will be established. Its establishment would represent an acknowledgement that the power balance between centre–region has shifted somewhat toward the region, and it could prove a useful forum for further adjustments. No such Assembly is likely for Wales unless it is established as part of another 'Home Rule all round' without a referendum. Even in this case its competence would not be extensive. Expressions of nationality in Wales are much more likely to be extra-parliamentary with sporadic bouts of violence (as in the burning of English vacation homes) which, however, the chapel tradition should keep restricted. No such 'militance' should be expected in Scotland.

These projections could be upset by a number of external factors; I shall mention three of the more interesting. First, the result of the 1979 General Election – Conservative Government with minimal representation from the 'Celtic fringe' – could become standard. (Mostly by chance it has not been so in the past.) Particularly if inspired by Thatcherian economic policies, this Government might be markedly less receptive to pressure from regional producer groups for a better deal. There could be institutional retrenchment as well; already the Scottish Trades Union Congress is complaining about the abolition of a few 'quangos' and the tardiness in replacing its representative on others. Politically, having ceded the devolution issue, there would be marked reluctance among Conservative leaders to establish an Assembly that would serve as a forum for the opposition. Reaction in Scotland and Wales is difficult to predict. More likely for Scotland than a turn to 'militant' tactics[47] would be a resurgence of the Scottish National Party. The key for Wales would be the willingness of the Government to make timely (and inexpensive) concessions on the language question.

The second possibility is described by Tom Nairn as the 'disintegration of Labourism'. Nairn states that:[48]

> The post-World War II consensus was more the work of the Labour Party than of the Conservatives. The latter accepted a good deal of it (until 1979), whereas Labourism was essential to it. The story of the 1964–79 period is how defence of the Keynesian compromise became more obviously doomed. The traditional right-wing Labour leadership lost its morale. The socialist left rebelled, and embarked upon its first really determined effort to control the party. As a result, the central pillar of post-war hegemony has broken apart, torn, between a rightest 'social democratic' secession on the one hand and a programme of (by British standards) extreme economic nationalism on the other.

It does not matter that the Labour split in Scotland and Wales is less pronounced. The 'disintegration of Labourism' in England alone would suffice. Now, in some respects this possibility complements the other – a split in the Labour Party could ensure Conservative domination. But because we are talking of 'labourism' as well, the situation could become more dynamic. In Scotland in particular – but similar actions in Wales cannot be dismissed – there could emerge a radical 'union of the left' that would combine industrial action (including factory occupations) with the assertion of national claims. The experience of 'Red Clydeside' after World War I offers an ambiguous model.

Our third possibility is that a British party might emerge that would have as its aim the alteration of the British system of governance toward more 'constitutional' procedures. Back in the recent past when it was not quite so staid, *The Economist* called this alteration 'Blowing Up a Tyranny'. As the paper explained in its leader of 5 November

1977: 'Guy Fawkes was discovered 372 years ago before he could blow King and Parliament up. Today he would be right to try again – to renew a democracy this time rather than a religion.' The journal then proceeded to label British government 'undignified, inefficient, undemocratic and, above all, unparliamentary'.[49] It must be emphasized immediately that to cast the current Social Democratic Party in the role of Guy Fawkes is risible. The success of the party, shown again at Hillhead, comes from presenting itself as the *safe* alternative to what it portrays as the wild leanings of Labour and the Tories. But this could be the point: structural reform is presented as a way to avoid 'wild' governmental alternatives. And, as in France, such a reform could have as a component the establishment of 'devolved' representative institutions, not just in Wales and Scotland but in English regions as well. The question of devolution would then be mixed with the reform of British constitutional procedures.

NOTES

1. See Norman Furniss, 'The Political Component of Scottish Nationality'. In Raymond Hall (ed.), *Ethnic Autonomy – Comparative Dynamics* (New York: Pergamon Press, 1979) pp. 152–79.
2. Ibid. and Norman Furniss, 'Internal Colonialism: its Utility for Understanding the Development of Higher Education in Scotland', *Development and Change* 7 (1976) pp. 445–67.
   The major groups studied were the Scottish Council (Development and Industry) and the Scottish Trades Union Congress. The general orientation on the role and significance of 'producer groups' is drawn from the work of Samuel H. Beer, *British Politics in the Collectivist Age* (New York: Knopf, 1965); see also the extensive and useful discussion by Stephen Blank, *Industry and Government in Britain: The Federation of British Industries in Politics, 1945–1965* (Lexington, Mass.: Lexington Books, 1973).
3. Michael Keating and David Bleiman, *Labour and Scottish Nationalism* (London: Macmillan, 1979).
4. Quoted in Furniss, 'The Political Component of Scottish Nationality', p. 155.
5. On this last see William Miller, *The End of British Politics? Scots and English Political Behaviour in the Seventies* (Oxford: Clarendon Press, 1981).
6. *Hansard*, vol. 939, p. 51.
7. Provisions from the *Scotland Bill* and the *Wales Bill*. British Sessional Papers, House of Commons 1977–78, vols IV, V.
8. *Hansard*, vol. 939, p. 447.
9. *Hansard*, vol. 939, p. 506.

10. *Hansard*, vol. 939, pp. 400ff.
11. Quotations from *Hansard*, vol. 939, pp. 1329, 1330; vol. 943, pp. 378, 335; vol. 944, p. 1488; vol. 942, p. 316 respectively.
12. In general, as the remarks of Francis Pym also illustrate, a large number of British politicians and political commentators fail to comprehend how a system of overlapping and competing jurisdictions could work at all, let alone how such a system might work well. To combine this incomprehension with a belief that there is something called 'parliamentary sovereignty', which, according to Michael Foot, is the 'most important precious possession of the British people', is to arrive at the conclusion that devolution is 'the end of Britain'.
13. *Hansard*, vol. 944, p. 1528.
14. Miller, *The End of British Politics?*, pp. 247–54.
15. For two useful interpretations see William Miller, 'Class, Region and Strata at the British Election' and Peter Pulzer, 'The British General Election', both in *Parliamentary Affairs*, 32 (1979) pp. 361–75.
16. Quotations from *Hansard*, vol. 968, p. 1376; vol. 968, p. 1350 respectively.
17. The first remark is by George Foulks, MP, in *Hansard*, vol. 968, p. 1385; the second by the *Daily Telegraph*, 9 Mar. 1979; the third by Vernon Bogdanor, 'The 40 Per Cent Rule,' *Parliamentary Affairs*, 33 (1980) pp. 249–63.
18. Quotations from Bill Spiers, Chairman of the Labour Working Party on Devolution, as reported in *The Scotsman*, 22 Mar. 1982.
19. *Scottish Marxist*, no. 23 (1981) pp. 6, 7.
20. *The Times*, 6 Oct. 1981.
21. Henry Drucker, 'Hillhead: Politics in the Dark', *New Society*, 1 Apr. 1982, p. 9.
22. The above is from *The Scotsman*, 11 Mar. 1982.
23. Reported in *The Scotsman*, 27 Mar. 1982.
24. Longer accounts of national institutions are given by James Kellas, *Modern Scotland* (London: Allen & Unwin, 1980) and Alan Butt Philip, *The Welsh Question* (Cardiff: University of Wales Press, 1975). The 'Kilbrandon Report', Royal Commission on the Constitution (London: HMSO, Cmnd 5460, 1973), presents useful material. Comparisons are made by H.M. Drucker and Gordon Brown, *The Politics of Nationalism and Devolution* (London: Longmans, 1980).
25. On the concept of 'internal colonialism' see Michael Hechter, *Internal Colonialism: The Celtic Fringe in British National Development 1536–1966* (Berkeley: University of California Press, 1975). A vivid and, I believe, fair assessment of the emerging 'Welsh aristocracy' is provided by Gwynfor Evans and Ioan Rhys, 'Wales', in O.D. Edwards, ed., *Celtic Nationalism* (London: Routledge & Kegan Paul, 1968) pp. 52–77.
26. For two exceptions see Philip, *op. cit.* and Ruth Pitts, 'The Nonconformist Influence in Welsh Nationalism' (M.A. Thesis: Department of West European Studies, Indiana University: 1981).
27. Ibid., p. 16.
28. Quotation from Prys Morgan in ibid., p. 21. The Eisteddfod, a competitive arts festival emphasizing singing had had a long tradition, but at the time was not in its most creative period.

29. Patricia Elton Mayo, *The Roots of Identity* (London: Allen Lane, 1974) p. 68.
30. Data from the 'Kilbrandon Report', op. cit.
31. See Furniss, 'Internal Colonialism: its Utility for Understanding the Development of Higher Education in Scotland'.
32. From Furniss, 'The Political Component of Scottish Nationality', p. 160.
33. See the discussion in Dennis Balsom, 'Plaid Cymru' in H.M. Drucker, ed., *Multi-Party Britain* (London: Macmillan, 1979) pp. 131–54.
34. William Miller, 'The Connection Between SNP Voting and the Demand for Self-Government', *European Journal of Political Research* 5 (1977) p. 100.
35. The disinterest, nay antipathy, toward cultural revival among the leadership could be attribured to a number of factors: the class composition of the SNP leadership; the dead hand of the 'Kailyard' mentality; difficulties in associating with major contemporary cultural figures, in particular Hugh MacDiarmid; the (astute) realization that there being no single 'Scottish culture', any revival could be more divisive than unifying. An attempt to sort out these and other factors is beyond the scope of this chapter.
36. Furniss, 'The Political Component of Scottish Nationality', p. 174.
37. This from the party's Vice-President for Policy. Quoted in the *Scots Independent*, Mar. 1981.
38. For a hopeful assessment of the future of this 'left faction' see Graee Hyslop, 'The SNP', *Scottish Marxist* no. 23 (1981) pp. 3–21. I thank Bernard Crick for additional information.
39. William Mishler and Anthony Mughan, 'Representing the Celtic Fringe: Devolution and Legislative Behaviour in Scotland and Wales', *Legislative Studies Quarterly* 3 (1978) pp. 385–400.
40. Michael Keating, 'Parliamentary Behaviour as a Test of Scottish Integration into the United Kingdom', *Legislative Studies Quarterly* 3 (1978), p. 409
41. 'The not-very-radical party', *New Statesman*, 19 Feb. 1982, p. 2.
42. Philip Rawkins, 'An Approach to the Political Sociology of the Welsh Nationalist Movement', *Political Studies*, 27 (1979) pp. 440–57.
43. For further discussion see Ian McAllister, 'Party Organization and Minority Nationalism: A Comparative Study of the United Kingdom', *European Journal of Political Research*, 9 (1981) pp. 237–55.
44. Quoted in Pitts, op. cit., p. 62.
45. Ibid., p. 66.
46. In Norman Furniss, 'The Practical Significance of Decentralization', *Journal of Politics*, 36 (1974). The term 'administrative/spatial decentralization' is described on p. 966.
47. This possibility is offered by Miller in *The End of British Politics*?.
48. Tom Nairn, 'The Crisis of the British State', *New Left Review*, no. 130 (1981) p. 40.
49. 'Blowing Up a Tyranny', *The Economist*, 5 Nov. 1977, pp. 11–16.

7 The Referendum and the British Constitution

Harry Lazer

On 5 June 1975, Britain conducted its first countrywide referendum on the question of whether or not the United Kingdom should remain a member of the European Common Market. Why had Britain resisted so long the adoption of a device used in democracies throughout the world? What were the fundamental reasons, as well as the immediate circumstances, for this sharp break with the British political tradition occurring at this time? We shall examine these questions, as well as the continuing debate over the referendum and what implications use of the referendum has for the British constitutional system.

THE REFERENDUM IN BRITISH POLITICAL HISTORY

Although the referendum had never been conducted on a statewide scale in Britain until 1975, it had been proposed a number of times in this century and had actually been used in limited areas. Thus both its advocates and critics gave a somewhat misleading picture. The former insisted that its repeated mention and limited use justified its being considered within the British political tradition; the latter dismissed it as a totally alien instrument.

The interest in the referendum began in the mid-1890s in the wake of Gladstone's proposal for Irish Home Rule. Its leading proponents were two enemies of Home Rule, John St. Loe Strachey, a Conservative publicist, and A.V. Dicey, the most eminent constitutional authority of the time.[1] 'Under our modern English Constitution we cannot secure . . .' the latter wrote, 'that the House of Commons shall even debate the gigantic constitutional innovations which it is prepared to enact.'[2]

A more serious and powerful consideration of the referendum, however, came during the Parliament Bill controversy from 1909 to 1911, when the House of Lords, after having rejected the Liberal Government's progressive Lloyd George Budget of 1909, had its powers severely restricted. Attempting to forestall the eventual verdict, Conservatives presented a number of alternative plans whose common feature was submission to a popular referendum of major bills which the Lords had refused to accept despite their sponsorship by the Government and their support by a majority in the Commons. In March 1911, the Conservatives (then known as Unionists) supported a private bill in the Lords which contained a referendum mechanism and later reinforced this commitment by a proposed amendment in the Commons to the Parliament Bill. This amendment required that all bills involving the Crown, home rule, the franchise, and the powers of both houses of Parliament and their interrelationship would need a referendum before being presented for the Royal Assent.[3]

With the passage of the Parliament Bill, however, the Conservative preoccupation with the referendum seemed to fade away, and a countrywide referendum was realistically suggested only once between the world wars. In 1930, Stanley Baldwin, the Conservative leader, had proposed one on tariff reform primarily to check his own intra-party division on the subject as well as to secure the authority to institute such a program on being returned to power.[4] In taking this step, he was in good company, as the earlier Conservative leader Arthur Balfour, who had committed the party to the principle of the referendum during the Parliament Bill controversy, had also declared his willingness to submit tariff reform to a popular vote.[5]

The referendum, however, was not mentioned again from 1930 until 1945. After the defeat of Germany, Churchill was anxious to preserve the wartime coalition until the defeat of Japan. He proposed to the Labour Party a prolongation of the existing Parliament, an extraordinary measure which should be given moral authority by the 'direct expression of the nation's will'. The Labour Party, eager for an early election, rejected the idea. Attlee, their leader, not only stated his opposition to the extension of the Government, but outrightly condemned the use of the referendum to secure it since, recently used by Nazi and Fascist regimes, it was alien to British political thought and practice.[6]

Although his reaction reflected a common view, it was only partially valid. The referendum, as noted earlier, had not only been seriously proposed a number of times but in the process it had secured support from dominant political figures, especially Conservative leaders, as well as the official backing, at one time, of the party itself. Even though the total Conservative record on the subject during this century is in fact less impressive than an emphasis upon its high points would indicate, there has been significant support for the referendum, despite its questionable historical associations.

Even more to the point, however, the purportedly alien nature of the referendum in Britain is belied by the fact that it has actually been used in the country – but not on a large scale. Local referendums were held in the 19th century on the establishment of public houses and on municipally sponsored legislation; in the 20th century they were held for Sunday movies.[7] Generally, local referendums in this century have been confined to outlying regions. In Scotland since 1918 local polls have been conducted on liquor licensing; in Wales since 1961 the people have 'been asked to vote every seven years, at first by county and now by district, on whether they want their public houses to open on Sundays'.[8] Moreover, as we shall see, the proposal of another such regional poll, this time in Northern Ireland, turned out to be one of the decisive steps leading up to the eventual adoption of a countrywide referendum in 1975.

Despite these instances of local use of the referendum and its strong advocacy at certain periods, the fact nevertheless remained that there was a powerful resistance to the principle of a popular referendum. The reasons were a combination of the constitutional, the historical, and the social. Especially important were the preeminent role of Parliament in British history, the fundamental principle of Parliamentary sovereignty, and the strongly élitist character of its society. Thus, despite the democratic nature of its political institutions, tendencies towards populism and majoritarianism have been discouraged.

Nevertheless our historical sketch of the referendum controversy in Britain does point to certain persistent characteristics which have predisposed a number of individuals and groups to propose its use. The main generating force for this break with the normal operation of British government and politics derived from the feeling of significant sections of the political and intellectual community that the prevailing consensus was being seriously threatened. This fundamental distrust of what a parliamentary majority, present or future, could do called into question the foundation of the British constitutional principles of Parliamentary sovereignty and strong cabinet government. Britain's concentration of governmental power, unchecked by any written constitutional limits, was almost unique among democracies. It could only be tolerated – much less enthusiastically supported – in a society characterized by mutual trust between political parties and actors. The government of the day has full scope and freedom for its actions only because of the confidence of the opposition and the public that it will operate within well-understood limits and that the basic socio-political structure will not be fundamentally changed beyond a tacitly agreed-upon consensus. In the normal swing of the pendulum, the opposition will gain control and exert a similarly wide scope of power under a similar protective covering of trust and understanding. This is the kernel of Lord Balfour's famous statement:

> Our alternating cabinets, though belonging to different parties, have never differed about the foundations of society. And it is evident that our whole political machinery pre-supposes a people so fundamentally at one that they can safely afford to bicker, and so sure of their own moderation that they are not dangerously disturbed by the never-ending din of political conflict. May it always be so.[9]

When it is felt, however, that the Government is contemplating moving beyond the established consensus and crossing the assumed limits of its powers, alarm is expressed about the overwhelming extent of the executive sway in the British political system and attention accorded to the lack of a bill of rights in a written constitution. It is at such times that the intellectual ground is receptive to institutional reforms and innovations, such as the referendum.

Another circumstance which has cropped up as a precipitant of a referendum demand is the emergence of a particularly contentious issue of major proportions, one that bitterly divides the country in general and a party in particular. It is understandable why the political leadership, when confronted by an embarrassing and potentially explosive situation, could consider recourse to a referendum as a felicitous instrument for extricating itself from it.

The one feature, however, which has been common to the background of each previous possibility of a countrywide referendum has been its proposal by Conservative elements, and at times by the party itself. Indeed, some of the earlier versions in which the Lords could check the Commons were patently partisan and unfair. The prospects of the referendum eventually being accepted and put into practice did markedly increase when this partisan bias was eliminated. The fact remained, however, that the referendum still originated from Conservative sources and was thus considered by non-Conservatives as a reflection of their philosophy and interests. Thus, if one were to predict its eventual acceptance within the British political system, it was evident that its philosophical base would have to be broadened and that it would more likely have to be propelled by other than Conservative forces, especially, by elements within the Labour Party.

In the first two decades of the post-World War II period, however, little mention was made of the referendum except to dismiss it out of hand, and its chances of being incorporated into the British parliamentary system seemed almost non-existent. The basic motives behind previous referendum proposals, the apparent dissolution of the political consensus or the emergence of a divisive issue, seemed totally absent. At a time when the prevailing political philosophy was termed 'Butskellism', when moderates were in control of both major political parties and conducted political affairs with relative harmony and agreement, complaints about governments upsetting the established consensus were rare.

By the late 1960s, however, significant changes were taking place which transformed the atmosphere into one much more favourably inclined towards a referendum. A shift to the left in the leadership of the largest trade unions would eventually be reflected in the balance of power within the Labour party moving from centre-right to centre-left, with the prospect of even a more pronounced turn to the left developing. As this left movement was translated into more radical policy demands, many persons in all parties, especially the Conservative, believed that the prevailing consensus was being threatened and seriously contemplated constitutional and electoral reforms that would check the resulting 'elective dictatorship', to use Lord Hailsham's colourful phrase.[10] Although Hailsham himself limited mention of the referendum to the ratification and amendment process for the new written constitution he was advocating, the disillusionment of such a renowned constitutional authority and Lord Chancellor with the operation of the parliamentary–cabinet system gave a cutting edge to this increasing Conservative skepticism and projected it into public attention. In this atmosphere, others could turn to it as a cure appropriate to the diagnosis.[11]

POPULISM

Changes within the Labour Party not only furthered the prospects of a referendum by provoking a defensive reaction among Conservatives, but also encouraged a response favourable to it within the Labour Party. A new and unsettling force, populism, was emerging in British political life by the late 1960s and, in conjunction with the changing ideological orientation of the Labour Party, was creating a sympathetic philosophic base within it where none had existed before. In absorbing the impact of populism, Britain was but following a pattern common to other Western 'post-industrial' democracies at this time.[12]

Populism is admittedly an elusive concept, and the movements and parties which have reflected its discontent against the political system have generally perplexed both political actors and observers because of the vagueness and contradictions of their principles, the eccentricity of their programs, and the difficulty of fitting them into the traditional left–right political spectrum.[13] Although there are a multitude of definitions of populism, it can best be described as the belief that the majority opinion of the people is not reflected in political institutions, but rather checked by an élitist minority. The most common and salient characteristics of those committed to this viewpoint are parochialism, individualism, and social conservatism.

Populists are generally parochial because their natural tendency is to support and give primary allegiance to the smaller and more familiar unit, the locality over the region, the region over the country, and the country over supra-national entities. They are often suspicious of cosmopolitan elements and hostile to alien ones. They are individualistic because of their overriding fear of being manipulated and controlled by organizations and élites. They are fundamentally conservative because of their deep concern about the unsettling effects of large-scale economic, social, and political change.

Britain, because of the combination of its social system and its political structure and ethos, has been one of the Western industrialized countries considered most immune to populism. Respect for authority is a dominant national value and deference to leadership operates at all levels within the political system. Although all countries of necessity possess political élites, there are hardly any other democracies where it is so tight, homogeneous, and powerful.

Even in this hostile atmosphere, populism has emerged. It has, however, not manifested itself in a separate political party or movement as in some countries, but has rather been reflected in a variety of political developments, such as the declining vote for the major political parties and the demands for immigration control and for devolution.

Populism's most significant impact on the political scene, however, was probably in provoking a bitter division within the Labour Party between its working class and middle class members. This was accomplished by providing the former with a general social outlook which articulated their developing opposition to the prevailing liberal élitism of the party's right wing and leadership, both heavily middle class. Since the unions had traditionally supported the right within the party, the emergence of populism combined with the increasingly leftist orientation of some major trade unions resulted in a new dominant coalition of the left and the unions.

POPULISM, THE REFERENDUM, AND THE COMMON MARKET

It was within the context of Labour's power politics and ideological tangle that the referendum finally succeeded. Populist attitudes encouraged its projection because it was an instrument of government which exemplified populist values. Largely dispensing with the distorting influences of legislative middlemen, it allowed the voice of the people to be directly expressed on public policy.

Despite the fact that there were theoretical currents and political forces in both political parties favourable to a referendum, it was still highly unlikely that it would have been brought to fruition on a country-wide scale in Britain if another essential ingredient had been missing: a major contentious issue. A most unlikely candidate, membership in the European Common Market, did emerge and become the question which convinced first the Labour leaders, beginning with a minority of one, that a referendum was not only feasible but necessary.

The issue of whether or not to join the Market loomed so important, especially within the Labour Party, because it reflected almost the whole gamut of populist values and concerns. It appeared to be a project, championed by an élitist minority, against the opinion of the mass of the population and evoked the image of the common man being challenged by the political and cultural Establishment.[14] Although this seemed a threat to the populist characteristics of individualism and conservatism, it was particularly repugnant to its parochialism. It is thus easy to understand why, with its potential emotional force, the

Market issue reinforced the changes occurring within the Labour Party by solidifying the left wing's alliance with the unions and further weakened the right wing by dividing it and isolating its main corps. We will examine the highlights of how this major constitutional break occurred.

THE COMMON MARKET AND THE LABOUR PARTY[15]

The Labour Party had a shifting attitude towards British entry into the Common Market. As a rough rule of thumb, it was usually against membership when in opposition and in favour when in charge of the Government. Despite the apparent zig-zagging, Harold Wilson always insisted that he and his party were consistent, and that they were committed at all times to British entry 'on the proper terms'. Thus his opposition to Market entry in 1971 was not one of principle but rather that the terms were not proper – even though the ministers most involved in the negotiations, pro-Marketeers all, thought otherwise. The Wilsonian formula possessed another utility for the party, aside from justifying these switches: it allowed the party to become a 'broad church' on this issue, encompassing both the pro- and the anti-Marketeers, as well as the decisive floating middle.

The strains on party unity and the necessity of ingenious efforts to maintain it became evident during the October 1971 debate and its decisive roll call. Prime Minister Heath was successful in securing entry by an impressive margin of more than 100 votes, 356 to 244. The bulk of Labour members, 198, voted against membership. However, 69 members, led by Roy Jenkins, Labour's Deputy Leader, voted against their party and for the Government despite a three-line whip; 20 acted in a similar spirit by abstaining. As their party critics pointed out, since 39 Conservatives had voted against the Government, it was really the 69 Labour dissidents who allowed it to survive. The limits of tolerance had clearly been reached.[16] It was within the context of this tense intra-party rivalry that the referendum came to the fore and was implemented.

The first linkage of the referendum with Market membership, however, came from the Conservatives and its inadvertent source was Heath himself. In May 1970, he had stated that it would be wrong for Britain to enter the Market without 'the full-hearted consent of Parliament and people'.[17] This was a potentially damaging phrase to come from probably the country's most committed pro-Marketeer because, despite fluctuations of popular opinion on the Market, by the spring of 1967, public sentiment, which had generally been favourable, shifted its plurality to the negative side. This antipathy was especially evident when formal Market membership was discussed in Parliament and most of the time when the proposed referendum was on the agenda.[18] It was thus understandable why the phrase was picked up by anti-Marketeers, first by Conservatives but later by all opponents, and became the touchstone of their criticism of Britain's entry without some sort of popular approval. This proved to be the case even though he probably did not literally mean what his words indicated and during the campaign made it clear, when asked, that he thought parliamentary ratification would fulfil this requirement.[19] Moreover, both Thorpe, the Liberal leader, and Wilson agreed with him on his opposition to a referendum.[20]

Most of the pressure for a referendum came from the Labour side. Soon after the 1970 General Election, Douglas Jay, a former Labour minister and a consistent and resolute anti-Marketeer, proposed it in an article in *The Times*. The main thrust of his argument was that the anticipated British membership in the Market morally required an appeal to an electorate because it was a fundamental constitutional change.[21] The pro-Market *Times* questioned the constitutional impact of the referendum upon the British system of parliamentary government as well as the random nature of its proposed use.[22] Even a harsher judgment of this suggestion was made in a leading article in the *New Statesman* by the new editor Richard Crossman, a formidable political critic as well as a former Labour minister. His emphasis was upon the reactionary record of referendums in practice and the assumption that much progressive legislation, already being implemented in Britain, would have been killed if put to a popular majority vote. His advice to the anti-Marketeers, with whom he was in sympathy, was to avoid the lure of the populist referendum, despite the mass support behind them, and rather achieve their ends by exerting pressure upon the Labour Party and its leadership, thereby operating within the traditions and practice of effective parliamentary democracy.[23]

A turning point in the history leading up to the Common Market referendum – as well as in the history of modern British populism – occurred later in 1970 when Anthony Wedgwood Benn declared his support for such a referendum on populist grounds.[24] Benn became not only a leader in the fight for the referendum but the personal symbol of it and of the philosophy behind it. It was in this multiple capacity, as well as that of Labour chairman for the year 1971–72, that he intensified his efforts to secure a referendum on the Common Market through a binding commitment by the Labour Party. To appreciate his relentless energy and determination, we should remember that he began his task in the party councils literally alone. When he originally proposed this commitment to the Party's National Executive Committee (NEC) at the end of 1970, he was completely alone. James Callaghan did predict at that time, however, that Benn had given the party 'a rubber life-raft into which the whole party may one day have to climb'.[25]

He was slowly building up support in the beginning of 1972 when external factors played into the hands of the anti-Marketeers. Georges Pompidou, the President of France, announced just before leaving for a visit with Heath that his country would have a referendum on British entry into the Common Market. Thus the British, who were finding it increasingly intolerable that they could be the only population of the aspiring Market members without a vote on the issue, now seemed to be handed the insult that even the French would actually have a vote – denied to them – on their own fate.[26] This provoked a much more intense debate on the subject and a fundamental shift of view.

In this changed climate, Benn raised the question again with both the National Executive Committee and the Shadow Cabinet – and in each case was successful. The Shadow Cabinet was pushed further in this direction when Heath, of all persons, gave the referendum concept further legitimacy by announcing that border polls ('regular plebiscites') would be held in Northern Ireland.[27]

Wilson's shift was obviously the decisive vote and it was not without its serious cost to party harmony. The leading pro-Marketeers (Jenkins, George Thomson, and Harold Lever) had at last reached the limit of their patience and resigned from the Shadow Cabinet, even though Wilson was able to contain the damage by retaining nearly all their colleagues.

When the referendum came to a vote, it was defeated 235 to 284. What was significant for the future was that the bulk of the Parliamentary Labour Party, following the whips, supported it, even though 63 Labour MPs did abstain and none voted against it.[28] Despite the existence of a significant pro-Market minority, the party was now in favour of a popular vote on the issue, a position also reflected in the party conference.[29] Although Britain had become a full-fledged member of the European Community, its major opposition party was now committed to a renegotiation of membership terms along with a popular ratification either through a referendum or a general election.

A referendum was clearly preferable to most of the party as the most effective way to maintain party unity. A general election would have shattered it because the pro-Marketeers would have been forced into the dilemma of choosing publicly between their conflicting priorities of party and conviction. Even though the Labour Party was far from sinking, Callaghan's prediction about Benn's original referendum proposal was being fulfilled.

THE PASSAGE OF THE REFERENDUM

In 1974, Labour returned to power and, true to its word, entered into membership renegotiations with the other Market governments. Similarly, in January 1975, Prime Minister Wilson announced that the Government would propose a referendum, to be held later that year, on continued British membership on the renegotiated terms. Labour Party lines, however, did not hold when Wilson intensified the political tension by presenting the recommendation of his Cabinet (approved only by a vote of 16 to 7) that the country accept membership on the renegotiated terms. To Wilson and the other party leaders this stand was in line with their consistent position of being in favour of Market membership on the proper terms. To much of the party, however, this appeared to be another switch of position on the Market with the only element of consistency being that this was the latest of a number of such sharp turns.

As a result, the Parliamentary Labour Party was severely split by the leadership's new position. More Labour members (145) voted against the Government's recommendation than for it (137); even the junior ministers were evenly split.[30] Despite this remarkable defection from its own party, the overall margin of support for the Government in the House of Commons was a formidable 398 to 172. This victory was rendered even more impressive when the 261 to 20 vote in the House of Lords was included as well. 'There could be no doubt in the minds of the informed electorate', wrote David Butler and Uwe Kitzinger, 'how the Prime Minister, the Cabinet and Parliament all wanted them to vote in the referendum.'[31]

The day after the Commons accepted the Government's recommendation on the Market, it did the same for the referendum bill. By an anti-climactic vote of 180 to 41, it endorsed Britain's first countrywide referendum.

THE CAMPAIGN

Ironically for a referendum generated by populism, respect for and deference to élite opinion strongly influenced the campaign. This was largely a result of the division of support within the political parties on the question of Common Market membership. The anti-Marketeers, being primarily left-wing Labourites and right-wing Conservatives, were generally individuals who had over the years been regular targets of the other major party. The pro-Marketeers, on the other hand, tended to be among the more moderate, centrist groups within each party. As a result, the most respected members of the political establishment, as shown by the polls, were all on the pro-membership side, and the less respected and more controversial political figures were all on the other.[32] The campaign could thus be considered influential less for the arguments presented about the Market but rather as a means by which the public could link a Market position with specific politicians about whom they felt positively or negatively. This negativism was especially significant among Conservatives as Tony Benn, their *bête noire*, played the most prominent role in the anti-Market campaign.

The centrist political position of the pro-Marketeers gave them an additional advantage over their opponents because it facilitated cooperation and coordination between their different partisan elements. The anti-Marketeers, on the other hand, being generally on opposite sides of the political spectrum, had to overcome years of hostility and contentiousness.

The pro-Marketeers were further aided by the country's major periodicals and newspapers being strongly weighted towards their side. In addition, their umbrella organization had heavier financial support and was better organized than its anti-Market counterpart.[33]

THE VERDICT

The end result of the referendum, so vigorously advocated and pushed by the anti-Marketeers was, as the public opinion polls prior to it indicated, a victory for their opponents. Even more significant was the size of the pro-Marketeers' triumph, better than 2 to 1 (67.2 per cent to 32.8 per cent). Moreover, they not only won with a significant margin in every component part of the United Kingdom, but they carried every single district in the country as well, except for the Shetlands and the Western Isles. Even Labour Party voters were estimated to have voted yes by a margin of 52+ to 47+ per cent.[34] One result of the one-sided margin and the large turnout (about 65 per cent) was that 43 per cent of the registered electorate had voted yes[35] (a percentage which would have, as we shall see, later significance). There could be no argument as to what the voice of the people had said. Wilson could justifiably declare with a combination of pride and relief: 'Fourteen years of national argument are over.'[36]

THE DEBATE ON THE REFERENDUM

Although discussion of the referendum stretched on for years and the debate was conducted in many different forums, we can, nevertheless, discern a basic pattern of argumentation. In examining the case for and against the referendum, we shall see that the arguments presented on either side were usually differentiated in character, even though at times blended together. One type of argument was concerned with referendums in general and thus applicable to their use in any country. More often, however, the arguments were tailored to the specific context of Britain, in terms of its particular constitutional arrangement, political institutions and history. Since much of the debate about the referendum was intra-party, still another type of argument was aimed at Labour Party members and reflected their particular values and concerns.

THE NEGATIVE CASE

In examining the case against the referendum, both the particular British and Labour emphases are strongly evident. The most obvious national note was struck when the referendum was dismissed as a mechanism alien to the British people and their political traditions. Thus when Attlee rejected Churchill's suggestion of a referendum to legitimize an extension of Parliament his words were defiantly patriotic and appropriate for a country which had emerged victorious over European totalitarianism:

> I would not consent to the introduction into our national life of a device so alien to all our traditions as the referendum, which has only too often been the instrument of Nazism and Fascism. Hitler's practices in the field of referenda and plebiscites can hardly have endeared these expedients to the British heart.[37]

In more restrained language, one could justify the view that British political theory and practice hardly encouraged the use of referendums. In examining the dominant political behaviour syndromes in British political history, Samuel Beer lists for the last two centuries: Liberal, Radical and Collectivist (Socialist Democracy and Tory Democracy).[38] Although there are some aspects of Socialist democracy which impinge on populist themes, there is little doubt that the referendum comes closest in spirit to the Radical school with its emphasis upon the people and its disdain of parliamentarianism. Despite Beer's identification of this radical tradition, he also points out its weakness on the British political scene, especially when compared to the situation in the United States.[39]

The most significant argument against the referendum was also deeply rooted in British political experience even though it could be of relevance to parliamentary systems in general. This was the claim, often presented in the past by the political élite, that a popular referendum would undermine the power and legitimacy of Parliament and subvert the effectiveness of cabinet government. This position thus combined British pride in presenting a model of parliamentary representation as one of the major contributions to world civilization with a satisfaction about the way that the legal concept of Parliamentary sovereignty had operated in practice as a support for strong cabinet government. If the people were to be asked directly their view on a particular issue, what then would become of the role of their elected representatives and of the government which they supported?

It is thus understandable why John Mackintosh, one of the severest critics of the referendum, could have called it 'the most serious attack that could be made on the system of representation which has served this country so well over the centuries'.[40] Once the referendum would be accepted in principle, he felt, any group would urge its use if it believed that it could secure a popular majority for a measure which it advocated. Moreover, once in operation, it could easily be argued that laws lacked authority if they only passed through Parliament but were not ratified by a popular vote.[41]

This line of criticism emphasized that the issue at stake was, in the words of *The Times*, 'a choice between parliamentary government and direct popular referenda',[42] and that a make-shift hybrid with two sets of political decisions would render the parliamentary–cabinet system of government unworkable. During the discussion of the Common Market referendum, Mackintosh raised the spectre of how the cabinet – and indeed practically the whole political establishment – could function if their advice on entry was rejected: 'Do they dust themselves down and set off in another direction; one which they have just explained over and over again is disastrous?'[43] Similarly Anthony King in analyzing the impact of the 1975 referendum, speculated on what the probable results of a 'No' vote would have been. Aside from the difficult, 'perhaps impossible',[44] position in which it would have placed the Labour Government, the effect on Britain's political leadership would have been devastating:

> If the British people had voted 'no' on June 5, they would have been repudiating, consciously, both the House of Commons, which over a period of fourteen years had consistently voted in favour of EEC membership, and also the leaders of all three of the country's major political parties. They could have been saying 'no' . . . to almost all of those who had been the country's political leaders since after the Second World War. The moral effect of such a repudiation would have been tremendous. It would have called into question the way in which Britain's parliamentary institutions had functioned until then. It would have undermined the moral authority of any Government formed from among the country's existing political leaders. It would have strengthened the political positions of the extreme left and the extreme right. . . . Britain . . . would suddenly have seemed a very doubtful proposition politically.[45]

Although this criticism partially depended on the specifics of the Market question, it was really pointing to the potential dangers of a referendum *per se*. Its authors usually went to the heart of the populist motivation of the referendum by contrasting its simple popular majoritarianism with the more complex democracy of a representative system. 'Only a measure which has run the gauntlet of party approval and parliamentary routine really deserves to be called the people's will', wrote Richard Crossman.[46] Similarly, Mackintosh felt that representative democracy secured a valuable, but delicate, balance between public opinion and expert opinion.[47]

The dangers for the ship of state listing too far to the popular side were vividly spelled out in arguments which would appeal especially to Labourites. The crux of this position was that the referendum had proved in practice an illiberal and reactionary instrument of government and its use would have checked recent progressive legislation and would cast a negative shadow on the future. 'Better the liberal élitism of the statute book', declared Crossman, 'than the reactionary populism of the market-place. If democracy worked in an Athenian sense, this country would still exercise the death penalty, flog young criminals, forbid abortions, repatriate immigrants, punish homosexuals, ban strikers and abolish aid to poorer countries.'[48]

THE AFFIRMATIVE CASE

The case for the referendum, as the case against it, had a number of significant arguments covering different themes and usually aimed at different audiences. The first one was based on general political and constitutional practice, the second on the unique character of British constitutional theory and institutional practice, and the third was of primary relevance to members of the Labour Party, although by no means limited to them.

The first argument was a rebuttal to the charge that the referendum would weaken parliaments and Governments, and that the latter, in particular, might find the experience unsettling and, after a defeat, have difficulty in getting to the normal groove of 'governing' the country. They rejected these contentions by pointing out that the experience of other parliamentary democracies had shown that referendum results need not destabilize the legislature nor paralyze the executive. Surely the British, with all their political talents and their long history of compromise and accommodation, could do as well. This argument became especially important after the 1975 referendum because then speculation about the future was grounded in observable facts.

The basic 'British' argument was the fundamental constitutional one, proferred at various times by Conservatives, and based upon the absence of a written constitution. Since there is thus no written constitutional limit and no institutional check (not in the courts, the sovereign, or the House of Lords) upon the actions of a British Government supported by a majority in the House of Commons, it can do virtually whatever it wants no matter how extreme and permanent. This character of British parliamentary democracy has rendered it an 'elective dictatorship' according to Lord Hailsham.

We have already noted that this was the argument levied by Dicey in attacking Gladstonian Home Rule proposals even when the House of Lords was a more powerful body. 'The Referendum is the People's Veto', he declared, 'the nation is sovereign and may well decree that the constitution shall not be changed without the direct sanction of the nation.'[49] We have also seen that the Conservative Party had proposed in 1911 an amendment to the Parliament Bill which required a referendum before bills dealing with certain fundamental subjects could become law. It was the thread of this argument which Douglas Jay presented in 1970 when he asked for a general election or a referendum before British entry into the Common Market because the people should have the right to approve or disapprove such a basic change in the constitution.[50]

The other fundamental argument for the referendum is based upon the philosophy of populism. Although it had a primary appeal to Labourites, the significance of its argument went beyond the scope of one party. Since it was a fundamental criticism of the essence of representative government and was skeptical of its democratic authority, it was obviously more sweeping and comprehensive than the previous affirmative argument, one concerned only with limiting the power of a parliamentary-supported government. The populists, as did the supporters of representative government, tended to draw a sharp distinction between it and populist democracy. Even if a categorical choice was not necessary, there was little doubt among the populists that their ethos had to invigorate parliamentary democracy for it to survive. The gist of populism, which Robert Shepherd noted has markedly influenced the Labour Party in the 1970s, was that 'the ballot-box at a General Election is no longer sufficient in modern democracy – people must have a say in the affairs of their workplace and the people must be allowed to decide directly on British membership of the European Community'.[51]

In the years we are examining, the most consistent advocate in British politics of the referendum from a populist perspective has been Tony Benn. Benn had been strongly influenced by the spontaneous popular demonstrations which had erupted in France in May 1968. He then proposed that the British people at least reconsider the referendum because 'the five-yearly cross on the ballot paper is just not going to be enough'.[52] In reflecting upon the implications of this attitude, he became increasingly concerned with the gulf developing between the people and their legislature. Thus when the House of Commons debated the question of Market membership in October 1971, he was opposed to its acceptance less on the intrinsic merits of the case than because such a step in evident opposition to public opinion would imperil Parliament:

> What I warn the House of is this. If the people think that by a temporary coalition, which has never been tested at the polls, some members of Parliament claiming a divine right that we have denied to kings, deny the people the right to decide their own future, we are in serious trouble [Interruption]. . . . We live in a world where enormous and unaccountable powers are everywhere growing . . . and people see in this Chamber the one thread connecting them to a countervailing power. If we cut the thread that connects them to us I do not believe that this House can long survive.[53]

The most highly developed exposition of the populist defense of the referendum combined both an attack upon the existing state of parliamentary institutions with a spirited rebuttal of the points brought out by their defenders in the Labour Party. Tony Wright critically examined the persistent allegation made by Labourites that the referendum was illiberal and reactionary in practice. Even if that assertion were completely valid, he claimed, a referendum would still be preferred by a believer in majoritarian democracy: 'Even if it is accepted that there is a conservative majority on a range of issues (for example on penal policy), may there not be a case for confronting that majority directly, by argument instead of seeking to circumvent it by a comforting élitism?'[54] He noted, however, that the examples given as warning about the referendum only presented an incomplete case since they could generally be typed as 'liberal' rather than 'radical'. Thus he sought to intensify Labour's intra-mural conflict between populism and liberal élitism by sharpening the distinction between the two. Wright emphasized that the social reform issues of hanging, flogging, and immigration were liberal élitist concerns of only a minority of the population and quite distinct from the bread and butter concerns, the real 'gut' issues of the working class and of the population and the ones he felt likely to secure majority support in a referendum.[55]

By this analysis, the two sides in the Labour Party were deeply and fundamentally divided on the roles of the political élite and the people in the operation of a democracy. Although he accepted John Mackintosh's view of the necessity of a balance between the two, Wright felt that he had it weighted so heavily in favour of the élite that the system could almost operate 'with the total elimination of the elective democratic component of government'.[56] He did admit that Mackintosh could be correct in that the élite might be embarrassed by the results of a referendum but he could work up little concern about this.[57]

THE REFERENDUM ON SCOTTISH AND WELSH DEVOLUTION

Once the 1975 referendum had been conducted, the nature of the debate about it significantly changed. The combination of a restrained campaign, a smooth operation[58] and a consensual result which upheld the Government and the political élite resulted in a muffled impact upon the political scene. Thus the very ordinariness of the referendum's inauguration became one of the strongest considerations for its possible future use. It is true there were those who argued that the referendum was only justifiable in this instance because of the unique circumstances of the Market issue, and Wilson had promised a few days after the referendum that it would never be repeated.[59] Nevertheless it was obvious that once the constitutional principle had been breached and a new precedent established, it would be much easier to repeat the procedure. The relative difficulty of removing the first olive from the jar or cutting the first slice of salami is an established part of the world's folk wisdom. It could thus be assumed that British political practice would probably conform as well. Less than four years later, these predictions came true and Britain held another referendum, this time on the question of devolution in Scotland and Wales. Although it was limited to these regions, it was unquestionably countrywide in importance and at least as significant in its implications as British entry into the European Common Market.

The referendum placed in the Scottish and Welsh devolution acts required their repeal if at least 40 per cent of the total electorate in each area did not vote its approval. The results of the referendum held on 1 March 1979 were:

Scotland: 1 230 937 votes (32.5 per cent of the total electorate) 'Yes' and 1 153 500 (30.4 per cent) 'No', or 51.6 per cent to 48.3 per cent of the voting.

Wales: 243 048 votes (11.8 per cent of the total electorate) 'Yes' and 956 330 (46.5 per cent) 'No', or 20.3 per cent to 79.7 per cent of the voting.[60]

Thus devolution was halted – at least for a few years. As with the Common Market referendum, the results were satisfying, although for different reasons. In essence, the devolution plans as presented by the Callaghan Government were not popular in Parliament. They were considered, on sound evidence, to reflect less of a true desire on the part of the Labour Government to respond to the nationalist aspirations and demands of the Scottish people than a patently political concern of the Labour Party at the erosion of its electoral support in Scotland – and to a lesser degree in Wales – with the increasing vote for the nationalists. The historian Hugh Trevor-Roper, for example, in describing the devolution plan as 'Labour's shabby project' stated that its only purpose was to salvage the party's fortunes.[61] Similarly, another observer believed that an earlier version exuded 'a strong whiff . . . of expedience' which explained its failure to evoke strong enthusiasm even when it did receive majority legislative support.[62]

This lack of enthusiasm reflected the compromise nature of the Government's plans, which almost guaranteed that no solid popular clientele would be behind it. Devolution alarmed many because it was considered by them as the first step in the unravelling of the United Kingdom. On the other hand, it did not really satisfy the demands of the Scottish Nationalists because the new assembly's powers would be limited and the principle of Parliamentary sovereignty at Westminster remained. They were, however, in favour of devolution because the assembly, whatever the restrictions upon it, could still be a sounding-board for their discontents; and this voice, combined with the possibility of majority control, meant that further change would be probable. In light of the tension between these two fundamentally opposing groups, the Government was attempting to devise a proposal which balanced the minimum which the nationalists would be willing to accept with the maximum the centralists were willing to concede.

What probably allowed the devolution bill to get through Parliament was the insertion of the 40 per cent clause, to which the Government acquiesced reluctantly. The nationalists considered it an English trick (even though Scottish hands were involved in it as well) because it could only be obtained if the enthusiasm for it was truly widespread. Yet it is difficult to argue with the proposition that such a dramatic step should not have been taken with a narrow minority. The actual vote, admittedly, was markedly influenced by the unpopularity of the sponsoring Callaghan Government, which would soon be defeated on a vote of confidence. Yet even with this factor taken into account, the miniscule margin of the affirmative vote on Scottish devolution was hardly impressive. Even the *Guardian*, which believed that the 40 per cent rule was a 'shabby little exercise in political chicanery', felt that the referendum results could not be considered as providing the 'clear endorsement' or the 'reasonably full-hearted consent' of the Scottish people before attempting this constitutional experiment.[63]

As for Wales, there could be no question about the meaning of the results. The negative vote of 46.4 per cent (the only vote of the day that went over 40 per cent) to 11.9 per cent proved the wisdom of Parliament's decision to submit its legislation to a popular vote. 'If there had been no referendum an Act of Parliament concerning Wales would have been brought into effect with the support of only a very small minority of the Welsh people.'[64] The second referendum, therefore, reinforced the reception of it into the British political system.

A paramount reason for this apparent acceptance was that the pessimistic, even calamitous, predictions made before the 1975 Market poll about the weakening of Parliamentary sovereignty and cabinet government have not been borne out.[65] It is difficult to discern – admittedly at close historical range – any significant effect on the operation of either. Indeed, in the years immediately succeeding the first referendum, the power and authority of Parliament have markedly increased. Party discipline in the House of Commons has been repeatedly breached and dissent is more open. The input of the back-bench members in the legislative process has grown with the operation of specialized committees. The role of Parliament has thus become visibly stronger and its public image enhanced. These developments, of course, were purely coincidental with the occurrence of the referendum and were primarily due to other forces, such as the existence of minority governments and the innovation of establishing a full set of specialized committees. Yet they serve to belie the assumption of the critics of the referendum that its initial use would inevitably subvert the authority and operation of Parliament.

Arguably in these years modern cabinet government has been weakened, but, if so, this was primarily because of the aforementioned tendencies strengthening Parliament and only tangentially because of the referendum. Even the defeat of the Callaghan Government in the aftermath of the referendum vote on Scottish and Welsh devolution does not contradict this. Few modern British governments have existed so long on borrowed time. Not only had it been a minority government for 2½ years but Labour had originally 'come to power' 4½ years earlier with only a majority of 3 based on less than 40 per cent of those voting. (Indeed, its share of the vote in the elections of 1974, which it 'won', was less than in 1970, which it lost.) The Government had endured a particularly unpopular stretch in the winter because of an abundance of strikes. Thus it was less the adverse vote of the referendum which brought down the Government than the unpopularity of the Government guaranteeing the adverse vote.[66]

We can thus say that, on the practical level, the referendum has worked, and there has been general satisfaction with the results. This has probably been more significant in influencing public opinion than all the theoretical discussion and political speeches taken together. Although our historical account and analysis clearly show that it has been a product of political dissensus, its operation has tended towards consensus. In a Britain increasingly polarized, the referendum may become a healthy countervailing force to the trend of political currents.

THE CONTINUATION OF THE REFERENDUM DEBATE

With the successful breaking of precedent and the general realization that the referendum is a feasible instrument of British politics, the debate about it shifts to the circumstances when it should be utilized. In this debate, the philosophical coalition which was successful in securing the first referendum divides according to the differing fundamental values of its component parts.[67] The populists, with their broad concept of popular sovereignty, generally favour an extensive use of the referendum in the future in order to render representative institutions more reflective of popular opinion. They tend to be opposed to more traditionalist elements who want to limit British parliamentary government because of its potential threat to individual rights. According to the latter school of thought, the referendum is particularly valuable when the legislature and government act in the field of basic governmental institutions and fundamental constitutional relationships. In this category, a temporary parliamentary majority by itself can secure permanent and irreversible change without a referendum.

This debate is still in a rudimentary stage and the line between the two camps is not a distinct and clear one. Moreover, those committed to the second view have to grapple with another distinction that may not be self-evident, the difference between constitutional and ordinary political matters in a country without a written constitution. In addition, there are such troubling questions as whether all constitutional issues are really important and whether all really important ones are constitutional.

CAPITAL PUNISHMENT

Despite these reservations, one can secure some indication of the future contours of the debate about the referendum by examining the discussion on one issue, the return to capital punishment for murder. This is an excellent test case for referendum consideration because of the sharp contrast between popular and parliamentary opinion about it. There is unquestionably a heavy majority of the British people in favour of a return to hanging for murder, with some estimates running even higher than 80 per cent. Each parliamentary attempt to bring back hanging has failed and a reversal of form on this issue does not seem a reasonable possibility in the foreseeable future. The most recent (May 1982) was defeated in the Commons by a margin of 162 votes, as compared with one of 119 three years earlier.[68]

The gross disparity between what people want and what Parliament does has understandably aroused popular expectations about a referendum on the subject and has made the possibility of one politically attractive. Thus one of the most immediate reactions to the announcement of the results of the 1975 Market referendum was that of an old man in Hackney who wanted a referendum on 'stringing up murderers. They never gave us a vote on that, did they?' he asked.[69]

The Conservative leadership was tempted in 1978 by the prospect of such a referendum. Its leading advocate was Edward Taylor, a populist MP representing a working class district (a rarity in the Tory ranks). Taylor, as did other Scottish Conservatives, had argued that the party should take a tougher line against criminals and tend to the views of the public on crime and punishment. 'It seems difficult to explain to constituents', he said, 'why we should have referendums on devolution and the Common Market and not on this issue.'[70] Among the influences helping to dissuade the Conservative Shadow Cabinet from this course was the critical attitude of *The Times*, which had consistently exhibited a lack of enthusiasm for referendums before the 1975 one was held. It wrote:

> A referendum is quite the wrong way to decide the matter. It is for the government and Parliament to do so. If they pass the question back for determination by popular vote they shirk the responsibility which representative government clearly lays upon them. . . . And if capital punishment, why not immigration rules or grammar schools or wealth tax or abortion? . . . A parliamentary system of government cannot pick and choose its forays into populism and retain respect.[71]

Reginald Maudling strongly supported its opposition to a referendum on capital punishment since its only purpose 'would be to bring pressure on MPs to vote for a proposal which otherwise they would reject'.[72] Maudling's words here carried particular weight because he had consistently voted for capital punishment and because he was not against the referendum on principle, but was opposed to its use on this subject.

In contrast, populists could assume a position of being against the return of capital punishment yet in favour of a referendum. Stanley Alderson, for example, is critical of a situation in which the 'politicians have developed the tradition of doing good in defiance of public opinion, if possible by stealth'.[73] He feels that it would have been much healthier if a referendum had originally required the believers in the abolition of capital punishment to confront a hostile majority opinion and to persuade it through an educational campaign. Instead, the reformers aimed their campaign primarily at the politicians and the intellectuals. Although successful in their legislative efforts, the resulting abolition lacks both moral authority and a sense of permanence:

> Although the abolition of capital punishment must be acknowledged an absolute good, the fact that it was passed in the face of the known opposition of the electorate has created bewilderment and resentment which have diminished respect for democracy and increased resistance to other measures of penal reform – which have indeed brought about periodical demands for the restoration of capital punishment.[74]

THE FUTURE OF THE REFERENDUM

Our analysis in terms of the two different philosophic currents, one populist and one conservative, involved in the advocacy of the referendum can be extended to its future role. On the present evidence, one would have to assume that the conservative position is dominant and will probably remain so in the foreseeable future.

To the degree that the referendum has been incorporated into the British constitution and accepted by both élite and popular opinion, the consensus has been achieved on conservative terms. The referendum that the British people will use in the future will be a limited one, generally restricted to fundamental constitutional issues. Thus, *The Times*, in the same breath that it was declaiming against the referendum on capital punishment as well as a host of other seemingly popular issues, still acknowledged that it had a proper role on fundamental constitutional matters:

> The referendum as a device of government has arrived, and has so far been confined to constitutional questions of one particular kind: those entailing a change of status – of allegiance in the case of the Ulster border poll, of an external source of law-giving in the case of the EEC, of status within the United Kingdom in the case of Scottish and Welsh devolution. That is enough for the time being for our constitutional arrangements to digest.[75]

A similar position – although much more positively inclined – came from a Conservative Party committee named by Mrs Thatcher to study the question of future uses of the referendum. While the committee did not eliminate the possibility for referendums on general legislative matters, it nevertheless put its primary emphasis upon requiring, through a special statute, the holding of a referendum before the enactment of any fundamental change in the British constitution. By its recommendation, authoritative if unofficial, this new procedure would be used for bills in the following categories – a list of topics rather similar to those proposed by the party during the Parliament Bill crisis: the House of Lords, the unity of the realm, the Crown, the Bill of Rights, and the House of Commons.[76] By those criteria, both Common Market membership and devolution would qualify, but capital punishment and most applications of immigration control, another sensitive and emotional subject, would not.

This essentially conservative result for an episode in which populism figures so prominently might be unsettling at first appearance. It should not, however, be especially surprising. Despite the tension between populism and conservatism, we should not overlook the degree of their affinity. The hopes of conservatives and the suspicions of liberals about the conservative impact of the referendum is well-grounded in their assumption of a broad popular conservatism, especially in Britain. Indeed, both major British referendums can be considered conservative in effect since each maintained the existing constitutional arrangement – even though the first was relatively new and the second had been centuries in existence; the first, moreover, clearly reflected the sentiments of the political élite as well.

Whether the precedent of the referendum will provide the impetus for future constitutional reform is another speculative, but interesting, question. One can argue that if the conservative forces have been successful on this reform, they will be encouraged to attempt others for which they were even more committed than the referendum. They would, however, have to accept powerful opposition to their plans, not least among their former populist allies.

The one prediction that one can safely make on the basis of the referendum experience is that if constitutional change does come, it will be the result less of reasoned argument, the clash of theoretical forces, or a well-mapped propaganda campaign than of accident, personal encounters, and party politics. The British, earlier in their history, were reputed to have gained an empire 'absent-mindedly'. They might secure a written constitution or bill of rights in the same way.

NOTES

1. Philip Goodhart, *Referendum* (London: Tom Stacey Ltd, 1971) pp. 19–20, cited hereafter as Goodhart, 1971. This book is the main source for this historical section.
2. Ibid., pp. 20–1.
3. Philip Goodhart, *Full-Hearted Consent: the Story of the Referendum Campaign – and the Campaign for the Referendum* (London: Davis-Poynter, 1976) p. 211, cited hereafter as Goodhart, 1976.
4. Goodhart, 1971, pp. 40–6.
5. Goodhart, 1971, pp. 28–9.
6. Goodhart, 1971, pp. 48–9.
7. David Butler, 'United Kingdom', in David Butler and Austin Ranney, ed., *Referendums: a Comparative Study of Practice and Theory* (Washington: American Enterprise Institute for Public Policy Research, 1978) p. 212.
8. Ibid., p. 212.
9. Introduction by the Earl of Balfour to Walter Bagehot, *The English Constitution* (London: Oxford University Press, 1949) p. xxiv.

10. This was the title of his Richard Dimbleby Lecture, *The Listener*, 21 Oct. 1976, pp. 396–450. For an expansion of these views, see his *The Dilemma of Democracy: Diagnosis and Prescription* (London: Collins, 1978). In the same vein is his 'The Constitution: The Right Road to Reform' in W.J. Stankiewicz, *British Government in an Era of Reform* (London: Collier-Macmillan, 1976) pp. 94–7. For similar criticism from basically conservative sources, see O. Hood Phillips, 'Need for a Written Constitution' from his *Reform of the Constitution*, reprinted in Stankiewicz, op. cit., pp. 78–93; Lord Justice Leslie Scarman, *English Law – The New Dimension* (London: Stevens, 1974). James Douglas, 'Human Rights and the Sovereignty of Parliament or Does Britain Need a New Constitution?', (1978), is a valuable introduction to these proposed constitutional reforms as well as brief for them. *The Economist* has consistently taken a sympathetic attitude towards constitutional reform, i.e., 7 Aug. 1976, pp. 9–11; 30 Oct. 1976, p. 16; 5 Nov. 1977, p. 16. Vernon Bogdanor has expressed similar views in considering the ramifications of devolution. 'Devolution and the English Constitution', paper for the 3rd Annual PSA Work Group on U.K. Politics, Strathclyde, 1978; 'Regionalism: The Constitutional Aspects', *Political Quarterly*, 8 (1977) pp. 164–74.
11. See Conservative Research Department, 'The Referendum and the Constitution', *Politics Today*, no. 16 (12 Sept. 1978). The most definitive intellectual conservative acceptance of the referendum is Vernon Bogdanor, *The People and the Party System* (Cambridge University Press, 1981).
12. The author has written a number of articles and papers about populism in general and in Great Britain in particular, and is at present completing a book-length work on the latter. The articles are 'British Populism: the Labour Party and the Common Market Parliamentary Debate', *Political Science Quarterly* 91 (Summer 1976) 259–77, and 'Devolution, Ethnic Nationalism, and Populism in the United Kingdom'. *Publius, The Journal of Federalism* 7 (Fall 1977) 46–89. Papers are 'British Populism: the 1975 Common Market Referendum' (presented at the annual meeting of the Northeastern Political Science Association, Tarrytown, 11 Nov. 1978); 'Constitutional and Political Implications of Devolution' (presented at the annual meeting of the American Political Science Association, New York, 1 Sept. 1978); and 'The Development of Modern Populism' (presented at conference on Populism and Populist Movements, Rutgers University, 19 Oct. 1979).
13. The following definition and analysis of populism closely approximate the first page and a half of 'The Development of Modern Populism' (see note 12), which is a condensed version of my forthcoming book.
14. See Hugh Gaitskell's speech at the 1962 Labour Conference, *1962 Labour Annual Conference Report*, pp. 164–5, as well as his biographer's account and rationale. Philip Williams, *Hugh Gaitskell* (Totowa, N.J.: Barnes and Noble, 1980) pp. 730–73.
15. The relationship of the Labour Party to the Common Market figures prominently in the authoritative accounts of the Market's reception in British politics. Robert J. Lieber, *British Politics and European Unity: Parties, Élites and Pressure Groups* (Berkeley: University of California Press,

1970) pp. 226–35; Uwe Kitzinger, *Diplomacy and Persuasion: How Britain Joined the Common Market* (London: Thames & Hudson, 1973) pp. 352–70, cited hereafter as Kitzinger.
16. See author's 'British Populism: the Labour Party and the Common Market Parliamentary Debate', op. cit.
17. Goodhart, 1976, p. 25.
18. Lieber, op. cit., pp. 226–35; Kitzinger, op. cit., pp. 352–70; David Butler and Uwe Kitzinger, *The 1975 Referendum* (London: Macmillan, 1976) p. 12, cited hereafter as Butler and Kitzinger.
19. Goodhart, 1976, pp. 25–6, 11.
20. Ibid., p. 12.
21. Douglas Jay, 'Joining the Six – the Case for a Referendum', *The Times*, 1 Aug. 1970, p. 13.
22. *The Times*, 1 Aug. 1970, p. 13.
23. *New Statesman*, 80 (7 Aug. 1970) pp. 137–8.
24. Kitzinger, op. cit., p. 246; Butler and Kitzinger, op. cit., p. 12.
25. Butler and Kitzinger, op. cit., p. 12.
26. Ibid., p. 18; Kitzinger, op. cit., p. 391; Goodhart, 1976, pp. 39–40; Anthony King, *Britain Says Yes: The 1975 Referendum on the Common Market* (Washington: American Enterprise Institute, 1977) pp. 61–2.
27. Goodhart, 1976, p. 46.
28. Butler and Kitzinger, op. cit., p. 19. Goodhart adding the tellers has the vote 237 to 286. Goodhart, 1976, p. 59.
29. *Report of the Seventy-First Annual Party Conference of the Labour Party, Blackpool 1972,* pp. 195–222; Butler and Kitzinger, op. cit., p. 20; Goodhart, 1976, p. 71.
30. Butler and Kitzinger, op. cit., p. 52.
31. Ibid., p. 53.
32. Ibid., pp. 256–8; King, op. cit., pp. 111–3.
33. Butler and Kitzinger, op. cit., ch. 4, 5 and 7; King, op. cit., pp. 102–23; Goodhart, 1976, ch. 8.
34. Butler and Kitzinger, op. cit., p. 271.
35. Ibid., p. 264.
36. *The Times*, 7 June 1975, p. 1.
37. Goodhart, 1971, p. 49.
38. Samuel H. Beer, *British Politics in the Collectivist Age* (New York: Knopf, 1965) part I. Beer has recently analyzed the modern British political scene, with roughly half the book concerned with populism: *Britain Against Itself: The Political Contradictions of Collectivism* (New York: Norton, 1982).
39. Beer, *British Politics in the Collectivist Age*, p. 41 and 41 fn. For an illuminating comparison between late 19th century American populism and Liberal Birmingham radicals, see Vivien Hart, *Distrust and Democracy: Political Distrust in Britain and America* (Cambridge University Press, 1978).
40. John Mackintosh, 'The Case Against a Referendum', *The Political Quarterly* 46 (Jan.–Mar. 1975) 73.
41. Ibid., p. 75.
42. *The Times*, 1 Aug. 1970, p. 13.

43. Mackintosh, op. cit., p. 80.
44. King, op. cit., p. 141.
45. Ibid., pp. 140–1.
46. *New Statesman*, 80 (7 Aug. 1970) p. 137.
47. Mackintosh, op. cit., p. 79.
48. *New Statesman*, 80 (7 Aug. 1970) p. 137; italics added.
49. Goodhart, 1971, p. 21.
50. Jay, op. cit., p. 13.
51. Robert Shepherd, 'Leadership, Public Opinion and the Referendum', *The Political Quarterly* 46 (Jan.–Mar. 1975) p. 32.
52. Goodhart, 1976, p. 23.
53. *Hansard*, Commons 823 (27 Oct. 1971) p. 1762–3.
54. Tony Wright, 'The Referendum: the Case Against John Mackintosh', *The Political Quarterly* 46 (Apr.–June 1975) pp. 153–60, 158.
55. Ibid., p. 156.
56. Ibid., p. 158.
57. Ibid., pp. 158–9.
58. Butler and Kitzinger, op. cit., p. 286.
59. Ibid., p. 288.
60. *Manchester Guardian Weekly*, 11 Mar. 1979, p. 4.
61. Hugh Trevor-Roper, 'Labour's Shabby Project', *The Spectator* 1 (24 Feb. 1979) p. 8.
62. Ronald Faux in *The Times*, 22 Feb. 1977, p. 16.
63. *Manchester Guardian Weekly*, 11 Mar. 1979, p. 1.
64. Peter Bromhead and Donald Shell, 'The British Constitution in 1979', *Parliamentary Affairs*, XXXIII (Spring 1980) p. 143. The statistics of the poll results vary slightly.
65. Even one of the most vigorous advocates of populism in British politics had listed the Market referendum as one of the 'Milestones in the Weakening of the British Democratic State'. Stephen Haseler, *The Death of British Democracy* (London: Elek Brooks Limited, 1976) pp. 243–4.
66. Bromhead and Shell, pp. 143–4; Anthony King, 'Politics, Economics and the Trade Unions, 1974–9', in Howard Penniman, ed., *Britain at the Polls, 1979: a Study of the General Election* (Washington: American Enterprise Institute for Public Policy Research, 1979) p. 93; Ivor Crewe, 'Why the Conservatives Won', in Penniman, op. cit., p. 287.
67. The conservatives are included in the coalition, although their actual role was a passive one.
68. *Manchester Guardian Weekly*, 23 May 1982, p. 1.
69. *Observer*, 8 June 1975, p. 3.
70. *The Times*, 5 June 1978, p. 1.
71. Ibid., p. 17.
72. Letter, *The Times*, 7 June 1978, p. 191.
73. Stanley Alderson, 'The Referendum Under the British Constitution', *Contemporary Review* 233 (Nov. 1973) 247–50, reprinted in Stankiewicz, op. cit., p. 75.
74. Ibid., pp. 75–6.
75. *The Times*, 5 June 1978, p. 17.
76. Conservative Research Department, op. cit.

8 Britain and the European Community

Hans J. Michelmann

INTRODUCTION

Whatever Britons individually think about their country's membership in the European Community, there is no doubt that Britain's entry on 1 January 1973 is among the most important developments in British or European politics in the post-war era.[1] Seldom has there been a single event that has reflected such a reorientation in British foreign and domestic policy, and one that had, by itself, such a potential for affecting the conduct and content of the county's public affairs. It is not surprising, therefore, that the issue raised such strong and conflicting responses. These ranged from the strongly favourable assessment of Britain's decision to enter Europe by former *Times* editor William Rees-Mogg, viz., that '. . . Britain's entry into Europe under Mr. Heath (was) much the most helpful event of my time as editor, and one that I believe will prove to be historically the most important',[2] to the loud condemnation of British membership at various times by Labour Party leaders like Michael Foot and Tony Benn.

Much of the debate about Community membership has centred around the loss of sovereignty British governmental institutions were alleged to have suffered upon British accession to the Community. I shall argue that, given the experience of the past ten years, it appears safe to conclude that fears of a loss of British sovereignty were unfounded, and that in some important respects, Britain, through Community membership, has actually been strengthened in her ability to affect the shaping of issues of vital importance to her. In the same vein, I shall argue that the impact of Community membership on the functioning of British governmental institutions has not been dramatic, but that this cannot be said of economic and foreign trade matters. Yet the sovereignty issue is alive in the anti-Community rhetoric of that portion of the Labour Party leadership opposed to Britain remaining in Europe. Its opposition to British membership helps to keep the Community a controversial issue in British politics.

Notwithstanding the controversy over the issue, British membership in the European Community has received only limited attention in the academic literature, and much of that literature, though excellent, focuses primarily on some of the more dramatic specific events in the history of the relationship between Britain and the Community. For this reason and also because of space constraints, I shall spend rather little time on the historic dimension of Community membership. Also, I shall make only passing reference to the 1975 referendum subsequent to the so-called 'renegotiation' of British membership terms by the Labour Government under Harold Wilson because that event is covered in another chapter in this book. Instead, I shall examine the impact of Community membership on contemporary British politics and public policy beginning with a brief historical overview that introduces a number of themes that have remained relevant to the present day in any discussion of Britain in Europe.

BRITAIN AND EUROPE: POST-WAR RELATIONSHIPS

By and large, British attitudes toward participation in the movement toward European integration were negative in the 1950s. Britain's economy, social structure and political institutions had survived the war in much better shape than those of the continental European states actively negotiating and then building the three communities. Traditional British hostility to any but intergovernmental schemes of international organization made the British government suspicious of the communities' supranational features. Added to these reasons for British non-participation were considerations of foreign policy. In the late 1940s and early 1950s, Britain's declining world role was not as evident, certainly not in British eyes, as it was subsequently to become. The Commonwealth, the Empire and ties with the United States, a traditional ally, were of primary importance, and association with European organizations whose main concerns appeared narrowly inward-looking seemed unrewarding and out of character. Thus the ECSC commenced operation in 1952 without British participation.

Britain's reaction to the proposal for a European Defence Community and the associated European Political Community was based on similar considerations. British unwillingness to participate was a major reason for the failure of these schemes and the ensuing temporary interruption in the movement toward European integration. By the mid-1950s, however, negotiations which led to the creation of the EEC and Euratom were underway. Britain declined to join these organizations for broadly similar reasons that had kept her from participating in the ECSC, and when the treaties initiating the EEC and Euratom were signed in Rome in 1957, only six ECSC member states, France, Italy, the Federal Republic of Germany, Belgium, the Netherlands and Luxembourg, were present.

Before long, Britain's decision to remain outside the Community began to appear questionable when the premises upon which it was made were challenged by domestic and international developments. The British economy entered a period of cyclical swings that proved difficult to manage, and though the average economic growth rate was at a respectable 3.9 per cent between 1958 and 1964, this was eclipsed by a mean growth rate of 5.6 per cent in the newly-created EEC, whose member states were reaping the benefits of progressively lowered barriers to intra-Community trade.[3] The rival European Free Trade Association, established by Britain and five other non-EEC states in competition to the Community, could not make up for the loss of British trading opportunities that resulted from being outside the progressively emerging common external tariff established by the EEC. Attempts at negotiating free trade in industrial commodities between the two trading blocs failed, and it became clear that Britain could achieve unimpeded access to the EEC market only through direct membership. A further economic reason for a change of attitudes toward Community was the increasingly threatening prospect of losing investment capital of American and other non-EEC firms wishing to establish European branch plants within the Community's common external tariff wall.

By the early 1960s, international political developments were also favouring a reappraisal of British attitudes toward the Community. The American government began to encourage British Community membership in the interests of a united Europe for political and particularly security reasons. The nature of Commonwealth and Empire had undergone changes that led to a decline in Britain's international leadership role and a concomitant decrease in ties with the developing world; thus trade and political links with the developed world, particularly the increasingly prosperous Community countries, became more important. Although some participants in the contemporary British debate about Community membership seem to forget them, these fundamental changes in Britain's economic and international situation from her position earlier in this century continued to provide a powerful impetus and rationale for British membership in the European Community.

Whatever the effective cause that finally induced the British government to change its orientation, Prime Minister Harold Macmillan announced in the House of Commons on 31 January 1961 that Britain planned to apply for Community membership. Supporting him in this decision were a substantial section of industry and much of the informed British public.[4] The story of the ensuing twelve years – of the humiliating rebuffs by France's Charles de Gaulle of British membership applications and the final success of negotiations under Prime Minister Edward Heath – has been expertly told in a number of places and does not need retelling here. Britain and the Community signed a Treaty of Accession in January 1972, and the European Communities Act, enabling legislation spelling out how Community legal measures and decisions would be incorporated into British law, was passed by Parliament in the ensuing months. On 1 January 1973, along with Denmark and Ireland, Britain became a member of the European Community.

ECONOMIC AND DIPLOMATIC IMPLICATIONS OF EC MEMBERSHIP

With formal membership, the most controversial issues associated with British entry into the Community seemed to have been settled. Firstly, Britain had committed herself to accepting Community laws and decisions, both those predating 1 January 1973 and those made with her participation subsequently. This had obvious implications for the touchy issue of British sovereignty, as we shall see presently. Secondly, as a member of a Community with common policies, Britain had to accommodate a number of economic and political practices to conform with those of her new partners. It is to some of the more important adjustments in policy that we now turn.

A major difference between the Community and Britain in economic policy lay in the key agricultural sector, a sector whose importance in the Community is evidenced by the fact that it continues to consume more than two-thirds of Community spending. Before entry, Britain subsidized the farm sector directly from government revenues to provide farmers with an adequate income, and imported the difference between British food production and demand at low world prices. Once in the Community, she had to accept the Community's policy of high prices (normally substantially above world market levels) for agricultural commodities, which entails protection of the Community market through import levies and intervention buying of surpluses that threaten the desired price level. A five-year transition period was negotiated for the implementation of the common agricultural policy (CAP); during the first year, the farm remuneration system was introduced and Community farm price levels were implemented in six steps over the life of the transition period.[5] The CAP has remained a major irritant in Britain's relationship with some other members of the Community since she, in her position as food importer, consistently and often raucously opposes large increases in farm prices demanded by France and other producer states at the annual agriculture ministers' marathon price-setting meetings. The agriculture policy has also contributed substantially to Britain's large net payment to the Community, and hence to the friction that issue has engendered over the years.

Britain's adjustment to the Community's customs union was also eased by a transition period. Abolition of barriers to British imports was, of course, the major reason for entry into the Community since it meant unrestricted access to a huge market and promised to provide a major stimulus for British exports. In the event, Britain's trade with the Community increased greatly in the first eight years of her membership. Exports grew by 560 per cent in dollar terms, while her exports to the rest of the world increased by only 290 per cent.[6] Fully 43 per cent of British exports now go to Community countries compared to 30 per cent before 1973. Over 2.25 million British jobs are dependent on Community trade, and Germany has supplanted the United States as Britain's most important export market.[7]

This, however, is only part of the story because in many of the first eight years of British membership, Britain's imports from member states of the Community grew more rapidly than exports. That resulted in a negative balance in her transactions with the Community. Fortunately for Britain, this deficit in visible trade was reversed in 1980, when she experienced a £700 million surplus in that category with Community members. Petroleum products composed the largest single category of British exports, and will in the future probably help to keep Britain's trade with her EC partners in surplus.

But even were her trade with other member states to swing into deficit from time to time, other economic arguments for continued Community membership remain. Britain received 58.8 per cent of direct American investment in the Community in 1980, twice her share of 28.7 per cent in 1973. Half of Japan's Community investment goes to Britain. This stimulus to British industry, amounting in 1979 to about a billion dollars from the United States alone, would be considerably reduced were Britain to withdraw from Europe and therefore to move outside the common external tariff.[8] Of equal importance is the increased leverage in world trade negotiations that comes from membership in the Community. On her own, Britain would not receive the favourable terms she does as member of the world's largest single trading bloc in trade negotiations involving such powerful economies as the United States and Japan.

Full integration into the Community customs union and agricultural policy had additional implications for change in British trading patterns because the provisions of these two policies discriminate against non-Community states. Such discrimination was potentially most harmful to the interests of the developing Commonwealth states whose largely agricultural exports to the former mother country might henceforth be at least partly replaced by commodities procured from Britain's Community partners and/or from the developing states associated with the Community. Entry negotiations and the provisions of the Community's accord with member states' former colonial dependencies (the Yaounde Convention and its successors, Lomé One and Lomé Two) have settled these issues to the satisfaction of the affected states. With some exceptions, Britain's former colonies have become associated with the Community as members of the ACP states, which receive very favourable terms of access to the entire Community for practically all their exports.[9] The Commonwealth countries covered by Lomé Two also became eligible for the substantial aid programs provided by the Community, a programme that is much more generous than that associated with the Commonwealth. These terms are not enjoyed by the South Asian members of the Commonwealth; their exports are covered by other, less generous provisions, which, none the less, allow them preferential Community access over non-Commonwealth countries' products. The Far Eastern Commonwealth countries, also not eligible for full Lomé treatment, have benefited from the Community's generalized preference system for developing countries. Overall, then, British membership in the

Community has caused comparatively little dislocation for the underdeveloped countries of the Commonwealth, and they have received benefits (aid and access to the entire Community) which they otherwise would not have had.

The old Commonwealth countries have gotten off less well than their developing country counterparts. Their industrial products are subject to the common external tariff, and their agricultural products to the CAP's variable levy which has cut in a major way into their food exports to Britain. New Zealand still exports some dairy products to Britain, though at a much reduced rate, and Canadian as well as Australian sales of beef and grain to Britain have fallen off.[10] The adjustment to Britain's new status, then, has affected the older Commonwealth countries to a significant extent, but they were in an economically more sound position to adjust to these changes than were the Commonwealth's more recent members. For Britain, the atrophy of trade links with the old Commonwealth and the dilution of the trading relationship with her former colonies in the third world (who have now diversified their trade links and have access to the whole Community) have inevitably contributed to a reorientation of her attention and energies toward a new international forum in which she does not play the leadership role that was hers in the old Commonwealth.

This reorientation in the field of international relations and diplomacy involves participation in a foreign policy framework known in the Community as political cooperation. The heart of this process, not officially part of the Community institutions and therefore operated by member state ministers and officials, is consultation among member state representatives with a view toward cooperation in relations with third countries and world problems generally. Since the inception of political cooperation at roughly the time of British entry, the member states have met at designated times, and often in response to emergencies, to discuss what can be achieved through joint action. The process takes place at the highest levels when heads of state and government discuss world affairs at their quarterly summits; it is institutionalized in the regular meetings of Community foreign ministers and those of their chief civil service deputies concerned with political affairs; it involves the member state ambassadors to the Community, the permanent representatives; and it leads to frequent consultation among member state diplomatic representatives in third countries as well as in the United Nations. At the UN, the foreign minister whose country holds the Community presidency customarily speaks for the ten member states in major debates.[11] In part because not all member states are at the same time members of NATO, defence matters, strictly speaking, are not discussed in the context of political cooperation, but the related areas of security and disarmament receive attention without objection from Ireland, the only non-NATO member of the Community.

A brief overview of other foreign policy issues treated in the context of political cooperation provides some insight into the extent to which Britain has been affected by this facet of Community membership. One of political cooperation's first success stories was the Helsinki Agreement where the (then) nine member states forged a coordinated approach and spoke as a unit; in the follow-up meetings to the Helsinki Accord, most recently held in Madrid, Community member states again coordinated their positions. In recent years, the Ten have consulted closely on the various Middle East crises and have taken joint positions on them, often separate from those of the American government. Member states cooperated on Iran and they continue to take a common approach to the troubles in Poland, in part because of the international trade ramifications of that issue.

A recent development of major importance to Britain in the context of political cooperation is the support provided her by her Community partners in the Falklands dispute. The other member states suspended commercial transactions with Argentina and provided political support by siding with Britain in public statements and in the United Nations. While Italy and Ireland subsequently watered down their support of Britain, the other member states retained solidarity with their Community partner. Her participation in the framework of political cooperation has provided Britain tangible benefits in the conduct of foreign policy; it is a forum which will continue to affect Britain's conduct of relations with the world, and it will provide her with some of the leverage that she lost with the decline of the Commonwealth.

SOVEREIGNTY OR DEPENDENCE?

Britain's trade and international political relations, then, have clearly been affected by her membership in the EC. It is time to assess the effects of her Community membership for domestic politics. The single most controversial issue in this regard concerns the implications for British sovereignty of the Community treaties and British participation in, and subjection to, the outcome of the Community decision making process. The issue surfaced in the debates preceding accession. It was a major theme in the public debate during the renegotiation period in 1974–75 and the ensuing referendum campaign. And, although it might appear that the issue was settled when British voters supported continued Community membership in 1975, it is still raised by advocates of British withdrawal from the Community, most notably those on the left wing of the Labour Party.

The concept of sovereignty is not a straightforward one. It is used differently by various theorists, it was used with different meanings in the British referendum campaign, and it has connotations for domestic politics as well as an international dimension. It is useful, in this chapter, to distinguish between two meanings which broadly parallel the distinction between its domestic and its international connotations. The first usage, pertaining to the domestic context and the more legalistic use of the word, has to do with what has often been referred to as the supremacy of Parliament; for our purposes, the right of the British government exclusively to make decisions for Britain. The second, less legalistic and more comprehensive usage has to do with Britain's ability to affect action impinging on her, including those originating outside her borders. It is a use of the concept of sovereignty which recognizes that in the contemporary world of interdependent states Britain, with continuing high levels of international involvement but less of her former power, could in the short run limit infringements on her sovereignty in the narrow, legalistic sense of that term by keeping aloof from the commitments involved in participating in international organizations, but would lose in the long run because decisions made in these fora affect her welfare. Not participating in these organizations means not having an impact on these important decisions, and hence limiting sovereignty in the broader sense of the word. This point is exemplified by the argument, made earlier, that Britain's membership in the European Community allows her leverage she would not otherwise have over decisions affecting the regulation of international trade.

Now there is little doubt that British sovereignty in the narrower, legalistic sense of the word has been affected by membership in the Community, although certainly less strongly than is implied by most critics of the Community in Britain. The European Court, the judicial institution empowered to make binding decisions of a legal and constitutional nature pertaining to the Community, has made the following ruling:[12]

> The Community constitutes a new legal order of international law, for the benefit of which the states have limited their sovereign rights, albeit within limited fields, and the subjects of which comprise not only member states but also their nationals.

The implications of this ruling are that the member states are bound by Community law and decisions in those policy sectors which have been transferred to the jurisdiction of Community institutions, and also that, in contrast to the practice in other international organizations, Community laws and decisions are legally binding on individuals in member states without member state enabling legislation in every case.[13]

The previous statement requires some explanation in the British case. In Britain, the Crown negotiates and signs treaties. This procedure was followed in connection with the European Community when the British government negotiated entry provisions and signed the Treaty of Accession. But before the provisions of a treaty (in the case of the Community, not only the content of the treaties establishing the three communities but also all relevant Community laws meant to have affect in member states and passed prior to British entry) can effect private rights domestically, that is, before British courts will enforce the relevant provisions, Parliament must pass enabling legislation. In connection with British Community membership, this was the European Communities Act, 1972. It mandates that directly applicable rights and duties provided for in Community law are to be given effect in British law, that the British executive be given power to enact delegated legislation (subject to some important limitations) to give effect to the obligations of the United Kingdom arising out of Community membership, and that interpretation of the meaning or effect of the treaties is to be determined according to Community law (and, therefore, if necessary, ultimately by the European Court). It also makes alternations to statutes and common law to affect Community provisions in the main policy areas under Community jurisdiction.[14] The Act further provides that British acts, precedent and subsequent, be in accord with Community law. This makes it possible to amend British legislation inconsistent with Community law.

The provision that subsequent British acts be in accord with Community law might appear to bind a subsequent Parliament and therefore violate a fundamental principle of the British constitution by drastically undermining the supremacy of Parliament. Collins argues that this is not the provision's effect. Rather than 'denying effectiveness to subsequent legislation inconsistent with Community law', he states, 'the provisions only express a rule of construction which must give way to contrary intention'.[15] In other words, the British Parliament has not given up its powers to legislate in a manner contrary to Community law. British courts 'should interpret subsequent British legislation in such a manner as to be consistent with Community law and may read subsequent inconsistent legislation as subject to Community law'.[16] However, the European Communities' Act does not entrench any of its provisions and thus make them unrepealable. If it should choose to do so, Parliament can amend or repeal any provision of the Act, or the entire Act; in that sense, the British Parliament has not in any way ceded its legal sovereignty. Parliament can, in other words, choose to withdraw from the Community and make null and void any or all Community provisions that apply in Britain. In the meantime, with Parliament's acquiescence, Community decisions prevail in areas of Community jurisdiction.

The powers of Community institutions to which Britain is subject by virtue of its membership include the right to tax. The Treaty of Paris establishing the ECSC allows the Community to levy a tax on coal and steel producers. In the context of the EEC, Community decisions affect the level of customs duties, the magnitude of the levy on imported agricultural commodities by virtue of the institutions' powers to set agricultural prices, and the level of value added tax collected in the member states going to Community coffers.

Without any pretence at being exhaustive, it is possible to provide a further indication of the extent of Community decision making to which Britons have become subject by noting a number of examples. The important agricultural policy need not be further discussed in this context. In the transport field, one that is considerably less developed at the Community level than is the CAP, Community decisions affect the hours of work allowed in road transport; however, progress in such matters as deciding the maximum weight per axle of lorries transporting intra-Community trade has been unbelievably slow. Community institutions have been busy with product code harmonization across national frontiers, since varying safety and/or health standards within the Community can create barriers to unfettered intra-Community trade, the prime objective of the customs union. Distortion or interruption of the free flow of trade can occur, also, through such governmental actions as subsidization of national firms or discriminatory government procurement policies which exclude non-national firms. In the private sector, trade and free competition can be interrupted through the collusion by firms to carve up markets, or by the overconcentration of industrial power. To control these and similar practices, the Community's Executive Commission has a competition directorate general with powers to investigate and prosecute offenders.

In recent years, the Community has passed legislation allowing such Community professionals as doctors, dentists and nurses to establish themselves in practice throughout the Community without regard to national frontiers. This freedom to work in member states other than one's own was much earlier accorded through Community agreement to most non-professionals. The Community's social provisions ensure that member state migrants receive pension and other social welfare benefits from their state of employment. Its regional policy provides grants for use in the Community's poorer regions.

In order to keep this discussion in proper perspective, and to assess its significance for the issue of sovereignty, a number of qualifying observations must be made. First, it must be remembered that the Community's jurisdiction extends over only a fairly narrow range of subject areas. Member states have not, in the context of the Community, pooled jurisdiction over defence or such highly controversial policy sectors as education, the great bulk of social welfare policy, or even over the most important instruments of economic policy, notwithstanding their association in an 'economic' community. In many respects, it is still quite appropriate to refer to the Community as a customs union with an agricultural policy – it is the policies related to these two areas that are most highly integrated at the Community level. Even in the Community policy par excellence, the CAP, member states together spend more on subsidies than does the Community. In other sectors covered nominally by the Community, for example, industrial, energy or regional policy, the lion's share of decision making and policy expenditure is still controlled by member state governments, whose sovereignty over these sectors, then, remains almost fully intact.

Secondly, when assessing the implications of Community decision making for British sovereignty, it is important to take into account the way in which Community laws are made. It is quite true that decisions made prior to British entry were not affected by representatives of the British government, although one might add that they were accepted by Britain when she joined. Since that time, however, Britain has been represented in all Community institutions, and consequently, British views were heard on every decision. Britain, like the three other major member states, has two commissioners in the executive Commission, and there are Britons at all other levels within that organization. The Commission solicits input for its proposals from all affected interest groups in every member state. Eighty-one Members of the European Parliament are elected in British Euro-constituencies, and there are representatives of British unions, industries and professions on the Community's advisory Economic and Social Committee. A British justice sits on the European Court, and Britain has been very ably represented on the Committee of Permanent Representatives, an institution composed of member states' ambassadors to the Community, who collectively do much important preparatory and support work for the Council of Ministers, the most powerful Community institution.

The rules of procedure of the Council are the single most important safeguard of British sovereignty in the Community context. The Council has final authority over most important decisions made in Brussels. There are provisions for majority decision making at the Council level, and some of that institution's decisions are made that way. Were all its decisions subject to majority vote, the implications for member state sovereignty would be quite significant. But since 1966, when France blocked proposals to widen the scope of majority decision making in Council, there has been an informal, but none the less fully operative, convention (the Luxembourg Compromise) that any member state can block a decision which it feels adversely affects its vital interests. This convention means, in practice, that on all decisions of importance, there must be unanimity.[17] In this decision making rule, Britain, or any other member state, has an effective means of safeguarding its sovereignty.

There is a third way in which British sovereignty can be safeguarded in Britain's dealings with the Community. The Community has no field service, hence all Community decisions must be enforced by member state officials, acting, of course, under instruction of member state governments. This feature of Community governance provides scope for member state non-compliance with Community decisions and has been used occasionally. Such non-compliance almost invariably leads to action against the offending country in the European Court, but again, there are no enforcement provisions for its judgments. In the past, member states have, although sometimes only after quite some time, complied with Court decisions. But the interval before compliance is sometimes sufficient to nullify a Community decision (if it applies to a temporary matter), or is used by the offending country to obtain, through political means, concessions that make an unpalatable decision more acceptable. This approach, used by France in a recent Community controversy over trade in mutton, could be used by Britain were a decision unacceptable to her government to somehow slip through the process, or were the Commission's limited delegated powers to result in action judged sufficiently harmful by London. So far, Britain has been among the more 'communitaire' of member states when it comes to complying with Community law.

She has, however, been less 'communitaire' in another sense, and thereby demonstrated yet a fourth way to safeguard her interests and to protect herself from decisions that are considered undesirable or harmful. The most dramatic demonstration of this approach was the renegotiation undertaken by the Wilson Government in 1974–75, in which it obtained alterations in the terms of membership agreed to by the Community and the Heath Government, for example with regard to British budgetary conditions. Some four years later, the much more openly pro-Community Thatcher Government undertook essentially similar action, although this time there were no explicit threats to withdraw from the Community in the absence of action favourable to Britain. In the 'second renegotiation', as some members of the French government characterized the British action, the budget was again the central theme.[18] By threatening to halt Community decision making through boycotting the Council and by holding up decisions much wanted by her partners, Mrs Thatcher managed to persuade the other governments to grant Britain a substantial refund for the years 1980 and 1981. In 1982, the process was repeated, and Britain again received a generous refund.[19]

These displays of stubbornness, as some would call them, or *Realpolitik*, as they would be characterized by others, are not guaranteed to yield Britain the desired results, and insofar as the British government must inevitably compromise in such situations to some degree, one might argue that use of these methods provides no assured safeguard of British interests. However, other countries, France in particular, have resorted to similar tactics on occasion; thus they have almost become an accepted part of the Community process.

The fact that the Community accommodates member states who take a determined stand on issues about which they feel strongly indicates the extent to which the Community is not about supranationalism, or at least increased supranationalism, and all that implies for sovereignty of member states. The Community process is still essentially intergovernmental, especially with respect to the extension of Community jurisdiction. Step-level extensions of the institutions' powers, or even comparatively minor adjustments to existing programmes that may have the effect of extending common decision making or increasing the powers of a Community institution, require the assent of every member state. Alternatively, member states are allowed to opt out should they feel their country is unready to accept the consequences of a new step toward joint decision making. This was best exemplified recently by Britain's decision to remain outside the framework of the European Monetary System (EMS), a Community programme which, in seeking to achieve exchange rate stability among member states, requires a considerable degree of member state discipline over economic policy.[20]

Such flexibility of approach is reflected, as well, in the implementation of existing Community programs. The Commission, which, as 'guardian of the treaties' has the responsibility of supervising the implementation of treaty provisions and Community programmes, has often been very lenient in some policy areas, for example, allowing (or at least not preventing) Britain and other member states to implement subsidization schemes for shipbuilding and to give regional subsidies whose provisions were contrary to Community policy. Such leniency can sometimes be explained as resulting from the inability of the Commission, because of resource or staffing restraints, to police adequately a Community now composed of ten member states. But it also reflects the political reality of a community of sovereignty-conscious member states and a Commission which is reluctant to challenge a member government head-on in all but exceptional cases.

Given these considerations, it might seem odd that the sovereignty theme should continue to fuel the rhetoric of British opponents of the Community. This reveals more about the political ideology and partisan political strategy of those professing the view that British sovereignty is endangered by membership in the Community than it does about the issue of sovereignty itself. In the political debate over the issue, the supporters of British membership have used the term in its broad sense and argued that Britain in the Community has more influence over matters that affect her interest than Britain outside. Those arguing for withdrawal continue to deplore the alleged loss of sovereignty that Community membership entails, in large part because their strategy for the conduct of British affairs entails sheilding Britain from external economic and political forces. An overview of major British groups' positions on the Community will help demonstrate this point.

THE CONTINUING DEBATE ON THE EC

The most consistent support for the Community has come from the centre in British politics, with the Liberal Party espousing British participation in the movement toward a united Europe as early as 1957. That party's continuing favourable attitude toward the Community is shared by its Alliance partners, the Social Democratic Party, whose leader, Roy Jenkins, was president of the EC Commission for four years until 1980. He and his colleagues in the SDP leadership, particularly former Foreign Secretary David Owen, have repeatedly warned against British withdrawal from the Community because they agree with the Liberals that Britain must trade to survive and that narrow protectionism will exacerbate rather than solve British economic difficulties. The SDP has had to downplay its support for the Community somewhat because among its present and potential supporters there are a considerable number unfavourable toward the EC. None the less, while the SDP leadership's reasons for quitting the Labour Party go well beyond that party's attack on the EC to include opposition to unilateral disarmament and disagreement over matters pertaining to internal party democracy, dissent over the Community and the related issue of disagreement over Labour's increasingly protectionist stance on foreign trade contributed to their decision to create the SDP. In that sense, the Community issue has had an impact on a recent significant domestic political development which could possibly lead to a realignment of the party system.

British industry has shared the centre's enthusiasm for the Community, at least since the time of the Macmillan Government, and it contributed heavily to the pro-Community campaign during the 1975 referendum. Its representatives have participated actively in Community decision making through the instrumentality of UNICE, Community industry's umbrella group, by direct lobbying and by membership in the Community's Economic and Social Committee. Because it views the protectionist policies advocated by Labour as disastrous for British economic well-being, it has attacked that party's Community stance vigorously. British industry insists that Britain must have a voice in determining the policies of the Community, the world's major trading entity, and is therefore a strong proponent of continued EC membership.

Industry's political ally, the Conservative Party, also supports Community membership, although not as strongly. Pockets of anti-Community sentiment remain in the party membership, and the party must, of course, remain sensitive to shifting public feeling concerning the EC. Moreover, Mrs Thatcher is distinctly less committed to the Community than was her predecessor, Mr Heath. This orientation was reflected in Mrs Thatcher's behaviour during the Community dispute over British budget contributions when she threatened to disrupt the common institutions' functioning. None the less, there is a reasonably broad consensus in Conservative ranks, not for movement toward closer European integration, but in support of the principles underlying most EC policies, particularly the principles of intra-Community free trade. Where Conservatives disagree with Community policies, as they do on CAP and Community financing, they express their opposition frankly and drive a hard bargain with their European partners, sometimes sufficiently vociferously to make other Europeans doubt Conservative commitment to the common enterprise.

There is no doubt, however, concerning the attitudes held toward the Community by most British trade union leaders, and in effect, by the Trades Union Congress. This hostility kept TUC representatives from filling the positions reserved for British unions in the Brussels institutions for the first three years of British membership until the referendum results made such a policy seem futile. Even when the Labour Government did its best to live up to its Community obligations, many TUC leaders and TUC-dominated party structures like the NEC sniped at the Community and British participation in Europe. At the September, 1981 TUC congress, a motion calling for British withdrawal from the Community without a prior referendum was carried by an overwhelming majority. The TUC position is the result of a combination of leftwing ideology which sees the European Community as a capitalist club with an economic analysis that prescribes a protectionist policy as a way of saving British jobs and curing Britain's economic ills. This position is unlikely to change dramatically in the future, although predictions about union politics are notoriously risky in Britain, given their susceptibility to alteration with changes in leadership.

The Labour Party has vacillated in its attitude toward the Community since the 1960s, but in the years since its loss of power in 1979, it has become steadily more opposed to Britain's continued membership. Even during its period in office, a majority of the Labour Government's backbenchers were hostile to the Community. Only about a third of the Labour caucus remained pro-Community, seeing no incompatibility between their moderate brand of social democracy and participation in a Community whose member state socialist parties are among the most enthusiastic supporters of European integration.

Labour opponents to the Community predominate in many constituency party organizations and in the NEC, which continued in the late 1970's to urge British policies inconsistent with Community membership. A discussion paper developed for the 1977 Annual Conference demanded reforms of the Community that were in line with the radical social and economic changes the Labour Party advocated for Britain, reforms that were clearly unacceptable to Britain's EC partners.[21] The paper criticized the Community for being based on and operating according to liberal–capitalist principles which interfered with the Labour principles of public ownership and subsidies, with planning and with import controls.

The parliamentary party, however, did not publicly go so far. Its manifestos for the 1979 British and European elections were surprisingly moderate, arguing not for British withdrawal from the Community but for critical opposition from inside. However, after the Conservative victory, the restraints of office no longer served to discipline the party, and with the inevitable drift leftward that characterizes the Labour Party in opposition, the anti-Community sentiment grew stronger. Soon there was growing support for Tony Benn's advocacy of withdrawal from the Community after a Labour election victory without another referendum, and this despite Benn's argument 1974–75 that a referendum should be held at that time to allow the British people to have a say, once and for all, on the issue of Community membership.

With the departure from the Labour caucus of the SDP dissidents, support for the Community in the parliamentary party was further diluted. The party's deputy leader, Denis Healey, remained one of only a handful of MP's willing to support continued British membership. Although spokesman on foreign affairs, he was hindered from making an effective public case for the EC when Eric Heffer, a committed proponent of withdrawal, was made spokesman on the Community. Party leader Michael Foot persisted for a time in his advocacy of withdrawal.

By late 1981, however, there were some signs of change in Mr Foot's position. Withdrawal without a referendum was hard to sell to the public, given Labour's position in 1975, and advocating such action made the position of the remaining pro-Community members untenable.[22] Furthermore, a TUC-sponsored report completed early in 1982 argued that withdrawal from the Community would involve unexpectedly, perhaps unacceptably, high costs for Britain.[23] At about this time, Mr Foot, in a Brussels speech, indicated that British withdrawal from the EC would be accorded a low priority by a Labour Government. Presumably, anti-Community party members could continue their advocacy of withdrawal, but the party would not, should it form the next Government, be bound to a specific date for leaving the EC. It is possible to conceive, therefore, of a Labour Government attempting to defer withdrawal indefinitely. Whether the Bennite faction would stand for such tactics is questionable. Undoubtedly the issue of Community membership would under such circumstances become part of a major showdown between those in the Labour Party who advocate radical socialist and protectionist policies for Britain, policies incompatible with Community membership, and those who, partly for electoral reasons, support more moderate policies that would not be incompatible with continued British membership in the EC.

THE BRITISH PUBLIC AND THE EC

The position any future Labour Government would take on British Community membership will be affected by then-prevailing public attitudes toward the Community, although it is more accurate to argue that public opinion has followed, rather than led, élite opinion. British public opinion has fluctuated widely on the issue of Community membership, being substantially favourable in the period from 1961 (at the time for the first accession attempt) until mid-1967 after de Gaulle's second veto of British membership,[24] then negative, except for a brief period just after accession in early 1973, until just before the 1975 referendum.[25] During the campaign, the majority of respected political leaders advocated a vote favourable to continued British membership in the Community, and the referendum results gave evidence of the majority's willingness to support that stance.

After that peak in support for the Community, public opinion concerning Europe gradually but steadily cooled, reaching its nadir in early 1980, when 71 per cent of those polled reported they would vote to leave the Community if another referendum were held then.[26] This low point in British support for the Community came just before Mrs Thatcher's success in obtaining a refund on Britain's contributions to the Community, and at a time when some of her rhetoric against the Community was bitter and almost abusive. Since that time, support for Europe has increased steadily; by October, 1981, supporters and opponents were almost evenly matched (49 to 51 per cent, respectively).[27] Observers attributed this trend toward a more favourable public opinion to a variety of factors, including Britain's success in the budget refund controversy and subsequent support for, even praise of the Community by Government spokesmen, the rise of the pro-Community Social Democratic Party, the increasing unpopularity of a Labour Party identified in the public mind with anti-Community rhetoric, and an increasingly favourable press.[28] But opinion on the EC remains volatile.

One reason for the increase in popularity of the Community may well be a gradual increase in the public's knowledge about Europe. Repeated surveys have found that those most knowledgeable about the Community were also most supportive of it. However, the degree of ignorance about the Community in Britain is still surprising, given the prominence of the debate of British membership ever since 1961. In a 1980 poll, for example, more than half of those polled believed that Britain's expenditures on the Community exceeded those for social security, education, or defence, which in 1979, a year in which British Community contributions were high, were larger than Britain's Community bill by factors of 17, 8.5 and 8.2, respectively.[29]

From another perspective, the lack of knowledge concerning the Community is not surprising. Polls have shown that the Community is not a highly salient issue; that explains, in part, the volatility of British public opinion on the subject, and it also suggests, of course, that the public is not interested in learning the details concerning the Community's functioning. These details are, anyway, complex and technical, having to do with qualified majority votes, value added tax and fixed exchange rates, monetary compensatory amounts, import levies, export restitution and other esoterica that is hardly the stuff of empassioned debates in the neighbourhood pub.

It is also extremely difficult to personalize Community politics. Before 1979, there were no directly elected Members of the European Parliament; British representatives to that Community institution, like their counterparts in other member states, were selected from among Members of their home Parliament and did double duty at Westminster and in Strasbourg. Elections were fought on British, not Community issues, and Euro-MP's hardly had time to do justice to both sets of responsibilities.

The situation did not markedly improve in 1979, when Britons for the first time had the opportunity to vote for a representative to a Community body. The campaign preceding the election was lacklustre, following shortly after the previous month's general election. Prospective Members of the European Parliament had difficulty in explaining the significance of the poll, given the institution's primarily consultative role and its lack of any significant powers. None of the drama associated with a possible change of government attended the election, and given the huge size of constituencies, each with an average of half a million constituents, it was hardly possible to become acquainted with the candidates. In the event, the average turnout for Britain, 33 per cent, was by far the lowest for any member state and just slightly more than half the average 61 per cent Community participation rate.[30] It was probably a good indication of the degree of British interest in the Community.

Little has changed in the ensuing years to heighten British interest in the European Parliament. The great majority of Britons still do not know their Euro-MP, nor do they really understand his role. In the future, their identification with Community representatives may be lessened because in March 1982, the European Parliament decided on a common, that is, Community-wide list system of proportional representation, with from three to fifteen members per constituency for the next Euro-elections. While such a system would undoubtedly lead to fairer representation of political parties in the British contingent to the European Parliament, it would attenuate even further the already very weak personal and representational ties that Britons have with the Community institutions.[31] At any rate, it is likely that Mrs Thatcher's Government will veto the use of proportional representation for the Euro-elections in Britain because her Government, like the previous Labour Government, is adamantly opposed to the introduction of that method of election in any context to Britain, for fear that its use may lead ultimately to its introduction for general elections.

British voters, then, have only very limited influence over decision making in the Community because of the weakness of the European Parliament. They have another, indirect and not very effective lever over the Community process by virtue of parliamentary committees set up to scrutinize Community legislation, especially the House of Commons' Select Committee on European Secondary Legislation. It was created to allow the Commons some influence over that area of decision making transferred to Community institutions as a result of British membership. The committee receives, through the British Government, all Commission documentation pertaining to a policy proposal, reports on the legal and political ramifications for Britain of the proposed legislation, and recommends whether the full House should take up a matter.[32]

The procedure has had its problems. First, if the House is to have any influence on Council decision making, it must act before the Council decides. This is difficult for some matters, especially those falling in the agricultural sector where decision making often moves quickly. It is also difficult for less hurried decisions because Parliament has no control over the Council timetable and because finding time on the parliamentary schedule, already overcrowded with domestic legislation, is no easy matter. Further, Commission proposals change, often quite fundamentally, before they reach the final decision stage in Council, especially during discussions in the Committee of Permanent Representatives. The House does not often get a second look and thus could find itself having discussed a proposal which is not the basis for Council deliberation. Finally, decisions in the Council of Ministers are affected by ministers of all member states, not only the British representative. Thus even if a British minister wishes to represent the will of the House, he may not be able to if the Council is to come to a decision; clearly that institution would become deadlocked if every minister were bound by his legislature. Representatives must have a good deal of discretion, and this is especially true in cases where member states trade concessions on separate matters in order to arrive at a decision. In these cases, the influence of Members of the House of Commons is very indirect; that of the ordinary voter practically nil.[33]

The upshot of all this is that the European Community decision making process remains élite dominated, bureaucratic, and not very susceptible to democratic control. The British organized interests have learned to make their influence felt in the Brussels institutions and indirectly through lobbying the British government. For them, British membership in the Community has meant adopting new tactics or refurbishing old ones for those policy sectors affected by the Community. For the average British voter, however, the Community will probably remain of secondary interest at best, unless substantially greater jurisdiction is transferred to its institutions. That seems very unlikely for the long term, even should Britain elect an SDP–Liberal Government, certainly not if Britain has a Conservative, let alone a Labour Government.

CONCLUSION

I have argued that the impact of Community membership on British politics and political institutions has, with the obvious exception of the 1975 referendum, been minor. Parliament's discussion of Community affairs is but a very small part of its business and of no great importance. Lack of public interest in Community matters is not difficult to explain along similar lines: the issues that engender public interest and public debate are still decided at Whitehall and Westminster, not in the Berlaymont or in Strasbourg. The stuff of Community politics is of limited scope, and generally in the control of state political executives because, by and large, EC policy is considered in the realm of external relations. Domestically, the issue of Community membership continues to arise from time to time because there is still a substantial amount of opposition to membership among Britons, and politicians of the left seek to exploit this opposition for partisan purposes. It is unlikely, however, that withdrawal from the Community will become a major issue in the next general election; there are other matters of far greater importance to British voters. It is very unlikely that the future will bring much change in this state of affairs because some member states, Britain foremost among them, will continue to rebuff efforts to increase Community powers in politically sensitive areas.

That is not to say membership in the Community has not made a difference to Britain: it has had a very important effect on British trade and is having an increasingly important impact on the conduct of her foreign policy. Britain's membership in the EC is a direct result of her need, given her export-oriented economy, to have unimpeded access to the Community market. Moreover, because of the loss of her formerly prominent world position, Britain had to anchor herself in an international subsystem in order to have more leverage over international economic and political forces than she could have on her own, or as a member of any other conceivable regional grouping of states. The price of EC membership is the loss of exclusively British control over matters falling under Community jurisdiction, and, therefore, some loss of sovereignty in the narrow, legalistic sense of the word. But Britain, as a member of the Community, is able to affect Community decisions, and, of course, retains the right to withdraw should that appear desirable. Previous cabinets have been unwilling to do so, even though they have made their concern over the financial burden of membership, accruing largely as a consequence of the CAP, known to their EC partners. British governments have, in other words, found the price of Community membership worth paying, given the resulting increase in trading opportunities and influence over international events, and given the alternatives of non-membership.

Whether future British Governments will persist in this attitude remains to be seen. It appears very likely that Conservative Governments will keep Britain in Europe, and a Liberal-SDP Government almost surely would, though the likelihood of such a government in the near future appears rather slight. Prospects for continued British membership are considerably less certain should a Labour Party Government come to power. It is conceivable, given continued high unemployment in Britain, that the public mood will shift and radical solutions become popular. Under such circumstances, a left wing Labour Government could seek fundamental changes in domestic policy and protection of the home market, which would both be incompatible with Community membership. British withdrawal would then be sought both by the British Government and by her Community partners. Should this come to pass, all that has been discussed here would become history very quickly, and British politics and economics transformed beyond recognition.

NOTES

1. Strictly speaking, there are three European Communities, the European Coal and Steel Community (ECSC), the European Atomic Energy Community (Euratom) and the European Economic Community (EEC). Since the merger of their executive institutions in 1967, it has become customary to refer to them collectively as the European Community (EC), a practice I shall follow in this chapter except where reference to a specific community is required.
2. Quoted in Euroforum, *Europe 81*, May 1981, p i.
3. Anthony King, *Britain Says Yes* (Washington: American Enterprise Institute for Public Policy, 1977) p. 8.
4. Ibid., p. 10.
5. Dennis Swan, *The Economics of the Common Market* (Harmondsworth: Penguin, 1978) p. 37.
6. *The Economist*, 28 Nov. 1981, p. 11.
7. Rt. Hon. Francis Pym, MP, (then), Leader of the House of Commons, in a speech to the House, 6 May 1981, quoted in *Europe 81*, July 1981, p. 6.
8. *The Economist*, 28 Nov. 1981, p. 11.
9. *The Economist*, 16 Jan. 1982, p. 38.

10. New Zealand has been most adversely affected by British membership in the EC, and continues to plead for preferential treatment of its food exports.
11. About 300 meetings are held annually by member state representatives to the UN to coordinate Community positions, and member states voted the same way on about 80 per cent of UN resolutions in recent years. (*The Economist*, 18 July 1981, p. 60).
12. Case 26/62: *Van Gend en Loos v. Nederlandse Administratie der Belastingen*, quoted in Lawrence Collins, *European Community Law in the United Kingdom* (London: Butterworths, 1980) p. 2.
13. One type of Community legislative instrument, the directive, requires enabling legislation by national governments, but member state legislation pertains only to the practical means of implementing the intent of the directive and hence does not leave member states a great deal of discretion with respect to its substance.
14. Collins, op. cit., p. 19.
15. Ibid., p. 20.
16. Ibid., p. 20.
17. A May, 1982 resort to majority voting on a farm price settlement may have led to a modification of the Luxembourg Compromise. Previously, majority voting had been used only in connection with the annual spending budget and with staff regulations. Britain, supported by Denmark and Greece, argued that the farm pricing decision was a matter of important national interest and, therefore, subject to the veto. However, other member states argued that Britain had attempted to block the decision on farm prices to force her partners into concessions on another matter, viz., a rebate of British contributions to the Community budget. It seems that such tactics will now no longer be acceptable. But Britain has been assured that the Luxembourg Compromise is in effect for other types of decisions of major importance to individual member states. Rules for use of the veto were the subject of high level negotiations in summer and fall of 1982.
18. Britain, notwithstanding her status as one of the poorer member states, was close to becoming the largest net contributor to the Community budget. This was so because Britain has a comparatively small farm sector and most Community spending is on agriculture, because of Britain's relatively high propensity to consume and therefore raise value added tax, a percentage of which must be forwarded to the Community, and because of her still comparatively large trade with third countries and the resultant high British tariff payments going to the Community.
19. *The Economist*, 5 June 1982, p. 55.
20. This the British government was unwilling to accept, especially given the volatility of the pound at the time the EMS was initiated.
21. *The Economist*, 10 Sept. 1977, p. 68.
22. *The Economist*, 15 Dec. 1981, p. 58.
23. *The Economist*, 13 Feb. 1982, p. 48.
24. King, ibid., p. 20.
25. Ibid., pp. 90–1.
26. *The Economist*, 9 May 1981, p. 80.

27. *The Economist*, 19 Dec. 1981, p. 29.
28. One of the most recent to make this finding is the Survey Unit's Study 'Britain and the Common Market', excerpted in *Europe 81*, Apr. 1981, pp. 8–9.
29. Ibid., pp. 8–9.
30. *The Economist*, 16 June 1979, p. 25.
31. In Britain, the Conservatives' share in the 1979 Euro-elections of just over 50 per cent of the vote gave them 60 of the 81 British seats; Labour received 17 seats on the strength of its 33 per cent poll, while the Liberals, the most enthusiastic Europeans of all, received no seats with their 13 per cent of the vote. The remaining seats went to one Scottish Nationalist, and to three Northern Ireland candidates of various persuasions.
32. The Hansard Society, *The British People: Their Voice in Europe*, (Westmead, Farnborough, Hants.: Saxon House, Teakfield Ltd., 1978) p. 33.
33. The House of Lords has established a Select Committee on the European Communities which has made a valuable contribution in a technical sense and held numerous hearings concerning Community issues. It is not, of course, an instrument of popular control either over the British government or the Community.

9 Change and Rumours of Change: Courts and the Rule of Law

Jerold L. Waltman

There is a growing feeling in Britain that the role of law requires to be reassessed.

Nevil Johnson

That the actions of those who govern are as subject to control by the law as those of ordinary citizens is an idea which was first planted in English soil. With the establishment of Parliamentary sovereignty, though, as a consequence of the Glorious Revolution, it receded into the background, in this the land of its birth. Through nearly three hundred years now, untrammeled Parliamentary supremacy has been the touchstone of constitutional theory.

In the last decade and a half, however, there have been serious discussions about resurrecting the role of law in English public life. Any movement in this direction, whether generated by the judiciary or as the result of action taken in Parliament, will inevitably alter the internal life of the judiciary as well as affect the courts' relations with other institutions. Some of the changes will have at most only a minor impact while others are pregnant with materials which go to the heart of the political structure of the country. For the most part, the attention has centred on three fronts: administrative law, civil liberties, and devolution.

Before examining each of these issue areas, it is important to stress some salient features of the British courts.[1] Firstly, the Scottish and

Northern Irish court systems are separate from England's. However, an appeal is available to the House of Lords from the highest Scottish and Northern Irish courts. Secondly, in the English judicial system the justices consider themselves part of an integrated judiciary. That is, the idea of a layered court system is not the proper metaphor. While there is a hierarchy of courts, the English do not think of a higher court 'overruling' lower courts in quite the same fashion as elsewhere. Rather, it is more the giving of advice. Judges, moreover, do not sit on only one court, making the system take on even less the look of a layered one.

Thirdly, the courts are not dependent on Parliament. Originally, their jurisdiction derived from the monarch's power to dispense justice. Consequently, the judiciary has long maintained that it is an 'independent' organ of the Crown's authority devoted to administering justice 'without fear and without favour'. The next point is that the judges consider the judiciary to be the guardians of the common law. In the English view, the common law is ever in evolution, but always touching a bedrock of unchanging principles. While most of the common law's substance relates to contract, tort, and criminal law, its 'great principles' sometimes touch the actions of administrative agencies.

Fifthly, English law has put the accent on 'wrongs' rather than 'rights'. The common law seeks to restore persons to the position they occupied before the wrong was committed. Naturally, therefore, there has been a heavy emphasis on remedies. Often, if a case cannot be brought within the scope of a common law remedy, it will be dismissed.[2]

Lastly, in fact, though not in form, the judicial function of the House of Lords is divorced from its legislative function.[3] A Lord Chancellor and eleven Law Lords are appointed to exercise the judicial function, into which no other Lord may inject himself. Further, these same persons, for practical purposes, now constitute the Judicial Committee of the Privy Council. Hence, in effect, the Law Lords are the Supreme Court of the United Kingdom.

ADMINISTRATIVE LAW

The power of the courts clashes with that of Parliament most directly in the area of public administration. When Parliament enacts a law, it will of course provide for its administration. Civil Servants are thereby given authority to carry out the law. In order to ensure Parliamentary control, Civil Servants are responsible to a Minister, who is in turn responsible to Parliament. Abuses of administrative power are checked therefore by vigilant MP's, aided if need be by the Parliamentary Commissioner for Administration, who bring the matter before a Minister during Question Time.[4]

Even if this mechanism served to correct all abuses, it is still true that administrators are dealing with law. In many cases, questions of interpretation necessarily arise, which as far as the aggrieved citizen is concerned might as well be maladministration. Does therefore such an aggrieved citizen have access to a court of law for redress? If he does not, the courts have given up the power to interpret the law; if so, can a court overturn an administrator's decision on the grounds of misinterpretation?

In any country with even a semblance of adherence to legality, the answer to the above question can only be affirmative. In fact, English courts have always assumed the authority to rule any action *ultra vires*, that is outside the law and therefore void. While judicial review as practiced in the United States, Canada, and Australia is out of the question, a judicial review of an administrative action to see whether it accords with the law is wholly appropriate.[5]

In essence, Parliament may make whatever law it chooses, but interpreting statutes is the business of the courts. As with all acts of interpretation, there is considerable room for discretion. Courts may, in the first place, constrain their jurisdiction within very narrow limits, refusing even to hear certain types of cases. Then, when they do consent to hear cases, they can place the same construction on the statute that the administrator in question gave it. The alternative strategy is to open the jurisdictional channels and also to inquire more deeply into the issues behind a decision. It is only a difference of degree, but it is an important degree.

Until the mid-1960s the courts had opted for the passive role, issuing rulings that made administrative action, for all practical purposes, unreviewable in the courts.[6] For example, it has always been held that only judicial acts of administrators are reviewable at all, not administrative ones. 'Administrative' was then interpreted so broadly as to encompass almost all Civil Service decision-making. Furthermore, the courts were operating under an 1861 House of Lords rule that forbade courts from overruling their own precedents, making them operate in a precedential straightjacket.[7] Once these narrow views were taken, therefore, they could not be set aside.

By the 1960s though there was an embryonic movement to broaden the scope of judicial review of administrative action, especially through use of the doctrine of 'natural justice'. The doctrine shares a philosophical affinity with natural rights, along with an inherent ambiguity. Its ambiguous character, however, does not deprive it of its strength. Lord Reid has stressed

> In modern times opinions have sometimes been expressed to the effect that natural justice is so vague as to be practically meaningless. But I would regard these as tainted by the perennial fallacy that because something cannot be cut and dried or nicely weighed and measured therefore it does not exist.[8]

Unlike natural rights, however, natural justice 'may . . . be used not as a standard for criticizing the content of legal rules but to refer to the principles which must be followed in the *application* of rules whatever their content'.[9] Generally, in the matter of public administration, the courts have held that natural justice requires two conditions: (1) That everyone is entitled to a fair hearing and (2) That no person may be a judge in his own case.[10] If these conditions are not met, the action which resulted from the procedure will be held *ultra vires*.

The reasons for the reorientation were several. For one thing, the Left had begun to share some of the doubts of the Right about the benign nature of bureaucracy.[11] Moreover, as the sheer size and complexity of administrative structures grew, the adequacy of Parliamentary oversight was increasingly called into question.[12] Freed from oversight, the state bureaucracies provided enough instances of abuse of power to arouse concern. Another factor was that law reform became an 'in topic', one result of which was the establishment in 1965 of a Law Commission, whose function it is to analyze and recommend changes in the legal system as a whole. A year later a Royal Commission, headed by Lord Beeching, was appointed to study and suggest ways of overhauling the court system.[13] (Its recommendations were largely adopted in the Courts Act 1971.) Once begun, this broad movement for law reform snowballed, and it was only a matter of time before administrative law came under scrutiny. Of equal importance was the role of leading individuals, especially Lord Denning, who served as Master of the Rolls until 1982.[14] Though usually outvoted 2-1 in his advocacy of expanded judicial power, his speeches (opinions) chided his fellow justices for allowing clear administrative abuses to stand up in the name of deferring to Parliament. Like dissenting opinions of American Supreme Court justices, his views provided an intellectual frame of reference for many on and off the bench.

The first hint of a reorientation of judicial attitudes occurred in the 1964 case of *Ridge* v. *Baldwin*.[15] The Chief Constable of Brighton was charged with conspiracy but acquitted, an episode that was reported thoroughly in the newspapers. The local watch committee nevertheless removed him from his post without a hearing. He thereupon filed a suit charging that the failure to grant him a hearing at which he could defend himself violated natural justice. The original judge threw the suit out, saying that the newspaper reports contained enough information for the committee to take both sides into account. After the case followed a tortuous route through the courts, the House of Lords held that the dismissal was *ultra vires* since the constable had had no opportunity whatever to be heard in his own defense. He was therefore ordered reinstated.

In the following years, several other cases served notice that the upholding of administrative action was not automatic. An especially important example was *Anisminic Ltd.* v. *Foreign Compensation Commission* (1969).[16] The Anisminic Company owned property in Egypt which was seized after the Suez invasion. Some years later the Egyptians gave the British government a lump sum compensation to be distributed to all such claimants. Parliament turned the matter over to the Foreign Compensation Commission (which had been set up earlier to settle such problems) whose enabling statute provided that its determinations 'shall not be called into question in any court of law'. Anisminic, denied its full claim by the Commission, appealed to the courts, contending that the Commission had misread the law in its case. The courts agreed to inquire into the matter in spite of the statutory wording. The Commission may have autonomy, the judges said, but only the courts can make a final reading of the law.

A more expansive challenge to administrative authority can be seen in *Congreve* v. *the Home Office* (1976).[17] A television owner applied for a renewal of his license but was turned down. The Home Office was on firm legal ground for a statute gave it clear authority to deny licenses. However, it refused to provide the disgruntled applicant with any reasons. The court startled more than a few persons with its holding that for the administrator to give no reasons must imply that he had no good ones. The denial therefore was 'unreasonable', making it *ultra vires* since Parliament could not have intended such an outcome.

A final example is especially pertinent since it, unlike the cases discussed above, involved the courts in a controversial area of public policy.[18] For some time a lively debate has been going on over the structure of secondary education.[19] Many, including most Conservatives, favour maintaining the three-track system established by the Education Act 1944 while others, including most Labourites, favour comprehensive schools. The position of the Government has changed several times since the early 1960s, in tune with the changes in party. Each time the policy has changed, the Department of Education and Science has run into recalcitrant local authorities controlled by the opposite party. In the mid seventies, the Labour Secretary of DES ordered in unmistakable terms such a footdragging Conservative authority to close its grammar school. A court case ensued. The decision went against the Secretary on the grounds that the power to close grammar schools was not specifically contained within any statute regarding the Minister.

Most of the conflicts everyday citizens have with administrators are settled through the mechanism of tribunals.[20] These are panels set up inside agencies to hear complaints and make administrative determinations. The proliferation of administrative agencies has led to a concomitant increase in the number of tribunals. (In fact, no one even knows how many there are. An admittedly conservative estimate is 2000.) In 1957 the Franks Committee was appointed to study the organization and procedures of these bodies.[21] The resulting Act of Parliament erected the Council on Tribunals to provide some oversight. Now, however, after two and a half decades of experience and the proliferation of tribunals on an even wider scale, there is another chorus of dissatisfaction and calls for reform.

The basic elements of concern are twofold. First, should the procedures of tribunals be infused with legalism? In the absence of established procedures akin to common law proceedings can there be an assurance that the citizen is given a fair hearing? Part of the virtue of tribunals is that the proceedings are informal and nonadversarial, making the average citizen (supposedly) more at ease. On the other hand, the tribunals are made up of civil servants who may be hesitant to overrule their colleagues. Also, without representation, a citizen may be at a disadvantage when arguing the technical points of his case. Too, many tribunals do not require the following of precedents. Two persons with similar situations may receive different treatment, with the adversely affected one having no redress.

The second problem concerns the type of avenue that ought to be available for an appeal to the courts. Since it is clear that tribunals are applying law, should a court be empowered to begin the case *de novo* and decide it on the merits? Or, should the courts only hear cases that involve procedural errors which deviate from the statute? The doctrine of natural justice enters the picture here; for in deciding a given case, say denying a welfare benefit, and then upholding that reading of the law, are not Ministers and their subordinates acting as judges in their own cases?

While everyone admits that informality in tribunal proceedings is a desirable state of affairs, there seems to be a growing feeling that some regularized procedures need to be introduced. One reform which has been widely adopted is to have a lawyer chair each one. Other proposals call for providing legal representation, establishing formal procedures which approach adversary ones in character, and creating binding rules of precedent. One problem with introducing any of these reforms is that all tribunals are not alike. The scope and importance of the issues they handle offer, as one observer put it, 'a window onto the panorama of modern life'.[22] What would ensure fair procedures in a tribunal dealing with large corporations might have the opposite effect in a tribunal setting rents in council houses. Moreover, if the procedures are made more formal and representation provided for, the decisional process will undoubtedly become more time-consuming and more costly. Access to tribunals then will be more difficult for people of limited means, defeating much of the purpose of having them in the first place.

As for the courts, one proposal which has been seriously discussed, but not implemented, is to create an Administrative Section of the High Court, whose function would be to hear appeals from tribunals.[23] If done, this would create a corpus of case law on administrative matters. It would also create a sensitivity to general principles of administrative law throughout the tribunal system. Serious abuses of citizens' rights might therefore be checked by the classic preventive cure – fear of appeal to a higher authority. However, it would in all likelihood seriously undermine the informality of the proceedings. As with the legalization reforms, the resulting cost and intimidation might keep those who need tribunals most from using them.

Another adopted reform has been to make appeal to the courts a little easier procedurally. Five common law writs have always been available as remedies to implement natural justic.[24] The party petitioning the courts, however, had to begin by stating the writ he sought and then showing how his case fit its application.[25] The Law Commission was asked in 1971 to study the matter, resulting in a recommendation, adopted in 1978, to subsume the five writs under a new writ, 'application for judicial review'. Now, a petitioner may simply show why the action in question was illegal and then let the court determine the proper remedy from among the five specific writs. The door to the courtroom is now open, therefore, a hair wider.

A BILL OF RIGHTS

The British have never seen fit to follow American practice in writing civil liberties down and encasing them beyond the reach of ordinary legislation. One reason is that the common law was long considered a bulwark against arbitrary executive power. Cases such as *Entick* v. *Carrington*[26] stood as examples of what the common law could accomplish in its shining moments. A member of the Privy Council ordered a citizen's house searched for seditious material. The homeowner then sued for trespass and was awarded damages. Moreover, Parliament has by statute enumerated the rights of British subjects on several occasions. Examples include habeas corpus, the Petition of Right of 1628, and the Bill of Rights of 1689.

The legal status of the citizen's protection remains, however, tenuous. In a given case, the courts might look to other precedents and not protect the individual.[27] As for the rights granted by Parliament, it is obvious that what is given may also be taken away.

Political checks and conditions become, in practice, therefore, the crux of the matter. According to one argument, the 'character of Englishmen' militates against the abuse of governmental power. The political culture assures that those who exercise power will do so in a libertarian fashion and that the infrequent departures will only be tolerated in a period of genuine emergency. Another approach, usually from the Left, is that the maintenance of the democratic nature of a sovereign Parliament is the key to accomplishing political good.[28] The people will grant the power to govern to a democratic social movement that will utilize this authority to expand the freedom of the many while judiciously guarding the essential liberties of the few.

The complacency generated by these contentions has given way in the last few years. Under the conditions of political stress which have recently arisen in the United Kingdom, new interest in civil liberties has been aroused. It is not at all clear that the common law and Parliamentary enactments have and can prevent untoward violations of civil liberties.[29] Nor has the faith in the genteel tradition and the enlightenment of the electorate emerged unscathed.

Furthermore, as the rosy belief in the steady progress of the welfare state has begun to wane, an omnipresent government also makes for unease. The size and scope of governmental activities multiples the opportunities for maladministration broaching on civil liberties. In addition, the sheer scale of government in the UK makes such policies as the Official Secrets Act of more consequence than formerly. That is, when there were only a handful of agencies and Civil Servants who could hide behind its shield, it did not matter much to everyday citizens. But when everyone's life is touched each day by public bodies, its ramifications become important indeed.

Moreover, it has become increasingly evident that the expansion of the welfare state has eroded some areas of individual choice. Rights to a private education and the private practice of medicine, for example, collide with the ideology of equalizing services. Such rights can be limited without much danger, to be sure, but should they be extinguished? At the moment, the accomplishments of the welfare state, impressive as they are, stand close to a threshold level of seriously curtailing opportunities for diversity. On top of this feature of the welfare state, there is the fact that it has transformed many private organizations into public or quasi-public bodies. Can, in the name of carrying out one desirable public policy, these groups violate basic civil liberties? For instance, if under colour of law, a closed shop arrangement is established, is there a threat to the right of association?

Most specifically, though, the issues have been brought to the forefront by the actions of extremist groups. The continuing political debacle in Northern Ireland is the most obvious and most tragic example. However, the National Front can share in this limelight. By stretching traditional civil liberties to the extreme, and by provoking strong counteraction, the old questions of liberty versus order and the limits of freedom of speech have been resurrected. In the same vein, the usually benevolent behaviour of the police has also been subject to question, especially at recent National Front rallies and during the summer riots of 1981.[30]

In sum, several streams have converged to make the issue of a Bill of Rights one for serious discussion. Two basic questions are immediately presented for its advocates. One is what the content of such a Bill should be; the other is how to go about enacting it, especially if it is to be secure from ordinary Parliamentary repeal.[31]

The issue of content revolves around the question of whether to include social and economic rights along with the more traditional legal and political rights. The arguments for limiting the Bill to the latter stress their longer historical lineage and their primacy in libertarian thinking. To include social and economic rights in any such document might serve to diminish the vitality of the basic legal and political freedoms. On the other hand, it is averred that deprival of minimum standards of material and spiritual well-being can render legal and political rights meaningless. Human rights as a whole are cut from the same philosophical cloth and to sever them artifically into legal and political rights and social and economic ones is improper.

Whatever the philosophically appropriate position, the case against including social and economic rights is a strong one. For one thing, the list of economic and social rights, given their amorphous quality, is bound to open up fissures of all sorts in the adoption process. Since there is not a universal political consensus on even including these rights, such a step might endanger the adoption of the document itself. Far more preferable, it is argued, would be drawing up a well-drafted Bill of legal and political rights (an intricate enough task) and securing its adoption. Then, if the proponents of social and economic rights wish them likewise enshrined in some type of basic law, a public debate can be held on that and the matter resolved. To burden the discussion initially, though, would probably be counterproductive.

The second objection to an inclusive Bill of Rights lies in the area of remedies. The traditional legal and political rights normally require a government *not* to do something. A court may then simply hold the action in question *ultra vires*, allowing everyone to go on about his business as before. With social and economic rights, however, the requirement is for a positive act. Only a *mandamus* would appear appropriate to secure the denied right. Since the wording of such rights would have to be somewhat vague, issuing writs with any meaning would be exceedingly difficult. In the process, the courts would either have to develop definitions of such vague terms or accept legislative definitions. If the former stance were taken, a barrage of litigation could be expected seeking ever clearer definition and broadening application of such definitions – similar to, one suspects, reapportionment cases in the United States. If the courts simply deferred to Parliament, the so-called rights would become legally meaningless. The latter outcome might also serve to detract simultaneously from a vigilant posture in safeguarding other rights.

Sir Norman Anderson has proposed a compromise solution which seems eminently reasonable.[32] Both sets of rights could be included in a document but they would be divided into those which are legally actionable and those which are to serve as goals for substantive policy. Such a move would obviate the problem of remedies but, unless different methods and timetables were used, might not overcome the first difficulty. None the less, it is a sensible approach to accomplish a blending of the eighteenth and twentieth centuries.

The United Kingdom is a signatory to two international documents which bear on the question at hand, the United Nations Universal Declaration of Human Rights (1948) and the European Convention for the Protection of Human Rights and Fundamental Freedoms (1950). Treaties have no legal status within the UK, however, until Parliament passes implementing legislation, which it has not seen fit to do in either of these cases. In 1978, though, the House of Lords, under the guidance of Lord Wade, passed a bill to make the European Convention actionable in British courts. While there was (and is) little chance the Government will push the measure in Commons, the debate did arouse public notice and comment. Such a move shows clearly that the question of a Bill of Rights is indeed on the agenda.[33]

If the expedient of making the European Convention actionable were chosen, the question of enactment would be settled. However, the sticky question of the sovereignty of Parliament would arise because the Convention provides for an enforcement (or at least litigative) mechanism. Could a loser in a British court appeal to the European institutions? Only by initially spelling out in the implementing legislation that such a move is allowable could Parliament assure that in the future it could legally undo it.

In short, the principle of Parliamentary sovereignty presents a riddle to anyone advocating any type of Bill of Rights. Of course, because of its very sovereignty Parliament could enact the most pristine Bill of Rights this side of eternity and make all of it actionable in the courts. But Parliament's sovereignty is such that no future Parliament's authority may be hobbled in any fashion. Thus, a mere subsequent statute would suffice to undo nirvana. The real question is finding some way to 'entrench' the Bill of Rights.

Legally, there are several ways to accomplish this. The easiest and surest way is to terminate the sovereignty of Parliament. This would have to be done if any type of written constitution were ever adopted. A document spelling out the creation and operation of institutions would automatically mean beginning with a clean slate, and Parliament could only derive its authority after such date from the document itself.

In the more likely alternative of a piecemeal approach, all hope for entrenchment is not lost. One possibility is to require by Standing Order that any breach of the Bill of Rights be done with an extraordinary majority (two-thirds or three-fourths are the usual suggestions). Since Parliament would be free at any time to repeal the Standing Order, its sovereignty would remain intact. Another expedient is a Derogation Clause. The Bill of Rights would specify that it had precedence in courts of law over all other statutes, pre and post dating its passage, unless Parliament specifically provided otherwise.[34] Parliament would then remain free to overturn a court judgment or offer an overruling clause in a draft bill.

The genius of these solutions is that they combine legal entrenchment with political insight. A Government which chose, under the special majority variant, to instead repeal the Standing Order, would open itself to charges of undermining the political consensus that civil liberties are sacrosanct. In any real emergency, it is inconceivable that the Opposition would not co-operate in granting whatever powers were necessary to the Government of the day. But in the intermediate levels of political conflict, political calculation would probably prohibit seeking an easy repeal of the Standing Order. Jacob Janelli has spelled out in clear fashion the delicate political maneuvering a Derogation Clause would introduce.

> Whether such a clause should be added to any particular measure will be a nice question of political judgment in each case. On the one hand the Government will thus be rendering its legislation immune from judicial review, but at the expense of holding out political ammunition to the Opposition. On the other hand, by omitting the derogation formula, the Government for the moment is relatively safe from criticism. If the legislation is never challenged in the courts or (better still) if it is unsuccessfully challenged, the Government's gamble will have succeeded. But if the legislative measure is successfully impugned, various consequences will follow. The Government will incur the same odium as if it had used the derogation machinery in the first place, but now in addition will be vulnerable to the charge that it has misled the country.[35]

DEVOLUTION

It is important to remember that the contemporary Parliament is the result of absorption, merger, and nondivestiture. Parliament's role in the political system was established but uncertain when Wales was absorbed in 1536. An undeveloped political entity sharing a crown with England, it was administratively united with England by Edward I. The Welsh received an allotment of seats in Parliament as a result. In 1707, after sharing crowns for over a century, Scotland and England agreed to merge their Parliaments. Each, however, was to retain its own legal system and established church. In 1800 Ireland ceased to be governed as a satrapy (legally at any rate) and was also given seats at Westminster. Never a satisfactory arrangement, this set-up was dissolved in a series of steps after World War I. In the process of terminating the Parliamentary connection with Eire, though, Ulster was retained as part of the United Kingdom.

What, in effect, has happened is that the English Parliament has become through these amalgamations a governing institution for the United Kingdom. It developed a dual role of domestic legislator for the disparate parts of the Realm and the curator of foreign and defence policies for a sovereign state. Because of the continuing political dominance of England, however, the domestic aspect of its attention tended to centre there. Moreover, since the relationships of England to Wales, Scotland, and Northern Ireland are quite different, no coherent approach to non-English components of the polity was possible.

Devolution, or the granting by Parliament of certain powers to a subordinate body, is not new.[36] In one sense, the establishment of assemblies in the Canadian provinces, and later the British North America Act (1867), represent devolution. So too does the similar legislation for other Commonwealth countries. Yet the type of devolution considered for the British Isles has always been of a qualitatively different character. For one thing, the Commonwealth countries never sent voting delegates to Parliament. For another, there was not, after the American Revolution, much bickering over financial powers. Still another factor is that the political relationship with the Commonwealth countries was always seen to be both remote and tenuous. Their political evolution towards independence was always assumed.

The structure and sovereignty of Parliament present several legal dilemmas for the devolutionist. While Parliament's sovereignty gives it unlimited flexibility in establishing subordinate bodies, the inability to make any type of permanent agreement casts a pall over devolution. The legal standing of the regional body is perpetually an inferior one, and a majority at Westminster may undo in an instant what painstaking negotiation may have created. On the other side of the coin, it means that those political interests which come to dominate the devolved institution may always attempt to wrest more power from the centre, since the centre is in a position to give it at any time.

Technically, the conflict of laws problem, so common to federal systems, would not exist. The statues or administrative acts of the inferior body would have to give way to UK statutes. In practice, however, the only type of legal and political conflict this would avoid are cases in which a regional majority which is a national minority tries purposely to use its regional institutions to frustrate a national policy.

Ambiguity being a universal trait of human language, the devolved assembly's grant of power will be open to varying interpretations. A continual check can be maintained by setting up a person or group to scrutinize legislation to see whether it conforms with the creating Act.[37] However, unless Parliament is willing to invest this person or group with unlimited authority, reference to the Judicial Committee of the Privy Council is almost unavoidable.

No matter how narrowly the enabling act is drawn, therefore, political reality is going to make the Judicial Committee into an 'umpire'. To be sure, Parliament could simply override any act sharply at variance with the wishes of a sitting majority. However, crowded political agendas will assure that matters of intermediate saliency will end up in court. Furthermore, it is likely that issues will arise between purely domestic groups which lie at the fringes of the regional body's power. A disgruntled loser in the political process might well file an individual suit challenging a statute's legality. Conceivably, the majority at Westminster could be, for any of several reasons, neutral, forcing the Judicial Committee to decide. Inevitably, too, there will be conflicting trade regulations emanating from London and the devolved body. Suits by business interests caught in some type of regulatory vise fill the courts of federal systems. In most cases, the stakes for the participants are fairly low; however, often these cases pose a fundamental question of constitutional law. Once decided, they tend to become precedents for cases in a variety of other, often completely unrelated, areas.[38]

The result of all this litigation is likely to be a corpus of case law dealing with the division of powers. It will become a habitual part of the frame of reference of political élites and form part of the givens of ordinary politics. If these rules are not challenged by Parliament acting in a major crisis of some sort, they will acquire a legitimacy which will transcend their legal status. They will become, then, as with other customs and conventions, part of the constitution.

Gladstone's various proposals for Home Rule for Ireland point to another dilemma.[39] If the entire United Kingdom is not covered by devolved institutions, Westminster will be in an anomalous position. Whatever domestic policies are transferred to the subordinate body for its area will be maintained at Westminster for England. The UK Parliament will be both England's domestic Parliament and the institution in charge of national defence and foreign policy. In this case, should the devolved region continue to send MPs to London? If they do not, they will be deprived of a voice in foreign policy, clearly an undemocratic outcome. If they do, though, they will have a voice in purely English matters which are devolved to their region. One solution offered would be to allow devolved-region MPs to vote only on non-devolved matters. While attractive, this idea would be difficult to implement since what is a devolved power will necessarily be ambiguous. Although the courts or the Speaker (as in the Parliament Acts 1911 and 1949) might make rulings, only Parliament could decide definitively. In this decision even, would the MPs in question be allowed to vote?

Reconciling devolution with the sovereignty of Parliament and its special links to England present vexing legal questions on all these fronts. If implemented, any form of devolution will convert the United Kingdom into a species of a federal state. In polities representing this genre, law and politics become inextricably intertwined. Who decides will have a great impact on what is decided, leading to a continual pull and tug over jurisdictions. Perhaps the marriage of law and politics will be marked by less cohabitation in the United Kingdom than elsewhere, but there will be no divorce.

CONCLUSIONS

Judicial activism in administrative matters must be considered separately from questions emanating from adopting a Bill of Rights or devolution. Administrative law represents evolutionary change, with no single event dramatically establishing new dimensions. Furthermore, it poses no fundamental challenge to political institutions. When a statute is construed in a manner displeasing to the majority in Parliament, simple legislation will suffice to undo the decision. Even procedural matters – the establishing, modifying, and revoking of writs – are within Parliamentary hands.

The Bill of Rights and devolution are qualitatively different. Parliament would be divesting itself, at least temporarily, of some of its authority. Either one would transfer policy-making in certain areas to a new configuration, of which the courts would be a major part. While an umbilical cord would still run to Westminster, the semi-autonomous character of the new rules and structures would thrust the courts into a politicized arena. There could then be no retreat to an isolated courtroom. This would be especially true in cases involving devolution, for Parliament would seldom be even an indirect litigant.

Hence, the potential for change in administrative law is not major as far as the politicized role of the courts is concerned. An activist judge may here and there snipe at arbitrary government, altering perhaps the substance of administrative law in marginal ways, but because the judiciary itself must usually generate these changes and because the results are so easily undone, little of long-lasting significance seems likely. The character and style of the 'judicial role' in England go far in assuring little change.[40] Judges are schooled almost exclusively in the private law. In addition, the habit of deferring to Parliament, supported by the legal philosophy of John Austin, is deeply ingrained.[41] Moreover, there is a strong custom of absolute nonpartisanship in making judicial appointments. The professional reputation of candidates within the legal fraternity is weighed much more heavily than any other factor.

The judiciary that all this produces is one that is characterized by internal cohesion and a high degree of technical competence. It is also doggedly committed to maintaining its independence by steering clear of the political fray. Patrick Devlin is more typical of English judges than Lord Denning.

> I appreciate that radical reformers may take a fundamentally different view from mine about the function of the judiciary. They may see it not as arbitrating between citizens and as holding the balance between the state and the individual but as one of the three branches of government. They may see the need for social reform as demanding that all three arms of the government should smite in unison for its achievement. Judges should give social leadership, they say. What if they are harnessed to an Act of Parliament? They are still free to gallop with it towards the social millennium, treating the sections that rumble along behind as but the wagons that are packed with fodder for progressive judgments.

> If judges were men endowed for such a task they would not truly be judges. . . . The judges are the keepers of the law and the qualities they need for that task are not those of the creative lawmaker.[42]

It is this attitude that led J.A.G. Griffith to remark:

> It is as difficult to imagine the judiciary in the United Kingdom handing down judgments like those sometimes handed down by the Supreme Court of the United States, based on radical and reforming principles, as it would to imagine such judgments being handed down by the Supreme Court of the Soviet Union.[43]

On the other hand, enactment of a Bill of Rights or a restructuring of institutions along devolved lines would be an outside force for change. The option of refusing to decide a case, especially in the devolution scenario, simply would not be available. Much political conflict would in essence become legalized – in turn politicizing the courts.

Because they would often be choosing winners and losers in political jousts, the courts could expect increased public scrutiny. The press and interest groups would pay much closer attention to the nuances of litigation. Along with the scrutiny would come a continual barrage of criticism and praise. For a judiciary used to being insulated from the tides of public debate, learning to live with criticism would take some getting used to. The challenge would be to develop a sensitivity to social and economic changes ('following the election returns') without being swept away by them.

Another reality to which the courts would have to become accustomed is frequent collisions with other institutions. Naturally, those who lose in court would carry the battle to other forums, seeking to modify, delay, or frustrate the results of court decisions. Winners would probably return to court, requesting injunctions or other writs to have their previous victory carried out. In these circumstances more than a mere legal question would be presented. It would be one of choosing strategies and tactics in institutional conflicts. The judges would need to acquire an instinct for when to fight and when (and how) to back off gracefully.

If these events come to pass, it is the Law Lords especially who will need to exercise the greatest judicial craftsmanship. Not only would they set precedents for the other judges, but they would create a style that would be emulated. Furthermore, as a constitutional court for the various parts of the United Kingdom, they would be handling some very delicate questions. An appreciation of the legal and political realities, historically and at the time of decision, would be absolutely essential. If on the whole, for instance, the Lords adopted the strategy of asserting broad jurisdiction but then deciding the early cases for the most powerful litigant, they would build a reservoir of power to be drawn upon later.[44] If, however, they challenged politically potent forces early in the game, their authority might suffer an irreparable blow.

How much of a rein Parliament could keep on the new policy-making configurations, and hence how easy it would be to checkmate controversial court decisions, would depend largely on whether the major parties can regain their dominance of Commons. If they do, overturning a court decision not favoured by the leadership of the moment would be simple. If, however, the politics of Commons becomes more pluralistic, whether through a loosening of the whips or through non-majority Governments, there would be less chance for direct overturn. The saliency of issues will normally be different to different groups of MPs and putting together a coalition to override a specific court decision would be more difficult.

The appointment process too would likely undergo a metamorphosis. Non-partisanship in judicial selection was only begun during Lord Haldane's tenure as Lord Chancellor (1912–15), and became settled practice only with Lord Sankey's Chancellorship (1929–35). This was possible, of course, because little of political consequence was being decided by the courts. But if the law becomes more political, partisan pressures are likely to return. The Lord Chancellor, sitting as he does in the Law Lords and the cabinet, is the perfect conduit for these pressures. Factions within the governing party would begin to take a keen interest in appointments, trying to see that judges with the 'proper' political views were put on the bench. To believe that the Prime Minister and other party leaders would not be pulled into this fray seems naive.

The result would more than likely serve to broaden the base for judicial recruitment.[45] If the route to the bench led at least partially through MPs, those with a political base would be more likely to be considered than now. Too, if the courts were playing an enlarged policy role, then it would seem likely that the politically ambitious would discreetly seek such posts. Over time, then, the judiciary would exhibit a greater diversity of backgrounds and personality types. This would not, according to several schools of thought, be entirely unhealthy.

Naturally, though, there is always the chance that making judicial appointments rather more political would mean the degeneration into a system of cronyism and downright corruption. The law itself then would lose public respect. (The experience of some American states offers ample proof of this proposition.) However, it is at this juncture that political culture and political tradition enter. By and large Britons who participate in politics are not corrupt. The fact that parties may exercise discretion in judicial appointments does not mean they would be sold to the highest bidder. There is a long tradition of the sanctity of the law and it is not likely incompetents or party hacks would be appointed to administer it. Further, people change when they become judges. In a political culture such as Britain's, one suspects that judges would continue to take their duties seriously. There would appear to be little cause for alarm on this front.

In the last three hundred years, the rule of law has slid from its once central place in the English political constellation. Democracy in the form of mass participation in electing a centralized Parliament, however, has not secured the blessings once held out for it. The labyrinth of the modern state has created occasion for abuse of power which legislatures seem unable to check, no matter what their legal authority. It is here that the rule of law cannot be severed from the process of governing. 'It is perhaps too often forgotten that one of the merits of the rule of law is that it is a curb on power – irrespective of the person or institution who wields it.'[46] Citizens of the United Kingdom may discover that they need curbs on power as much as they need the right to participate.

NOTES

1. Structural details can be found in Fred Morrison, *Courts and the Political Process in England* (Beverly Hills: Sage, 1973) chs 1 and 2 and, in more complete form, in R.M. Jackson, *The Machinery of Justice in England*, 7th edn (Cambridge University Press, 1977).
2. See J.A. Jolowicz, *The Judicial Protection of Fundamental Rights under English Law* (London: Kluwer, 1980) 5–6.
3. See Robert Stevens, *Law and Politics: The House of Lords as a Judicial Body, 1800–1976* (Chapel Hill: University of North Carolina Press, 1978) and Louis Blom-Cooper and Gavin Drewry, *Final Appeal: A Study of the House of Lords in its Judicial Capacity* (Oxford: Clarendon Press, 1972).

4. For a succinct overview of the problems of administrative justice, see Kenneth Wheare, *Maladministration and its Remedies* (London: Stevens, 1977).
5. A good compendium is S.A. deSmith and J.M. Evans, *Judicial Review of Administrative Action*, 4th edn (London: Stevens, 1980).
6. See Morrison, *Courts and the Political Process*, ch. 3.
7. This rule was overturned by a Practice Directive issued by the House of Lords in 1966.
8. *Ridge* v. *Baldwin* (1964) A.C. 40.
9. Paul Jackson, *Natural Justice*, 2nd edn (London: Sweet & Maxwell, 1979) 5.
10. A good discussion may be found in any standard text on administrative law. The most complete for this purpose is J.F. Garner, *Administrative Law*, 5th edn (London: Butterworths, 1979).
11. The earliest broadside was Lord Hewart, *The New Despotism* (London: Ernest Benn, 1929).
12. See Wheare, *Maladministration* and Nevil Johnson, *In Search of the Constitution* (New York: Pergamon Press, 1977).
13. See Morrison, *Courts and the Political Process*, ch. 2.
14. See Peter Robson and Paul Watchman, *Justice, Lord Denning and the Constitution* (London: Gower, 1981).
15. (1964) A.C. 40.
16. 2 A.C. 147.
17. Q.B. 629.
18. *Secretary of State for Education and Science* v. *Tameside Metropolitan Borough Council* (1977) A.C. 1014.
19. See Maurice Kogan, *The Politics of Educational Change* (New York: Praeger, 1978).
20. There are two excellent works on the tribunals. R.E. Wraith and P.G. Hutchesson, *Administrative Tribunals* (London: Allen & Unwin, 1973) takes an administrative approach whereas J.A. Farmer, *Tribunals and Government* (London: Weidenfeld & Nicolson, 1974) is more legalistic.
21. Committee on Administrative Tribunals and Enquiries, *Report of the Committee on Administrative Tribunals and Enquiries*, cmnd 218, (London: HMSO, 1957).
22. Wraith and Hutchesson, *Administrative Tribunals*, 14.
23. In a report of Justice, a non-partisan law reform society. See Garner, *Administrative Law*, 256.
24. The five are certiorari, prohibition, mandamus, declaration, and injunction. The first three are prerogative writs; that is, they flow from the Crown. Certiorari orders an inferior body (usually a court) to send a certified copy of a proceeding in order that its legality may be inquired into. Prohibition orders a lower court not to proceed outside its jurisdiction. Mandamus compels a public official to do his legal duty. The declaration and the injunction are equitable remedies. A summary can be found in Law Commission, *Report on Remedies in Administration*, cmnd 6407, (London: HMSO, 1976).
25. This is a good example of the aforementioned focus on 'wrongs'.

26. (1765) 95 Eng. Rep. 807. This case is analyzed in Louis Jaffe, *English and American Judges as Law Makers* (Oxford University Press, 1969) 22–4.
27. See, for example, *Liversidge* v. *Anderson* (1942) A.C. 206.
28. Labour Party, *United Kingdom Charter of Human Rights: a Discussion Document for the Labour Movement* (1976).
29. The major issues are discussed in Colin Campbell, ed., *Do We Need a Bill of Rights*? (London: Temple Smith, 1980).
30. Patricia Hewitt, *The Abuse of Power: Civil Liberties in the United Kingdom* (Oxford: Martin Robertson, 1982) contains a thorough, if somewhat polemical, discussion of these and related items.
31. This issue is discussed fully in J.R. Jaconelli, *Enacting a Bill of Rights* (Oxford: Clarendon Press, 1980).
32. Sir Norman Anderson, *Law, Liberty and Justice* (London: Stevens, 1978) 43–4.
33. Lord Wade, 'Introducing a Bill of Rights', in Campbell, ed., *Do We Need a Bill of Rights?*, 17–22; House of Lords, *Report of a Select Committee on a Bill of Rights*, House of Lords Paper 176 (1978).
34. Canada, for example, employed this expedient before the current constitution was adopted.
35. Jaconelli, *Enacting a Bill of Rights*, 284.
36. See Vernon Bogdanor, *Devolution* (Oxford University Press, 1979) and his 'The English Constitution and Devolution', *Political Quarterly*, 50 (Jan./Mar. 1979) 36–49.
37. This was done in the Government of Ireland Act 1920 which created the Stormont Parliament. The provision was also included in the ill-fated Scotland and Wales Acts of 1978.
38. See, for example, the discussions in Richard Johnston, *The Impact of Judicial Review on Federal-State Relations in Canada, Australia, and the United States* (Baton Rouge: Louisiana State University Press, 1969).
39. See Bogdanor, *Devolution*, ch. 2.
40. See the discussion in Morrison, *Courts and the Political Process*, ch. 2.
41. See John Austin, *Lectures on Jurisprudence*, 3 vols (New York: Burt Franklin, 1970; originally published, 1861).
42. Patrick Devlin, *Judge* (Oxford University Press, 1979) 17.
43. J.A.G. Griffith, *The Politics of the Judiciary* (London: Fontana, 1977) 52.
44. This was, for instance, the strategy employed by John Marshall in *Marbury* v. *Madison* (1803).
45. On British judicial selection, see C. Neal Tate, 'Paths to the Bench in Britain: a Quasi-Experimental Study of the Recruitment of a Judicial Élite', *Western Political Quarterly*, 28 (Mar. 1975), 108–29 and Alan Katz, 'Patterns of Judicial Recruitment of the English Judiciary: the Limits of Reform', paper presented at the 1981 meeting of the American Political Science Association, British Politics Group.
46. Sir Leslie Scarman, *English Law: The New Dimension* (London: Stevens, 1974) 68.

10 Conclusion: a Crisis of Participation?

Donley T. Studlar

The ideal of democracy continues to haunt institutionalized reality.
Raymond Grew, *Crises of Political Development in Europe and the United States*

THE DIRECTIONS OF CHANGE

Our survey of British political institutions has developed several common themes. This concluding chapter will discuss the major threads of argument in the foregoing analyses and will consider the models of change offered in the introduction in light of these findings.

How much change has really occurred in British political institutions in recent years? One's assessment of this question depends partly on one's frame of reference. Two-party politics has been the norm since 1935, but from 1885 to 1935 it was not. Social class as a basis for electoral cleavage reached its zenith in the post World War II period. Some commentators contend that British government has undergone perhaps too much change in the last twenty years[1] while others argue that no fundamental institutional reform has occurred since at least early in the twentieth century.[2] Our contributors incline toward the second position. They consider the British polity over-institutionalized at the central level, accepting of cosmetic change but resistant to fundamental change, and in need of greater accountability through a dispersion and sharing of power.

The British penchant for centralized rule through the doctrine of Parliamentary sovereignty is well known. Although Britain was willing to implement federalism for some of its territorially and ethnically diverse colonies, resistance to ideas for domestic devolution, decentralization, and federalism is still strong within the governing circles of the United Kingdom, as Furniss, Rasmussen, Ashford, and Lazer indicate. There are longstanding theoretical reasons for this devotion to centralization (the notions of national unity and even-handed treatment for all) and perhaps even stronger partisan reasons (maintenance of the two-party system, strong central leadership control of the political parties). In general these two arguments for centralization have reinforced each other. Labour Party social reformism, for instance, has been predicated upon Labour Party rule over all of the United Kingdom through obtaining a majority in the House of Commons and forming the Government. Like the Conservative and Liberal parties before it, the Labour Party talks decentralization and greater participation in Opposition, but rarely carries it out in Government.[3] Even when decentralization is attempted, the resistance is so great that it may be undermined by members of the proposing party. The Liberal split over Irish Home Rule is instructive, as is the Labour failure to implement devolution. Would even a Liberal–Social Democrat attempt at decentralization similarly founder? The tensions of a coalition government could make reform difficult to achieve.

Yet despite resistance to decentralization and the cautionary example of Ulster, more favourable attitudes toward this reform have been developed in recent years. Furniss contends that the end of devolution is not in sight and that a certain amount of back-door decentralization has already occurred. Although Ashford strongly argues the need for local government decentralization, he is not hopeful that it will occur. Rarely, however, have there been so many parties and groups advocating decentralization. In the long run, the prospects for change may not be that dim.

Related to the centralization problem are the problems of representation and participation. The latter two have taken several different forms in recent years – referendum, proportional representation, reselection of sitting MPs, and changes in rules for selecting party leaders being the most familiar. Lazer and Samuel H. Beer contend that populism has at long last made an impact on the political system. Beer, however, sees the significance of this populist trend as more far-reaching than does Lazer.[4] Few advocates of changes have advanced as thorough analyses of the defects of traditional British views of representation as has Rasmussen. What he recommends is a focus on territorial representation, not only in the form of decentralization, but also in how candidates and MPs are selected. Changes such as he proposes would remove power from the central party organizations and leaderships. More diverse, less cohesive parties would be the price paid for greater participation by the less powerful. This would have ramifications throughout the polity, perhaps encouraging some changes but obviating the need for others, such as proportional representation.

Rasmussen's emphasis on representation of local and territorial interests, seconded by Ashford and Furniss, stands in stark contrast to analyses which argue for the importance of functional representation in modern Britain, perhaps even including a reformed House of Lords representating corporate groups.[5] To be sure, some observers, Furniss in particular, do not see territorial and functional representation as necessarily opposed. Additionally, Christoph notes the inroads of trade unions into the Civil Service. Nevertheless it is noteworthy that our contributors find so little applicability for the popular ideas of corporatism, collectivism, and interest group pluralism.

What about more participation through use of the referendum? Under the Conservative Government of Mrs Thatcher, the referendum has fallen into disuse, despite her espousal of it in Opposition. Once again we witness the disjunction between Opposition affinity for more participatory modes of politics and normal Government satisfaction with the status quo. A broad view of the referendum, however, shows that is not a device that is used frequently in most states, Switzerland excepted. Even in the United States, long a repository of populism, there has never been a country-wide referendum.[6] At best, the referendum is an occasional device. If populism is gaining ground in the United Kingdom, then we can expect future referenda. As an irregular mode of greater participation, however, it is unlikely to be as significant a change as the others discussed above. Perhaps that is why the referendum was so easily incorporated into the British polity.

Along with the movements toward greater decentralization and participation, there has arisen increased concern with constitutional checks and balances and criticism of the narrowness of the British concept of law (Waltman, Lazer, Ashford). Waltman suggests that the British judiciary has been edging ever closer to judicial review. The conventional British élite view is that such a movement is even more objectionable than federalism; in fact, the two dangers are often linked, as in the devolution debate.[7] Greater judicial involvement in the political process, like use of the referendum, will probably be a matter of opportunity rather than deliberate, systematic encouragement. The flexibility of British constitutional arrangements, however, does not set definite limits to this development.

Michelmann argues that the constitutional impact of the European Community, like its economic impact, has been overrated. In several ways Britain has been the odd man out in EC political affairs – resisting proportional representation for the European Parliament, having a socialist party less than enthusiastic about the EC, and conducting a post-entry referendum on the subject being three examples. Similarly, of course, Britain has often been a dissenting state in EC economic affairs. There is little evidence here that supranationalism has checked the power of British central government to conduct its internal affairs as it wishes. In the proposed trilateral scheme of checks and balances, so far the central government has been able to resist encroachments from both the regional and international levels.[8] Furthermore, it appears to be in more danger from the well established pressures of the former (see Furniss) than from the latter.

It is interesting that our contributors place so little confidence in Parliament as an institution to check the others and act on behalf of the public. Only Michelmann identifies the House of Commons as serving the people's interests, but it is largely ineffective in this role against the remote EC bureaucracy. Others see Parliament more as part of the problem than as part of the solution. Parliamentary sovereignty is a fig leaf covering centralized, unresponsive rule, according to Ashford, Waltman, and Rasmussen. Only a Parliament willing to share its power with groups other than parties and the executive could contribute to a reformed British government, in their view. Christoph and Rasmussen are not impressed with the inroads that parliamentary select committees (or the ombudsman) have made on executive power. A decentralized, dissenting Parliament, however, might be able to help renew other institutions.

Richard Rose contends that there are two dimensions to authority, effectiveness and consent.[9] The contributions to this book place more emphasis upon the latter concept as the key point of current changes in British politics. In order to be more effective in its assertion of authority, British government needs to be able to generate greater consent for its operations. By sharing power through participatory reforms and decentralization, central government may wield its formally reduced power more effectively.[10] The price of resisting the sharing of power may be to lessen not only consent, but also effectiveness. Successful change assumes, of course, that the 'carriers of reform', to paraphrase Furniss, do not become mesmerized by the chimera of central authority when they gain control of it.

This again raises the question of political parties and the role of partisanship in bringing about change. Our contributors are generally suspicious of how dedicated parties are to fundamental institutional change. Ashford states this view succinctly: 'The overall result is a disjointed and sometimes irrelevant debate that may serve central partisan interests without providing policy solutions.' Examples of this tendency include not only local government reform, but also devolution and the European Community. Much may be promised, but little is delivered. Even that little may be subject to reversal when another party takes office. These practices have led, as Wald points out, to attempts to change British institutions by circumventing parties. As long as British government is majority party government, however, such attempts can have only sporadic success at best. The short-term vested interests of the two traditionally major parties are too intertwined with the centralized structures of government to allow much institutional change to be implemented.

That is why the hopes of reformers are tied to the encouragement of multipartyism and coalition government. Alone in office, the SDP or Liberals might be as incapable of change as the Conservatives or Labour, whatever their promises. Multipartyism, however, enhances the prospects of at least some parties taking institutional change seriously, and coalition government makes it more likely that such a party would have a role in government. Even if reform through parties failed, as it did in the short-lived Lib–Lab pact, then coalition government makes it more difficult for the government to quash movements for change outside the affected parties (Waltman).

If parties and partisanship always acted to inhibit change, little would ever occur. There are circumstances in which partisan institutional change can be accepted as either being in the general interest or too difficult or bothersome to reverse. The 1911 Parliament Act is an example. Nevertheless, the adversarial nature of the two major British parties in recent years makes such circumstances unlikely. As Wald and Ashford point out, however, the nebulous legal standing of British political parties makes changes *within* them more likely, for better or worse. Thoroughly decentralized political parties or a long-term multiparty system coexisting with a centralized form of government might be too great a tension to bear.

MODELS OF CHANGE RECONSIDERED

Where does this leave the models of change considered in Chapter 1? Although our contributors are reluctant to opt for one model over the others, their observations do fall into a pattern. As noted above, they seem more impressed with the change-resisting capacities of the British polity than with its ability to adopt change, at least in a fundamental way. Surprisingly little regard emerges for the incremental model of change. Both Rasmussen and Ashford see the British penchant for thinking in terms of piecemeal change as aborting more fundamental analyses and solutions of problems. Christoph, however, thinks that *ad hoc* change is about all that one can expect from the bureacracy and Lazer emphasizes the incremental (and conservative) method of adapting the referendum.

The reluctance of the British political system to embrace changes in recent years inclines our authors toward the grudging adaptation model of change. Despite the theoretical flexibility of the British constitution and the pressures for reform, decentralization has been resisted, the EC has been only reluctantly accepted, the House of Lords and the electoral system remain unreformed, political activism by the judiciary has been condemned, and the Civil Service has changed only slightly. Arguably, the most substantial changes have been those involving the House of Commons, the party system, and the referendum. Most institutional changes have only been able to advance a small way, if at all, before being stifled.

Beer appears to be correct in arguing that British political culture has changed more than British political institutions.[11] Rasmussen contends that institutions developed earlier are ill equipped to represent the better educated population of late twentieth century Britain. Trust in government, political parties, and leaders has declined.[12] These cultural tendencies have led to greater questioning of the assumptions on which political institutions are based. In an increasingly dissenual political culture, people are looking to the law and to participatory structures to protect themselves against perceived defects of leaders and institutions.

Some changes have been introduced, but the general pressure for change remains. The years of the 1960s through (at least) the 1980s appear to be a crisis period in British politics. Discontent has surfaced in many ways, and the polity is struggling to cope. Christoph notes, however, that politicians and reformers often have difficulty in sustaining interest in change. On the basis of the results of the 1979 devolution referenda, one might also question whether the British population, when put to the test, can maintain a desire for change. Fatigue and general conservatism might allow the system to continue with minimal alteration.

These comments are reminiscent of an earlier analysis by Dennis Kavanagh.[13] In examining the 1931 crisis of the British party system, he argues that the conservatism of the British population tolerates failures and missed opportunities by leaders to a greater degree than one might expect in a democracy. Furthermore, Kavanagh sees the incremental model and the archaic polity model as indistinguishable.

> Here, the élite reliance on intuition, ad hoc improvisations, and patching-up has in large part contributed to the intractable nature of the problems facing Britain. Commitment to a gradualist approach produces immobilism.[14]

Our contributers have little affinity for either the overloaded government or post-industrial society models per se. Nevertheless Christoph and Waltman view the overload of the welfare state as contributing to discontent with the Civil Service and with infringements of civil liberties. If this is a crisis period in British politics, then there may be an overload of institutional issues on the agenda, in addition to economic and other policy problems.

Although our authors are equally reluctant to embrace the post-industrial society model, their analyses indicate that some of its provisions are relevant. The desire for greater participation and the need for British government to meet this demand are frequently reiterated points. Wald is most explicit in application of the post-industrial model to British party developments. In a work which echoes some of the major themes here, Beer argues that populism is on the rise in Britain through its three component elements of quality of life, participation, and decentralization.[15] These analyses fit very well with Inglehart's findings on the attitudes typical of post-industrialism.[16] The problem, as noted in the Introduction, is to discover what forms of political institutions are appropriate for coping with these attitudes.

Over-institutionalization, the combination model which has gained considerable currency in discussions of British politics, does seem to be applicable, at least at the central level. Preservation of central control is a main goal of the various groups – partisan, executive, bureaucratic, and parliamentary – which feel their power threatened by various decentralizing and participatory reforms. The more of these groups there are, each with its well-entrenched institutional bulwarks, the less likely any significant change is to occur. Although studies emphasizing pluralistic stagnation or corporatism have been popular in recent years, nobody has thoroughly analysed the 'cozy triangles' of British politics, as has been done for the United States with considerable success. Bringing interest groups into consideration of why British political institutions often act to stifle change could be a fruitful endeavour which would amplify the notion of over-institutionalization.

In summary, then, the contributors to this book find some features of each of the five models to be relevant in understanding Britain's current political dilemmas. The archaic polity model, however, clearly dominates the discussion. Institutional change in Britain has not risen to the challenge of demands for increased participation and power-sharing. If the crisis is perceived to be severe enough, however, significant institutional change is possible.

BRITAIN IN AMERICA'S PLACE?

For a number of years commentators have been noting, usually anecdotally, a convergence of the British and American political systems. Most frequently this has involved the British system becoming more like its American cousin, however fervently many US political scientists wished for the direction of influence to be reversed. Our analysis suggests that this Americanizing of British politics has accelerated in recent years and that Britain is undergoing a crisis of participation, perhaps similar to one that has already occurred in the US or as part of a general post-industrial trend.

In this regard it is instructive to compare our findings with those of a systematic statement of the tendencies toward Americanization in the early 1960s, namely Thomas J. Carbery's 'The Americanisation of British Politics'.[17] Carbery argues that American influence has been felt in Britain in several areas – protracted election campaigns, increased attention to the candidates for Prime Minister, lack of ideological distinction between the parties, potentially stronger Parliamentary Committees, potential use of the party primary, possible political appointment of Civil Servants, discussion of fixed terms of office, and party conferences resembling American conventions. The incorporation of the first two points seems beyond dispute. On the third point, the two major British parties have grown more ideologically apart, but so have the American ones. Furthermore, the British party system has fragmented, a recurrent but usually temporary phenomenon in the US.[18] Wald's analysis indicates that the much-disputed internal changes in the Labour Party are not that remarkable in a comparative context. Making the leadership responsive to lower levels of the party is never completely solved in a democratic polity, as the recent experience of the US Democratic Party demonstrates. Britain may not yet have party primaries, despite Rasmussen's and Finer's advocacy of them,[19] but Labour Party reselection procedures and the Social Democrats' all-member selection of the party leader are steps that could lead further down that path. Deference toward party leaders is definitely in decline. The similarity of British and American party conferences/conventions, however, lies more in the rallying of prearranged support than in being the forum for leadership selection which Carbery claims. The rest of Carbery's analysis is concerned with possible (in early 1960s) governmental resemblances between the US and the United Kingdom. Parliamentary Committees are now an established part of British government. As Carbery predicts, they are not as strong as Congressional Committees, but they have given notice to the Government that they are forces with which to be reckoned.[20] The outbreak of cross-voting and other types of dissent in recent parliaments, not foreseen by Carbery, is another indication of convergence between the US and UK legislatures. Discussion of a fixed term of office has waned, although Rasmussen gives cogent reasons why it should be revived. As Christoph notes, political appointment of Civil Servants has not advanced very far, although some steps have been taken in that direction.

Proposed and in some instances implemented innovations that Carbery does not consider include proportional representation, devolution, local government reform, the referendum, judicial activism, a bill of rights, and lessened government secrecy, in addition to others previously mentioned. While we are not attempting to trace intercountry borrowing,[21] all of these additions to Carbery's list except PR have strong American pedigrees. If anything, Carbery underestimates the extent to which the British and American political systems are converging in the direction of the latter. This is not to deny the existence of substantial differences between the two systems or movement in American politics in a British direction – somewhat more responsible parties, greater governmental secrecy, and more leadership power in the Democratic Party, for instance. Moreover, as we have reiterated in this book, the forementioned institutional changes in Britain have not always advanced very far. Yet it is remarkable that serious discussions about these questions are now taken as a matter of course.

These movements toward the introduction of American-style modes of participation and governmental structures suggest that the United Kingdom is undergoing a belated crisis of participation.[22] Beer argues that populism has replaced deference, primarily because of cultural trends dating back to the romantic revolt of the 1960s.[23] Although not abandoning the incremental model, Vivien Hart argues forcefully that British debate over such changes as devolution, the referendum, and electoral reform harkens back to American developments of eighty years ago.[24] This does not mean, of course, that American-style solutions will necessarily be adopted, or that other institutional problems will not arise. The American formula itself seems to have become less stable in recent years.[25] Alternatively Wald, Lazer, and Inglehart argue that the crisis of participation affecting Britain is not the result of lag, but part of a general Western-wide trend. Although differing in several respects, the 'belated crisis' and the 'general crisis' interpretations are not completely contradictory. It could be, for instance, that the current crisis of participation in the United Kingdom is so severe partly because of lag factors.

The problem for political institutions is how to channel these demands for participation.[26] Extension of the suffrage would appear to have reached its limits with the lowering of the voting age to 18. New channels of participation are needed. Therefore proposals have emerged (1) for the referendum, devolution, and local government reform; and (2) for making institutions such as Parliament, the Civil Service, and parties more responsive to their less powerful members and to the public at large. If Britain has a more acute problem of participation than other democracies, it may be because Britain has a more centralized form of government.

The analyses in this book mark a profound change in the thinking of North American political scientists about British politics. Since at least Woodrow Wilson, political scientists on the Western side of the Atlantic have generally admired the British political system and argued that many of its features ought to be emulated. US political scientists have been especially impressed with the coherence of Britain's political parties and the fusion of legislative and executive policy-making in comparison to the incoherence and fragmentation of American parties and governments. Little evidence of that perspective is revealed in the previous pages. The perception of British decline has apparently affected North American political scientists as well as other observers. Not only do the contributers to this book recognize the problems facing the polity, they often advocate American-style solutions to these problems. There is no evidence of the residual nostalgia that Beer, for example, feels for class politics, strong leadership, Butskellism, responsible parties, and deference.[27] The abandonment of the British model in favour of an unacknowledged American model of politics is almost complete.[28]

If Britain achieves reasonable, workable solutions to its current dilemmas of governing, will the British model make a comeback? One wonders how the situation will look twenty or thirty years hence.

NOTES

1. Samuel H. Beer, *Britain Against Itself* (New York: Norton, 1982) pp. 25–6; Frank Stacey, *British Government 1966–1975* (New York: Oxford University Press, 1975) pp. 1–4.
2. Douglas E. Ashford, *Policy and Politics in Britain* (Philadelphia: Temple University Press, 1981) esp. pp. 10, 262–300.
3. Vernon Bogdanor, *The People and the Party System* (New York: Cambridge University Press, 1981); Richard Rose, 'From Steady State to Fluid State: The United Kingdom Today', in William B. Gwyn and Richard Rose (eds), *Britain: Progress and Decline* (New Orleans: Tulane University Press, 1980) pp. 129–54; L.J. Sharpe, 'The Labour Party and the Geography of Inequality: a Puzzle', in Dennis Kavanagh (ed.), *The Politics of the Labour Party* (Boston: Allen & Unwin, 1982) pp. 135–70.
4. Beer, op. cit., pp. 107–48.
5. Keith Thomas, 'The United Kingdom', in Raymond Grew (ed.), *Crises of Political Development in Europe and the United States* (Princeton University Press, 1978) pp. 72–74; Beer, op. cit.; Gordon Smith, *Politics in Western Europe*, 3rd edn (New York: Holmes & Meier, 1980) pp. 61–2.
6. David Butler and Austin Ranney, *Referendums* (Washington: American Enterprise Institute, 1978) p. 7.
7. Vernon Bogdanor, *Devolution* (New York: Oxford University Press, 1979) pp. 173–6.
8. Joseph R. Rudolph, 'Ethnic Sub-States and the Emergent Politics of Tri-Level Interaction in Western Europe', *Western Political Quarterly*, XXX (Dec. 1977) 537–57.
9. Richard Rose, 'The Nature of the Challenge', in Richard Rose, (ed.), *Challenge to Governance* (Beverly Hills: Sage, 1980) pp. 5–28; see also Stacey, op. cit., pp. 1–4.
10. See Dennis Kavanagh, 'Political Leadership: the Labours of Sisyphus', in Rose (ed.), op. cit., pp. 215–35.
11. Beer, op. cit.
12. Vivien Hart, *Distrust and Democracy* (Cambridge University Press, 1978).

13. Dennis Kavanagh, 'Crisis Management and Incremental Adaption in British Politics: the 1931 Crisis of the British Party System', in Gabriel A. Almond, Scott C. Flanagan, and Robert J. Mundt (eds), *Crisis, Choice, and Change* (Boston: Little, Brown, 1973) pp. 152–223.
14. Ibid., p. 218.
15. Beer, op. cit., p. 150.
16. Ronald Inglehart, *The Silent Revolution* (Princeton University Press, 1977).
17. Thomas J. Carbery, 'The Americanisation of British Politics', *Journal of Politics*, XXVII (Feb. 1965) 178–84.
18. See Ivor Crewe, 'Prospects for Party Realignment: an Anglo-American Comparison', *Comparative Politics*, X (July 1980) 379–400. Crewe argues that the decentralization and flexibility of US parties encourages dealignment but not realignment. In Britain the situation is reversed.
19. Samuel E. Finer, *The Changing British Party System, 1945–1979* (Washington D.C.: American Enterprise Institute, 1982) pp. 213–14, 230.
20. Beer, op. cit., pp. 192–4.
21. Jerold L. Waltman, *Copying Other Nations' Policies* (Cambridge, Mass.: Schenkman, 1981).
22. Raymond Grew, 'The Crises and Their Sequences', in Grew, (ed.), op. cit., pp. 21–2; Thomas, op. cit., pp. 90–2.
23. Beer, op. cit., pp. 107–48.
24. Hart, op. cit., pp. 201–2.
25. Ibid.; Arthur Miller, 'Political Issues and Trust in Government: 1964–1970', *American Political Science Review*, LXVIII (Sept. 1974) 951–72; Jack Citrin, 'Comment: the Political Relevance of Trust in Government', *American Political Science Review*, LXVIII (Sept. 1974) 973–88.
26. I am indebted to my co-editor, Jerold L. Waltman, for the insights in this paragraph.
27. Beer, op. cit., pp. 5–19, 96, 218–20.
28. Earlier analyses suggested that American political scientists' criticisms of the British model were highly selective. See Leon Epstein, 'What Happened to the British Party Model?', *American Political Science Review*, LXXIV (Mar. 1980) pp. 9–22; Dennis Kavanagh, 'An American Science of British Politics', *Political Studies*, XXII (Sept. 1974) pp. 251–70.

Name Index

Subject Index